COACHING SKILLS:
A Handbook

COACHING SKILLS:
A Handbook

Jenny Rogers

Open University Press

Open University Press
McGraw-Hill Education
McGraw-Hill House
Shoppenhangers Road
Maidenhead
Berkshire
England
SL6 2QL

email: enquiries@openup.co.uk
world wide web: www.openup.co.uk

and Two Penn Plaza, New York, NY 10121-2289, USA

First published 2004

A catalogue record of this book is available from the British Library

ISBN 0335213308 (pb)   0335213316 (hb)

Library of Congress Cataloging-in-Publication Data
CIP data applied for

Typeset by YHT Ltd, London
Printed in Great Britain by MPG Books Ltd, Bodmin, Cornwall

In memory of Bill Morgan (1903–2002)
and
Charlotte Davey (1973–1996)

Contents

Introduction

Like many others who now earn their living as coaches, coaching found me. More than a decade ago, I was newly back in the BBC, running its management development programmes. Soon, I began to get tentative phone calls: 'I've done all the courses, but now I'm in a new job and I need to get to grips with this or that issue – can you help?' Or, 'I've got this editor in my team. He's too senior for a course but he urgently needs help with his leadership style. Anything you could do?' Some of these queries had the air of 'Psst! I need help – but don't tell anyone!' Others just assumed that it was only right and proper that tailored and time-effective help was going to be available for some of the most senior people in the organization.

Significantly, there was no accepted word then for the process that people were requesting. I believe we referred to it as 'one-to-one sessions', in a fuzzy fumbling for a word or phrase that would accurately describe what would happen. This process was, of course, coaching, an activity that must be as old as human society but which has only recently emerged as a proper discipline in its own right.

This book represents the material I wish had been available to me then. Knowing then what I know now would have saved so much time and spared clients so many of my well-intentioned but clumsy early attempts at coaching.

I have written the book with a number of different readerships in mind, but they are all united by one thing: a wish to understand what coaching is, how it works and how to do it. This could mean that you are in a quite different job or role but are wondering what this coaching stuff is and whether you could make a living at it. You could be working in a professional role, such as training, that looks a bit like coaching, and may even think you probably already do it informally. You could be a trainee coach, already resolutely committed to the idea of improving your practice. You might be a therapist or counsellor, considering turning your existing skills to a different kind of clientele and wondering what that would mean for you in practice. You could be a much more experienced coaching practitioner looking for a benchmark to affirm what you already know.

Reading the book is no substitute for training and supervision as a coach, though my sincere hope is that it will support and boost the training that you do undertake. Only through training will you get to identify your own quirks, habits, strengths and weaknesses because the only real way to discover how to practise as a coach is to do it and then to get feedback on how you do it. We reckon in our firm that it takes about 1000 hours of working with clients to become reasonably adept as a coach – about the same as it takes to learn the basics of a foreign language or a musical instrument. To be able to work with more or less any client probably needs at least another 2000 hours obtained over a number of years of practice: a certain amount of real time needs to pass. This is why coaching is more than just learning techniques, essential though these are, especially in your earliest days of practice.

Writing this book has emerged from a number of strands of experience. First, I have now had fourteen years of working as a coach and many thousands of hours at it with many hundreds of clients from a wide variety of sectors. My experience has been as an executive coach – that is, I work more or less exclusively with senior people from organizations. However, the basic principles I look at here will apply whatever type of coaching interests you.

This experience has been hugely enriched by working over the last five years in training other coaches and working as a supervisor with people who are studying for their Diploma in Coaching. Seeing and hearing at first hand what newer coaches struggle with has been enormously valuable. It's so easy sitting placidly in your chair, listening to the recording of a coaching session, blithely free of the need to make those split second decisions that the coach had to make. The wrong turnings are so much more obvious than when you are in that hot seat yourself. It is also humbling – sometimes hearing wonderful coaching from naturally gifted coaches who need little in the way of direction. However, mostly this experience has shown me what the common difficulties are and has given me useful insight into how to guide people towards the approaches that will work.

I am often asked what it takes to be a great coach. There is a quick answer and a slower, more thoughtful one. The quick answer is that as a great coach you have a self-confident fascination with how people achieve their potential and a wish to go with them on that journey; unbounded curiosity about people; intuition into what makes them tick; a high degree of self-knowledge; the self-discipline to keep yourself out of the way, and the ability to resist giving advice or wanting to be right.

The slower answer is that you can't become a great coach by wishing to become a great coach. You will be trying too hard, an understandable and common trap for newer coaches. Coaching well means managing a constant state of ambiguity. You have to have everything I described in the previous paragraph, yet in practice there is so much more. For instance, you have to have curiosity about people, yet know when that curiosity is coming from your agenda and not the client's. You have to have intuition and yet know when to hold it back. You have to be able to resist giving advice and yet know when it is the one time in a hundred when it is not only appropriate but also vital to do so. You have to keep yourself out of the way and yet you have to be fully there and a real presence for your client – you are not a coaching cypher, self-restrained to the point of disappearing. You have to like people and yet be able to control much of your need to have them like you because you will often have to challenge and be tough. Coaching is a serious business, and yet, as one of my colleagues once pointed out, you will continually hear boisterous laughter emanating from our coaching rooms.

This is the territory I have covered in this book. I assume little or no coaching experience but I also assume your own curiosity and commitment. I discuss and describe coaching techniques but I also put forward some ways of transcending the techniques so that your coaching can attain the seamless and flowing quality that the best coaching has. Listening to or watching wonderful coaching sounds like hearing the only conversation that could ever have happened on that topic – and yet another equally excellent coach could have had another quite different and equally effective conversation.

Anyone writing this kind of book hits the problem of how to represent client experience. I want to bring the experience of coaching to life – for both coach and client – and the best way to do this is through real case studies. Yet, as a coach, I promise my clients confidentiality. I have resolved this problem through a rigorous and wholehearted process of disguise, often blending more than one client's story while staying true to the real-life themes. When in doubt, I have checked the disguise with the original client.

I do not believe that anyone writing a book on coaching can approach it as a blank sheet. Many of the influences which have gone into writing this one have probably disappeared into an internalized set of assumptions about human behaviour, going right back to my good fortune as a postgraduate student in encountering thinkers such as Henri Tajfel, Michael Argyle and other social psychologists of the sixties. The great Kurt Lewin, with his insistence on turning theory into action-centred research, has been a constant source of thought-provoking ideas.

My thinking has also been profoundly affected by the work of Carl Jung and Isabel Myers; by the humanistic–existentialist writers and practitioners such as Viktor Frankl and Irvin Yalom; by the Gestalt school; by Carl Rogers and his Person Centred Therapy; by Transactional Analysis; and by Gerard Egan's Skilled Helper model. Neuro-Linguistic Programming (NLP), which itself developed from therapy, has been an influence. All of us in the coaching field also owe a debt to the Coaches Training Institute in California for beginning the process of synthesizing coaching practice into a workable and elegant model. I have acknowledged these and other specific sources throughout the book wherever I am aware of them, which may not be in every case. My own blend of these and other ideas is eclectic, opinionated and personal. This is not a textbook.

I have also been profoundly affected by my luck in working with excellent colleagues and associates in our firm, Management Futures, and our sister company, Coaching Futures. Together we have produced an approach of which I am tremendously proud. I particularly acknowledge the superb standards set by Phil Hayes, Jan Campbell and Julia Vaughan Smith, all of whose ideas and commitment to coaching have been a constant inspiration to me, and the support of my husband, Alan Rogers. He runs the firm in a way that keeps all that annoying admin. at bay and gives us no excuses for not doing our best coaching work.

Being a coach is to have a wonderfully privileged job. It is never less than demanding and never dull. Clients ask you to walk with them at key moments in their lives and careers, sharing their triumphs and disappointments, their vulnerabilities, their hopes, their dreams. Coach and client work on making the substantial changes that will bring about the ideal world that the client wants. Major changes can prove to be possible in a relatively short time. The discussions have an openness, candour and directness that few other conversations are likely to have. The Chinese sage who pronounced that 'What we teach is what we most want to learn' was completely correct. As a self-development process *for the coach*, you can't beat coaching and yet you will never get to the end of it. There will never be a point where you can stand back and say, 'Well, I made it – I'm now the complete and perfect coach.' That is one of many factors which will make your likely learning lifelong.

I invite you through this book to learn how utterly stretching, fascinating and enjoyable this process is.

1   What is coaching?

This question can puzzle both coaches and clients. It's the question I get asked most frequently when new organizations approach my company about potential work and it's the one that we find we must get out of the way early on our training courses for would-be coaches. There seem to be a number of reasons, many of them arising because the word *coach* is used to mean so many different things.

'Coach' may suggest a teacher earning extra money by helping your reluctant children through a loathed Maths or French exam. Or it may suggest the pushy-parent figure in tennis who also acts as coach and manager to a prodigiously talented child. More attractive images may be from other kinds of sports coaching, especially perhaps in its more modern manifestations. Here a coach may be a clever, sophisticated and highly paid guru figure whose tantalizing and competitively sought coaching secrets are eventually revealed in books and newspaper articles.

This idea is still clearly alive and well, as I discovered to my dismay when I rang one client's office to hear his colleague shout, 'John! It's your guru on the phone for you!'

If not guru, there are also associations with management consulting which may not help. For instance, I often heard it alleged as a proven fact (needless to say it was no such thing) that one former Director-General of the BBC was merely the puppet of the McKinsey consultants who had a permanent office a few doors down the corridor. 'X [one McKinsey man] works his arms and legs and another works his mouth' was how it was described. I admit to having wondered if there was truth in this scurrilous rumour when, the only time I appeared before the great man and his Board, I was surprised to find X sitting smugly at his right hand.

In some organizations, having a coach is still unusual and is reserved for very senior people with performance problems. The underlying and unflattering association is with animals who have been insufficiently socialized. The intention can therefore be frank corrective training and to need coaching is then understandably seen as being a sign of shameful failure. These clients will not want others to know that they are having coaching. One client of mine invented a convoluted and entirely fictional dental problem to explain his absences from the office while he had his sessions with me because he was the first person in his company to have a coach and felt that he could not risk the assumption being made that he was therefore a weakling.

'Is this outplacement in advance?' another client asked me suspiciously. This was at a time some years ago when I was relatively new to the field. Alas, I came to see that in her case it probably was outplacement in advance, and that her company was seeking to show that it had done everything it reasonably could before sacking her. In this case I had been manipulated by the organization as much as she.

While these are recurrent concerns and confusions, it is probably much more common to be troubled by an underlying comparison with psychotherapy and counselling. Many potential and actual clients ask worriedly about this. When coaching is described to them, they may say, with visible suspicion, 'This sounds like counselling!', implying that if coaching is just counselling in disguise, then it's not for them, thank you. In spite of much more enlightenment in the way we view mental health, there are still many hugely unhelpful clusters of associations with needing help in this area of our lives.

It's clear, for instance, that even the most apparently macho men are likely to be affected by post-traumatic stress disorder after being directly involved in wars, disasters and their aftermath. Maybe it's especially the most macho men who are affected. Yet there is still shame associated with owning up to needing help. The thrum of underlying belief is that we 'should' be able to deal with these things on our own. These are not rational concerns. They have to do with fearing the power of our own emotions, of losing control, of the veneer of grownup-ness being ripped away and, even worse, the fear of florid insanity.

Some of the older traditions of the psychotherapy trade could also be unhelpful. In the earliest years of therapy, it was common for the therapist or analyst to insist on multiple sessions every week over several years. Those were, of course, more leisured days for the typically privileged clientele of the pioneers, but this practice has also been open to the charge of creating dependency. The racy way the early protagonists wrote about their work can also easily provoke scoffing and incredulity. Both Freud and Jung, for instance, wrote case studies which are really fabulously baroque mystery stories in which the analyst is the detective-hero, the puzzle of the patient's misery solved by finding a diagnostic label such as *neuroticism* or *narcissism*.

The themes that unite all of these concerns are basic to understanding what coaching is. Take it as axiomatic that all clients, whoever they are and however grand, successful and important they are, fear two things: vulnerability and loss of control. They are right in these fears because coaching is about change and to change you do make yourself vulnerable and you may indeed not appear to have the degree of control you want over your life while the changes are happening.

A definition of coaching; the six principles

My definition is a simple one that conceals complexity.

> The coach works with clients to achieve speedy, increased and sus-
> tainable effectiveness in their lives and careers through focused
> learning. The coach's sole aim is to work with the client to achieve all
> of the client's potential – as defined by the client.

Behind this definition there are six important principles which help differ-
entiate coaching from some other apparently similar disciplines.

Principle 1: The client is resourceful

The client has the resources to resolve his or her problems. The client has not
come to be *fixed*, though there may be others in the client's world (e.g. a more
senior manager paying the bill) who believe that this is the purpose of the
coaching. Clients may share this belief sometimes: 'Tell me what to do!' Or, 'If
you were me, what would you do?' Only the client can really know what to do
because only the client knows the full story and only the client can actually
implement the action and live with the results.

This does not preclude the coach from offering useful information, but it
is the client's choice whether or not to use it.

Principle 2: The coach's role is to spring loose the client's resourcefulness

It follows from the first belief that the role of the coach is not advice giving.
When you give advice you imply that you know best and that the client is a
lesser person. When you give advice you will invariably get sucked into the
'Why don't you' ... 'Yes, but' game:

> Why don't you give up smoking?
> Yes, I agree I should but I can't do it yet ...

Advice giving also leads to dependency – the opposite of what you are trying
to achieve as a coach. There is more about this in Chapter 2. The coach's role
is to ask the penetrating questions which take clients into territory they have
never previously considered. In doing this, clients will build on their own
resourcefulness.

Principle 3: Coaching addresses the whole person – past, present and future

Coaches working in the corporate field sometimes see their role as strictly being about work. I believe that this is a mistake. My experience is that difficulties in the professional life of the client are usually paralleled by difficulties in the personal parts of their lives. Also, relationship patterns formed in early life always have a bearing. Coaching is not psychoanalysis, but unless you know a little about early life and issues in current life beyond work, you are unlikely to be able to work with the client as fully as is possible when you and the client take a more rounded view.

Principle 4: The client sets the agenda

This is where there is a difference with teaching. There is no set agenda with coaching. The coach may indeed have a mental model of, for instance, effective leadership, but if this is not a concern for the client, then it should not appear on the agenda of the sessions. The agenda starts with the client. Where the client agenda is exhausted, then the coaching must stop, even if only temporarily.

Principle 5: The coach and the client are equals

The coach and the client work together in a partnership of equals. The model is colleague–colleague because it is based on total respect. Suspending judgement is essential. Where you cannot respect a client for some reason, or where the client does not respect you, it is unlikely that your coaching can be effective and you must end or not start it.

Principle 6: Coaching is about change and action

Clients come to coaching because they want something to change. Essentially they want to be more effective. The role of the coach is to help them achieve this increased effectiveness. It follows therefore that you cannot coach a client who does not want to change – so third party referrals should always be regarded with initial caution. Equally, if a client says he or she wants to change, but seems to be unable or unwilling to do so in practice, then the coaching may have to stop – or you could consider referring the client to another coach.

In our practice, we represent this whole approach to coaching in diagrammatic form, as in Figure 1.1.

My assumption is that as coaches we are dealing with both the being self and the doing self.

The being self is the inner personality and the sum total of the experi-

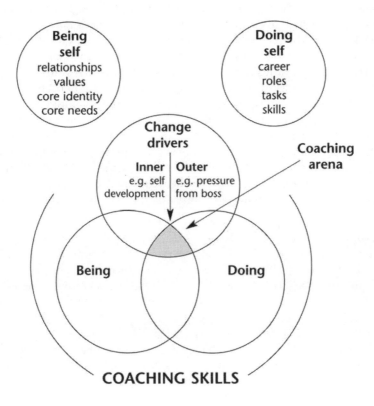

Figure 1.1 A model of coaching

ences, attitudes and roles that we play or have played in our lives. It is about core values, who we are rather than what we do.

The doing self is the externally focused person with tasks to accomplish and skills with which to do them. It is usually the doing self which initially presents for coaching. For instance, 'Please help me become more effective in my work'; 'Show me how to run a meeting better'; 'Help me write a proper CV', and so on.

The request for coaching is always triggered by change. If there is no change then it is unlikely that you have a genuine client. The change could be internally triggered – a being self area. Birthdays with a nought or a five on the end may well be cause for reappraisal of life and direction. So may a serious illness or a major change in personal status such as marriage, having children, the death of a parent or a divorce. Alternatively, or often in addition, there is externally imposed change. The organization may be losing or gaining staff, the client's role may have changed through promotion or restructuring. Skills that seemed perfectly adequate before may not look so impressive now. There may be a new boss who demands a different kind of performance with consequent pressure for change in individuals. The client may have actually lost his or her job or be threatened with doing so.

The crossover area in the middle creates the agenda for coaching.

This is why it is essential to take a whole-life perspective and to accept the client's initial agenda as merely the starting point for the coaching. The inexperienced coach often fails to act on the instinct which tells him or her that this is the correct way to go. As a new coach myself I was sometimes far too overawed by the seniority of my clients to ask them what felt then like impertinent questions about their backgrounds and childhoods. I quickly discovered what a mistake this was. One example will do.

Peter

Peter was referred to me by his HR Director. She had grave doubts about whether his promotion had been the right decision. Her description of him was that he was 'a very clever but shouty bully' and would not last long in his new senior role if he continued to use the tactics that were all too familiar to his previous staff.

We had two sessions before I realized that his conversation was full of 'musts' and 'shoulds'. Curiosity aroused, I did at last ask the questions about childhood and about his current personal life. Peter then readily told me that he was the elder son of famous, overpowering and very successful parents. Growing up, he had the impression that nothing he could do would ever be good enough but you had to keep on trying because one day you might get it right. You must never admit to a mistake because that showed your soft side and if you did that you would be attacked. The only way you could get people to do things was fighting constantly, keeping them up to the mark through pressure – the way his own outstanding scholastic and early work career had been managed by his parents and teachers. He had a happy though occasionally turbulent marriage.

I did not believe my role was to be his psychotherapist – there was no exploration of the all-too-evident damage his childhood had done to him. However, Peter himself quickly made the connections between this experience and his current behaviour. Previously he had assumed that shouting and putting people right was the only way you could get them to do things. Uncovering, naming and challenging those core assumptions created the turning point. My work with him was about linking the tender and patient behaviour he was able to show at home with some high-quality observation of how other managers at work got better results with less effort. I will not claim, and nor would he, that he is a reformed character, but he now operates with a great deal more subtlety and a great deal less negative energy.

What happens in a coaching session: an overview

Typically coach and client will meet on the coach's premises for a series of hour-and-a-half or two-hour sessions over a period of a few months. The most common pattern for me is six two-hour sessions over a four-month period. In the United States, most coaching seems to be delivered in hour-long or half-hour sessions by telephone and at more frequent intervals.

The client comes to the first session with a suggested list of goals for the work. Typically goals take two forms:

- *Dilemmas*: which of two or three paths should I follow?
- *Puzzles*: how can I make something or someone more comfortable, work better, be more focused, get past a block?

Examples might be:

- improve an important relationship;
- manage my time better;
- make more money;
- decide what I want to do as the next step in my career;
- tackle performance problems in my team;
- restructure my organization;
- learn how to make more convincing presentations;
- acquire the skills I need in a new role;
- launch myself into a freelance career;
- tackle the stress in my life;
- get a better balance between work and home.

Normally there will be two or three topics in each session. The client will leave with a plan of action around each of his or her goals. The first part of the next session reviews how the 'homework' has gone. This is an obvious point, but easy to miss: the changes themselves happen outside and between sessions.

As coaching grows in popularity and familiarity, it is developing a number of distinct branches.

Life coaches concentrate on whole-life dilemmas: personal relationships, life balance, planning for the future. Life coaching is now developing its own distinct branches, and we can expect this to continue as more coaches enter the market. For instance, I know life coaches who specialize in relationship coaching; relationship coaches who only deal with widowed or divorced women. There are coaches whose client niche is women returning to work after having had children and others whose niche is health and fitness. Some life coaches have also successfully blurred boundaries with executive coaching, specializing, for instance, in coaching small-business owners or professional service firms such as solicitors or architects.

Sports coaches increasingly work from the core coaching principles I describe in this book, an approach often described, confusingly, in the popular press as 'sports psychology'. They may work with individuals or with teams to improve sporting performance.

Executive coaches. Their work is generally concentrated on the most senior executives in large or medium-sized organizations. Clients expect familiarity with and track record in management. Potential topics for coaching include everything in the life-coaching agenda plus any and every aspect of running organizations. As with life coaching, executive coaching is also developing its own niches – new leaders, retirement planning for older leaders, stress and burnout, finance, careers, finding a new job after redundancy, interview preparation, presentation skills, voice, image, strategy, and many others. Fees for executive coaching are generally higher than fees for life coaching.

Differences between coaching and other disciplines

Coaching and psychiatry

A psychiatrist is a doctor trained in treating severe mental illnesses. Entry to the profession is strictly controlled by licensing after lengthy training, and practice is monitored and audited. If your licence is withdrawn, you cannot practise. Continuous updating is mandatory.

You might see a psychiatrist if your GP believes you could benefit from stabilizing medication prescribed by a specialist or if for some reason you felt you had temporarily lost your way in some form that felt serious. Psychiatrists also deal with disabling forms of mental illness such as schizophrenia, severe post-natal depression, drug and alcohol dependency or a chronic depression. Forensic psychiatrists specialize in people whose illnesses or personality disorders involve danger to themselves or others.

Successful therapy often involves drugs as well as a 'talking cure' where the patient would typically be referred to a psychotherapist. However respectfully psychiatrists treat their patients, and the best ones do, there is little doubt about who has the power. Even when psychiatrists refer to their patients as *clients*, and increasingly they do, the model is overtly medical. The patient – a telling word – is sick and the helper is a doctor whose role is to cure sickness. The doctor has the power of superior knowledge, the power to make a diagnosis, the power to prescribe drugs, and, in some cases, the legal power to restrain and lock up the patient.

As a distantly related discipline, psychiatry is about as far from coaching as it is possible to be.

Coaching and psychotherapy

The borderline with psychotherapy is probably the one that worries coaches most.

In Colin Feltham and Ian Horton's excellent *Handbook of Counselling and Psychotherapy* the activity is defined as

> ... addressing psychological and psychosomatic problems and change, including deep and prolonged human suffering, situational dilemmas and crises and developmental needs, and aspirations towards the realization of human potential.

Where there are persistent issues of self-esteem, unresolved grief, anxiety, depression, anger or severely dysfunctional behaviour and beliefs, then a psychotherapist may be able to help.

There is a huge spectrum of approaches to psychotherapy and a number of rival 'schools' using different models. Some people in the field claim that there are as many as 400 different schools and approaches. This probably accounts for the widely varying effectiveness reported.

My own experience reflects this in a small way. A few years ago a personal crisis left me needing psychotherapeutic help. I could not shake off the feelings of overwhelming anxiety which haunted me for months afterwards. My world seemed to be dissolving. In seeking psychotherapeutic help, I experienced first a very poor and then a profoundly helpful experience of therapy.

My doctor referred me first to 'Dr X' who operated out of an elegant private medical practice in the City. I probably alienated him from the start by asking if his doctorate was a medical one. This was a bit naughty as I already knew it wasn't but I was by now annoyed by the grandiosity of the way I had been kept waiting and treated as a petitioner. He sat at a world domination desk, sideways on, while I sat on a very much lower sofa on what felt like the very far side of the large room. It was a smart, black leather sofa, but in sitting so much lower I couldn't help but feel that I was meant to be literally sitting at his feet. He asked me about my 'symptoms' (sic) and dispensed a good deal of advice, all of which I had heard before. He talked about his 'patients', implying of course that we were sick. Perhaps I was, but I did not go back.

Instead, I sought help from Sue, a fellow coach who also operates as a therapist. Her steady, calm exploration of feelings and mutual exploration of practical strategies for dealing with them were just what I needed. If proof were required that a high price is no guarantee of high quality, her charges were about a third of those demanded by 'Dr X'.

Where is the boundary?
Some psychotherapists consider that there is no boundary with coaching. They deliberately position their 'offer' to clients as one where they can work flexibly across whatever boundary there is. For these people, coaching is the new psychotherapy. They consider that it is a respectable way for clients to ask for help without having to own up to anything being askew where their mental health is concerned. They also like the freedom that their double discipline gives. If and when a deep-rooted issue appears, they can ask their clients if they want to explore it in psychotherapeutic style. Among the associates in my firm there are some coaches who also work as psychotherapists, making a clear distinction between the two activities, and others who work as coach-psychotherapists making no such distinction. They will tell you that being able to toggle between the two causes neither them nor their clients any problems. These colleagues have no difficulty endorsing the six principles described above.

Other therapists are definitely at a different end of the psychotherapeutic spectrum. You would see them undertaking activities which would make most coaches want to keep well away – not necessarily because of doubts about the value of the activities in themselves but because of a feeling that if you go there you need to be very sure of what you are doing. This might include activities such as catharsis, rebirthing, regressive hypnosis, tackling phobias through progressive desensitization, looking in detail at early life and especially at relationships with parents and siblings.

The coach needs to know about earlier life and the impact of these important relationships, but does not dwell on them. If they need to be dwelt on, then you will refer the client to a trusted psychotherapist.

The contrast with coaching
In general when you compare psychotherapy and counselling with coaching you will tend to see a number of differences. The most important is the probable mental state of the client. A client for psychotherapy or counselling is far more likely to be in a distressed state than a client for coaching. Feltham and Horton's definition, quoted above, refers to 'deep and prolonged human suffering'. Many psychotherapists still refer to their clients as *patients*. Where this is the case, the underlying model is clearly the medical one of doctor–patient.

By contrast, I, in common with all the other coaches I know, assume that my clients are functioning normally and have robust mental health unless proved otherwise. I am looking to work with my clients on functional rather than on severe psychological problems. All schools of psychotherapy stress that therapy is a partnership. I believe that in practice this critical difference in assumed mental state will almost inevitably lead to a profound imbalance in power which makes a genuine relationship of equals a lot less likely in a therapist–client relationship than in a coach–client relationship. For instance, psychotherapists may be motivated by a sincere and profound wish to *help*, and by feeling pity for the suffering of their clients. They will describe their work as a *helping* discipline. The helper, almost by definition, feels as if he or she is in a stronger place than the helpee. Coaches are more likely to describe what they do as *working with* a client.

With executive coaching there are some further tweaks on the power relationship which are significantly different from therapy. These coaching clients are generally both well paid and powerful people and they – or their employers – are paying premium fees for their coaching. By contrast, therapy and counselling may sometimes be provided free or very cheaply to the user (for instance through the National Health Service, a voluntary agency or an employer through an Employee Assistance Scheme) and are potentially therefore subject to the peculiarly corrosive tendency to see such users as petitioners, lucky to get their rationed treatment.

Not all, but much psychotherapy looks to the past to explain the present, and the therapist is interested in answering the question 'Why?' Insight into cause and effect and the origins of emotions is a strong feature of some (though not all) schools of therapy. The coach may look briefly to the past but is more interested in the client's present and future and is probably more concerned with the question 'What?', as in 'What to do?' than in the question 'Why?'

There are also some differences in practicalities and mechanics. Coaches will see clients for an average of six two-hour sessions, probably spread over a period of months. Therapists will tend to suggest seeing their clients for a 'fifty-minute hour' every week. This gives a distinctly different timbre to the experience – for both therapist and client. Coaching may rightly be accused of being superficial by contrast.

There still are many psychotherapists who work with clients over periods of years with weekly therapy in the belief that this is the only way to achieve real depth. The plus here is the intensity and trust that can be created; the minus is the possibility of mutual dependency, much rarer when the relationship is more fleeting. Pressures of time and money mean that so-called 'brief therapy' is now much more common. However, 'brief' in psychotherapeutic terms still seems to mean that the therapist expects a longer commitment to the process than would be usual for a coach. Interestingly, acceptance seems to be growing among some therapists that impressive results can be achieved in only five or six hours, and that this is what some clients prefer.

As a further slant on how the two disciplines may be more similar than they appear on the surface, I, like some other coaches, also offer year-long, unrestricted access. This service, to a minority of clients, is aimed essentially at those just starting a new job which they know they are likely to find taxing.

It is also true that some coaching relationships can continue for a long time: one client astonished me recently by telling me that he and his former coach had been meeting every six weeks for ten years. While I do not have any clients with whom I have worked for such an extended period, I do have several who have come to me on and off for six years – signing on again for another run of six sessions when they are facing the challenge of yet another new role.

A properly qualified psychotherapist has university-based training over several years, submits to regular supervision from another therapist and is registered with one of the many bodies which trains and licenses. These controls are helping to raise standards. However, currently anyone may call themselves a psychotherapist in the UK and even if you are flung out of membership, you could still practise. Interestingly, in this field, it is still only the psychiatrists – that is, the professionals who are dealing with the most seriously ill people – who are obliged to be licensed in order to practise at all.

Chartered Psychologists may also do work which is very similar to psychotherapy. There are several relevant sub-specialisms here including Occupational Psychologist, Counselling Psychologist and Clinical Psychologist. To call yourself by these titles you must have a degree in psychology and have passed a number of other qualifying hurdles in order to be registered with the British Psychological Society.

None of these restrictions applies to coaching and at the moment it looks unlikely that they ever will.

Coaching and counselling

Counselling is sometimes described as the 'shallow end' of psychotherapy, though it is also sometimes used as a synonym for psychotherapy. Confusingly, career coaching is often still referred to as career counselling, even though, as with coaching, its clients are assumed to be in a stable mental state.

As with psychotherapy, heroic efforts have been made over the last forty years to control the quality of counselling through better training and through accreditation. However, in practice there are even fewer barriers to waking up one morning and describing yourself as a counsellor than there are to calling yourself a psychotherapist without benefit of training. For instance, I have heard people claim to have been 'trained' on the basis of simply attending a one-day course.

You would be unlikely to get a job as a counsellor at your local GP's surgery or as a full-time workplace counsellor without accreditation, but you could well work in an unpaid role for one of the many self-help groups which need skilled people to deal with distressed clients facing up to bereavement or serious illness. The Samaritans wisely call such people 'befrienders' and devote considerable effort in training them, emphasizing the limits of the role.

Counselling and psychotherapy are often used as interchangeable terms, but by custom and practice the word counselling seems now more likely to mean a short-term engagement around a particular crisis. Often, the client will have been managing perfectly well until the onset of this crisis.

Typical examples would be trauma counsellors who work with survivors of a rail crash; relationship counsellors who work with couples (the 'marriage guidance' area); spiritual counselling offered by religious groups; police officers who counsel rape survivors or the families of missing children; specialist nurses who counsel people newly diagnosed with life-threatening illness; or priests who counsel the bereaved.

More than any of the other approaches described in this chapter, counselling has come to carry with it an emphasis on the powerful comfort of non-judgemental listening in the moment. This means talking it through extensively, without either counsellor or client feeling any of the obligation to *action* which both coaching and psychotherapy may imply. Where action is encouraged – as it may be for instance with couple counselling – then the process may be a more consciously psychotherapeutic one.

The role of theory

This is a potentially confusing field. There are many possible entry points to the different professional roles, different training paths, and the same words used to mean often very different things or different words used to mean the same things.

Psychology emerged as a branch of philosophy. Psychotherapy was originated by doctors who were psychiatrists. It was presented originally as a science. These early beginnings are still telling. Essentially psychotherapy and counselling are part of the health sector, whereas executive coaching is a branch of management development, and life coaching an approach to personal development closely paralled by the popularity of the many thousands of self-help books. Depending on the type of therapy or counselling, there are also some other important differences. It is probably no coincidence that the early Austrian and Swiss pioneers of psychotherapy began their work in the late nineteenth century when religious belief was breaking down at an accelerating rate.

Psychoanalysis – the earliest form of psychotherapy – was one response to the big philosophical questions that this raised because it appeared to be offering a substitute belief system which could explain and then tackle human distress. Most of the serious training in counselling and psychotherapy involves a great deal of exposure to the theory of at least one of the great schools of psychotherapeutic thought, some of them complex and demanding in the frameworks they offer to explain human behaviour. Many of these quite consciously tackle the biggest issue of all: what, if anything, is the meaning of life? Others draw on ideas which seem close to those of the world's great religions. For instance, Carl Jung describes what he calls 'individuation' – becoming the person you were destined to be before events – or life – intervened.

At their most extreme, some of the theoreticians in this field appear to be more interested in fitting the patient to the theory of the particular school of therapy than in fitting the therapy to the patient. At the moment, the only comparable phenomenon in the coaching field is the many rival theories of organization behaviour, and you could be a perfectly adequate coach without ever needing to tackle those. Coaching, by and large, is a more pragmatic trade drawing on borrowed theory. Theory therefore tends to play a much smaller role in the current training of coaches. In coaching currently, practice leads theory. Depending on your point of view, you can see this either as a strength or as a weakness which needs addressing. Perhaps it is both.

The debt of coaching to psychotherapy

Coaching owes a huge and largely unacknowledged debt to many other disciplines, but particularly to psychotherapy and counselling. In our wish to establish ourselves as significantly different, we in the coaching field can often come across as ignorant, simplistic, mean and grudging where psychotherapy is concerned. I have been guilty of this myself.

There are some trends in the writing in both disciplines where an unwholesome kind of competition seems to be evolving. According to the rules of this game, therapists writing about coaching accuse it of superficiality and psychological crudity. This can undoubtedly be true: an ineffective coach will often miss the clues, both major and minor, that almost any psychotherapist would pick up.

Now that coaching is growing up, we can expect more assaults on the same lines. A light-hearted piece by a *Financial Times* journalist a few years ago mocked the coach's trade. The article described a fictional coach earning a fortune, sitting on her yacht enjoying uninterrupted sunbathing while giving her client platitudinous advice by phone. Steven Berglas, a psychotherapist, wrote a heartfelt attack on coaching in the *Harvard Business Review*, portentously entitled 'The very real dangers of executive coaching' (June 2002), comparing skilful psychotherapy with clumsy coaching. Naturally, the good psychotherapy came off better. Similarly, coaches writing about psychotherapy can often over-emphasize its shortcomings, concentrating, for instance, on the tiny minority of therapists who abuse their clients. Therapy has been around as a profession for more than a hundred years, so naturally there has been a longer time for examples of bad behaviour to accumulate. Coaching, too, is bound to produce its black sheep in time.

However, the truth is that without the early work of the psychoanalysts such as Freud and Adler, and the later twentieth-century pioneers of counselling like Carl Rogers and Gerard Egan, there would be no coaching. Even the minority of approaches which appear to come from management and organization development in fact mostly have their origin in therapy of one kind or another. For instance, team coaching descends in a straight line from 'T' groups – a therapeutic intervention – and thence from the National Training Laboratories in the United States after the Second World War.

Very many of the approaches I draw on in this book were first developed in therapeutic settings. For instance, to name just a few, 'empty chair' work is a feature of Gestalt therapy; catharsis is a technique described and used by Arthur Janov; tackling limiting self-beliefs is a special feature of Rational Emotive Behaviour Therapy. Coaches may remain largely unaware of the origins of these approaches because they have learnt them from others who had already turned them into second generation versions, but the parent technique is usually still visible.

When do you know that a client needs psychotherapy or counselling rather than coaching?

Coaching and psychotherapy are not necessarily either/ors. Clients can benefit from both processes happening in tandem or serially. An example would be this client:

Andrew

Andrew was a partner in an international accounting practice. He had just been promoted and now had to lead a significantly larger group of staff than before. He had attended one management training course which had not proved useful. He told me that he had always found it difficult to keep stress under control but now it was intruding into his life in a way that he found unmanageable.

After a few sessions it was clear to both Andrew and me that he needed two separate strands of intervention. One was to establish his team leadership through a set of new behaviours including more effective delegation and a more authoritative personal presence. I could work with him on this. The other was to look at why he set himself such impossibly high demands in every single aspect of his life resulting in chronic and ever-present feelings of panic and anxiety. This was psychotherapeutic territory beyond my competence and I suggested a colleague skilled in working with these conditions.

Andrew began the work with my colleague and we suspended our coaching while it was happening – his suggestion. After ten meetings for successful therapy, we returned to the leadership issues. We also had a useful handover session, again at his suggestion, where the three of us discussed progress and also the necessary linkages between the therapy and the coaching.

Here are some other examples:

Maureen

Maureen had lost her job and her former employer was willing to pay for five two-hour sessions. The request presented as something ultra-familiar: please help review my career choices so that I can get another job.

We have a well-honed suite of possible approaches on which clients can draw in such circumstances. At the first session Maureen got well into her story, describing persistent and gross sexual abuse in virtually all of her jobs, plus failed attempts at whistle-blowing to expose corruption, incompetence and fraud in the highest places. To my dismay I found myself increasingly doubting that any of it was true. There were many signals of glaring incongruity. I had already agreed that I would do only the first session as she had requested help from a colleague whose professional background was similar to her own.

At the time this colleague and I had the same professional supervisor. I brought this case to the mutual supervisor, worried that I was being unfair to a client who could have been telling the truth in spite of the apparent unlikelihood that this was so. He immediately told me that my colleague had brought exactly the same issue in her most recent session and on just the same grounds.

I could not have worked successfully with this client. A skilled therapist could very possibly have worked with her, raising the possibility of and then working on the probable fantasies, regarding such robust lying as fascinating material for the sessions. I, however, felt out of my depth as it seemed highly likely that Maureen had at least some severe underlying mental health problems and certainly needed a different kind of help from the sort I can provide.

I now trust my own instinct because with experience I can see that it has always been alerted early in the process.

Josette

Josette had been referred to me by her boss, a British manager running an aid agency operation in a third-world country. Unusually, I had no opportunity to get a briefing from him before my meeting with the client, in London for a conference. Josette was the first locally appointed person to do her job, and the first woman to hold the post. She told me she was struggling to do her job and wanted some help.

Within ten minutes I had been obliged to halt the conversation several times. Josette spoke in a whisper and I simply couldn't hear her. I had to draw my chair so close to hers that our knees were practically touching. Her story involved betrayals in literally every aspect of her life, starting with abandonment by her parents. In the few months she had been in her job she described the office as being full of enemies specifically targeting her reputation and sanity. Her partner had left her and she had no friends. She said she had no self-confidence and misery pervaded her life. The impression of impotence was palpable: she seemed entirely in the grip of feeling that she was everyone's victim. At the end of our first hour together, I told her very gently that coaching was not the place to start, but that therapy might be.

I knew without any doubt that I did not have either the skill or will to help her tackle such overwhelming feelings of helplessness, noticing also that her impact on me was to create exactly matching feelings of powerlessness and anger. Rarely has the clock moved so slowly as it did in that session. As her therapist I might have been able to use this data 'in the moment'. As a coach, I knew I would not and could not.

There is no one-size-fits-all way to pinpoint when a coaching client needs psychotherapy, but these are some rules of thumb that I find useful:

- The client cries: frequently, intensely and uncontrollably.
- The client returns over and over again to one relationship – typically with a parent, parent-figure or sibling.
- One major fear appears to dominate the client's life – e.g. abandonment, ever-present dread of complete catastrophe, rejection, loss of control.
- When the client tells his or her life story it features a major trauma. Examples from my own practice include: living through a major house fire; being the cause of a fatal road accident; being the apparent cause of the death of a sibling; childhood as a refugee; a mother leaving children behind after moving into a new relationship; being the survivor of child abuse; an entirely unanticipated divorce after a long marriage; the theft and destruction of a PhD thesis by a trusted colleague.
- The client is unable to move on from one incident – everything seems to be seen through the prism of that event. Typically the event will involve loss of some kind.
- The client frequently resorts to 'if only ... '
  - he/she/they would change
  - that hadn't happened
  - I hadn't done that
  - I wasn't the way I am
  - I didn't look the way I do
- There are serious issues of self-esteem which keep recurring.
- A bereavement has never been acknowledged and worked through.

- Inability to accept personal responsibility: victim-thinking has become a way of life.
- The client describes symptoms of frequent mental dysfunction which intrude significantly into everyday life: e.g. depression, anxiety, panic attacks, agoraphobia, obsessive-compulsive disorder, hypochondria.
- Denial of 'reality' – the client lives in a fantasy world.
- Substance misuse: drink, eating problems, drugs.
- Other kinds of addictive behaviour: e.g. gambling, compulsive risk taking, sexual promiscuity.
- The client behaves in troubling ways with you – e.g. heavy flirting, displays of anger, constantly fails to turn up for appointments.

Note that all of this behaviour could have other, more innocent explanations, but the more of them that are present, the more likely it is that you are in therapeutic territory. Sometimes I can feel as if I am probably in therapeutic territory, but I am uncertain. I may get this feeling when a client can make behavioural changes, some of them transforming, and yet his or her overall pattern of functioning still seems stuck in some significant way that is difficult to grasp.

Overall, probably the most important single indicator is your own feeling that *you are out of your depth or that something is wrong.* Trust that feeling.

Handling the conversation about referral

- Tell the client that you feel at the limits of your skills. Beware of appearing to blame the client for his or her problem.
- Stress your respect for the client and your desire to help.
- Explain the differences between psychotherapy and coaching; describe how psychotherapy can help.
- Ask for the client's reactions.
- Offer to refer the client to a trusted psychotherapist. Make it clear it is the client's choice to follow it up. Ideally, offer three possible choices, explaining the general approaches and styles of each therapist.
- Clarify the boundaries of the future coaching relationship.
- Keep stressing your support for the client.
- If you write a letter of referral to the therapist, copy the letter to the client.
- If you both agree that the coaching should cease, offer to contact the client at an appropriate future date for feedback on his or her progress.

It is also striking that many clients previously recommended for counselling or psychotherapeutic help might now be better off with coaching. Here is an example:

Iain

Iain was struggling with an increasing distaste for his work, running a franchised operation under the aegis of a company he had grown to dislike. He found himself testy and irritable with his partner, Sally – also a business partner – and knew that the relationship was under serious strain. Weariness and too much time spent in the pub were leaving him too tired to play football on Saturdays with his 8-year-old son. With Sally pregnant again, the need to earn a decent living for the family seemed overwhelming, yet he was beginning to hate every day he spent at work and to feel that he was a failure in every aspect of his life. Friends urged him to go to his doctor, suggesting that perhaps he was depressed and that Prozac might help, or that the doctor might refer him to a therapist/counsellor.

So far, then, both Iain and his friends and family know there is a problem. They have looked to a medical model for help. By this stage, Iain is so desperate that he is willing to take up any suggestion. His GP tells him there is a four-month waiting list for free counselling, but also sensibly spots that Iain is not depressed, only confused, worried and angry. This GP has been contacted by a local coach and is now referring people to her. These clients pay for themselves. After five sessions with his coach, Iain has worked out a new career plan, has reverted to being an occasional social drinker, has repaired his relationship with Sally and his son and describes himself as 'a "new man" – so energized it's unbelievable!'

Coaching and mentoring

This is an easier one.

The word *mentor* comes from the Greek myth of the king who asked Mentor, an older, wiser man, to look after his son during the king's absence. Pure mentoring still has this implication and is how the word is most often used. Typically, a mentor is a colleague in the same or a parallel organization who is not in a line management relationship with the mentee. Mentoring has sometimes been described as 'being a career friend', someone who knows the ropes in an organization and can act as sponsor and patron. That being said, there are many people who are commercial providers of what they call mentoring where there is no pre-existing knowledge of the organization.

An effective mentor will be able to endorse my six principles without difficulty and my definition of coaching could apply equally well to mentoring as there is nothing in it which says you should be working as a coach-mentor full time or in a paid capacity. Some organizations have introduced mentoring schemes, partnering mentees with mentors from inside the organization, normally people approaching the last ten years of their careers. I have noticed how often these relationships break down, usually as a result of a mixture of the following:

- chronic misunderstanding on both sides about obligations and expectations;
- the relationship is not a priority for either side;
- the mentee and mentor don't like or respect each other;
- the mentee is doing it because it seems like an obligation, not out of any wish to learn or change;
- the mentor is inadequately trained or has little natural aptitude for the role;
- the mentor sees his or her role as being to pass on the fruits of his/her experience.

All these, of course, are also common reasons that a coaching or therapeutic relationship can go wrong. For an amusing view of all of this, consult David Clutterbuck's articles, 'Twelve habits of the toxic mentor and twelve habits of the toxic mentee', on: www.coachingnetwork.org.uk.

In practice, mentoring does have the overtones of implying that the older and wiser mentors will be passing on their advice and also that they may be able to act as patron to the mentee. Where this is so, mentoring is a different activity from coaching – and, to my mind, a less effective one. Where coaching principles apply, mentoring and coaching are synonyms for the same process. In practice, *mentoring* is coming to seem like an older-fashioned word for *coaching*.

Coaching and training

If coaching is about learning, and it is, then how is it different from training? There are some major and some subtle differences.

A trainer has a set curriculum and rightly presents as an expert in his or her subject. Some trainers behave more like lecturers than coaches, doing a lot more of the talking than any coach would consider appropriate. There may be externally agreed standards involving accreditation or assessment which the trainee is expected to reach and on which by implication the trainer is assessed. So for instance, in schools, Standard Assessment Tests (SATs) *grade* the pupil but *assess* the school and its teachers against nationally agreed norms. On many training courses, the participants have been enrolled against their will whereas coaching is far more likely to be voluntary.

A coach definitely has no set curriculum and would rarely talk for more than a few minutes at a time, but may be an expert in his or her subject – for instance, negotiating, leadership, life-planning or human relationships generally. There is no equivalent of SATs in coaching. Coaches are rarely assessed other than at the beginnings of their coaching careers when increasingly they may undertake a qualification.

That being said, there are certainly times when you might see a coach acting a little like a trainer. Here is an example.

> **Jane**
>
> Jane was the newly appointed Chief Executive of a major hospital at the time she signed on to work with me. We looked at her presenting issues of how to manage a chronically over-busy life. This quickly established that she had already done her previous organization's time management course and knew that her problems were deeper than how to use an electronic diary more effectively.
>
> Further conversation revealed a number of hot spots: for instance, how to say no without causing offence and how to delegate. There are established protocols on how to do both these things. The trainer's answer would be to launch immediately into explanations of both. The coach's answer is to use his or her knowledge of these protocols as the template for the coaching discussion but to hold back from immediate advice. With Jane, for instance, I asked a number of questions about what was happening on the occasions when she *was* able to say no easily and effectively. There always are at least some examples of success, even if they are infrequent. This demonstrated that in the right circumstances she could set her own standards perfectly well; it was how to stick to them all the time that was the issue. This was what we focused on. I then flung some quick-fire role-played challenges at her, inviting her to use her own newly established 'rules' with me. The aim here was to embed the new rules through practice – something most trainers would also consider desirable.
>
> As she left, I arranged for her to have our standard handouts on both topics, just for reference. Again, this is something like what might happen on a training course. The difference is that the client had already established and endorsed her own procedures. If there were useful elements that our protocols might have added, I would have mentioned them, but, as so often happens, there were not. The client herself had already identified them.

As with mentoring, training is far more effective as a learning process when it proceeds from coaching principles.

Coaching as a line management activity

Interest in coaching as an alternative to command and control is growing. This is because in a non-authoritarian society, people reject control and control, i.e. the 'telling' mode, is very limited in its effectiveness. To become an employer-of-choice, it is clear that offering development is a considerable incentive: effective development is at the heart of innovation and coaching is one of the best ways to grow innovation and shared skill. Finally, experience shows that coaching works.

Here coaching is an approach to performance management which emphasizes the manager's role as *developer* rather than as *controller*. Line managers use a *coaching approach*, encouraging team members to develop self-confidence, resourcefulness, skills, belief in the value of their own decision making and so on through a process of accelerated learning. However, the line management responsibility puts a significantly different slant on how the line manager coach can work. For instance, it is always more difficult to promise confidentiality, encourage or expect complete disclosure, set aside your own considerations or remain detached from the possible outcomes.

Examples:

- An extreme one: direct reports are not very likely to confess to drug or alcohol misuse to a line manager, but they may with an external coach.
- Line managers may feel obliged to report such misuse if a direct report makes such a confession but an external coach would not.
- Managers may feel more compunction about working on personal issues (i.e. life rather than career) because it may feel and be intrusive.
- Line managers have their own targets to meet and may feel unable to take a detached view of a direct report's performance.

When done well, all the approaches I have described in this chapter have a great deal in common. When done badly all also fall into similar mistakes. So there are mentors who act indistinguishably from the best coaches and coaches who can fall into the traps of the worst mentors. On the positive side, there are coaches who do psychotherapy without labelling it as therapy and therapists who might as well be coaches. To be successful, all depend on respect for the client – the foundation stone of which is what the great Carl Rogers, one of the most significant thinkers of the twentieth century in this area, called 'unconditional positive regard'. All call on the practitioner to create and sustain a high degree of rapport and to act from the highest ethical standards. All need an extraordinary degree of self-awareness and self-management. All demand extraordinary levels of listening and questioning ability plus the capability to challenge appropriately – and an infinite curiosity about and interest in people.

2 Creating trust: foundation values and practices for coaches

A coaching conversation is unlike most other discussions. It involves an unusually high level of trust and candour on both sides. Creating and sustaining this unusual environment is what gives coaching its power. To do it as a coach involves abandoning many of the normal conventions of conversation in our society and replacing them with high-level, alternative skills, all of them about communicating acceptance and respect. In this chapter I look at some foundation principles that are necessary to create trust, returning to the topic in more detail in Chapter 8.

Coaching and advice

The word *coaching* is blessedly free from the supposed taint of mental difficulties associated with psychotherapy. However, it is also thoroughly saturated in assumptions made because of its presumed likeness to sports coaching. Both novice coaches and novice clients may still believe, perhaps at an unconscious level, that somehow the coaching process is about being told what to do, either because the coach actually knows best or because the coach thinks he or she knows best.

The concept of choice in coaching

One of the ground precepts of coaching that I described in Chapter 1 (page 7) is a belief that the client is resourceful. Underneath this belief are the fundamental principles of choice and self-responsibility. Making these principles explicit has been the great gift of mainstream twentieth-century psychology to the world. They are the foundation, for instance, of the Transactional Analysis (TA) school: that whatever misery and dysfunction there is in your life, you can transform yourself through conscious choice. TA has become a huge popular success, offering a structured way of understanding interpersonal relationships through books like Eric Berne's best-seller *Games People Play* (1964). Its underlying assumption is similar to many in other schools of psychological thinking: human beings, uniquely among animals, are able to look to the future, therefore we are not the prisoners of our past.

The American psychologist Will Schutz, the developer of the personality questionnaire FIRO-B™, also skilfully articulated these principles, though from a different perspective. Schutz took the concept of choice to its ultimate in his book *The Truth Option*:

> I choose my whole life and I always have. I choose my behaviour, my feelings, my thoughts, my illnesses, my body, my reactions, and my spontaneity.

Schutz's philosophy was that choice is not a moral concept, only one which has consequences. If you assume that you can make choices then you take responsibility for your life. You bring areas that are unconscious into the areas of consciousness. For instance, you may feel afraid of your own violent or sexual feelings but your overtly expressed values do not allow you to admit this to yourself. You conceal your fears in hearty condemnation of people who do indulge their violence or sexuality.

Similarly, if you express fear of your boss or a colleague, there may be no objective reason at all for the fear; your real fear is of being unable to cope. If you see others as the cause of your fear then you will spend a lot of time and energy criticizing, trying to change others or avoiding them. Equally, your life may be filled by anticipation of being humiliated, ignored or rejected, regardless of whether this is actually likely or not. Once you see that the fear is in you, you can work on your ability to cope: a very different strategy, and one that is at the heart of coaching. Essentially, coaching is about the client becoming and staying aware of and in control of their own power.

Avoiding the principle of choice always involves a pay-off. For instance, if I take a lofty line on people who abuse their power, then my pay-off is that I hope to be seen as morally superior. If I claim that the organization is causing me hideous stress by overworking me, my pay-off is that I am a victim and will attract sympathy, attention and possibly financial compensation as well. If I claim to be confused then people may excuse my inability to make a decision. Schutz stressed that accepting the principle of choice does not involve blame, either of yourself or others. At its heart it involves taking responsibility for yourself.

Similarly, you cannot take responsibility for others. I sometimes challenge clients to show me how they could actually *make* someone else happy or unhappy. No client has yet been able to show me how this could happen. We all choose how we respond to any stimulus, often at an unconscious level, but we choose none the less. When you take inappropriate responsibility for others, you will quickly get to burnout – something familiar to all experienced coaches whose clients describe the stress that accompanies believing that you have to do everything yourself.

If you really accept that people are resourceful then you have to believe in the concept of choice. It follows that you can't be a victim, or be brainwashed or manipulated. As Schutz commented, 'Nothing is stressful to me unless I interpret it as stressful.'

Schutz took a wholehearted view of choice, believing that every single event in our lives is the consequence of choice. Thus there can be no 'accidents' and we even, according to him, choose our own illnesses. You need not take this belief to such an extreme to see that even where you become caught up in a web not of your making, you have a choice about how to respond.

This concept has never been more powerfully illustrated than by the Austrian psychiatrist and neurologist Viktor Frankl in his deeply moving short book *Man's Search for Meaning*. Frankl was imprisoned in Auschwitz and other camps during the Holocaust in conditions that were at the most extreme edge of anything human beings can be asked to bear. He did not know whether his wife and family had survived (his wife, mother, father and brother in fact all died in the camps). He had been imprisoned purely on grounds of his Jewishness and stripped of his professional identity, his clothes and even the hair on his head by his Nazi captors. He was ill, cold, malnourished, surrounded by desperate and dying people, in constant fear of being killed and forced to do brutally hard physical work. Yet in his book he describes feeling that although his captors had physical liberty, he had more freedom:

> ... there were always choices to make. Every day, every hour, offered the opportunity to make a decision, a decision which determined whether you would or would not submit to those powers which threatened to rob you of your very self, your inner freedom; which determined whether or not you would become the plaything of circumstance.

Frankl chose to separate himself mentally from his surroundings. At one stage he had a vision of himself after the war, giving lectures and writing about his experiences. This sustained him and saved him from the 'give-up-itis' described by the Allied soldiers who eventually liberated the camps. They observed that many former prisoners simply lost their will to live. In Schutz's terms, they chose to die. Viktor Frankl chose to live. After the war he founded a still-thriving Institute devoted to his own version of psychotherapy, *Logotherapy*, wrote many more books and died full of honours in 1997 at the age of 92.

You insist, I resist

Coaching is about drawing out this intrinsic human resourcefulness. It follows, then, that if you do genuinely believe in the resourcefulness of your clients, you will have to find alternatives to giving advice. So the first step to establishing trust is to abandon advice-giving as a coaching tactic.

This is easy to say and to write, but it is probably the single most difficult task for an inexperienced coach. Many people who become coaches have had earlier jobs where they have been paid to give advice. Their professional training has positioned them as specialists and a great deal of their professional identity is invested in being an expert.

For instance, human resource specialists are trained to tell managers what the employment law is and to help them avoid making catastrophic mistakes when hiring and firing staff. Doctors are trained to know more than their patients about the human body. Accountants are trained to interpret balance sheets and to give clients the benefit of their advice on personal finance. So when confronted with the messy and sprawling issues that clients bring to coaching, inside, the inexperienced coach is thinking:

> It's my job to find the solution for this client – I'll have failed if I don't.
> I can't bear this client's pain and confusion. I need to help her by telling her what I think she should do.
> It's so obvious – he needs to do x or y.

If advice worked as a helping tactic, it might be possible to make a case for it as a prime approach to coaching. However, it doesn't.

Think for a moment about something you do which is generally acknowledged to be unwise. This might be something like smoking, drinking more than the recommended number of units of alcohol a week, driving too fast on the motorway, eating unwisely, being over- or underweight for your height, not taking advantage of health-screening services, or getting too little rest. Now imagine a good friend is giving you advice on the topic. This is what typically happens:

You:	I'd really like to give up smoking, but it's so hard!
Helpful friend:	Yes, you should you know, it's the one way we can reduce the risks of heart disease – and think of the money you're wasting!
You:	Yes, I know, but it's so hard to do.
Helpful friend:	The best way to do it is to go cold turkey.
You:	Mmm, I tried that four years ago and it didn't work so I don't think I can do that.

Helpful friend:	You could! My friend Emma went to a wonderful hypnotherapist and she stopped straight away. Has never had a fag since.
You:	Yes, but that's Emma. It may have worked for her but I don't think I could do it just like that.
Helpful friend:	Yes you could.
You:	Well I'm not ready yet.
Helpful friend:	(gives up in exasperation)

In this example, you and the helpful friend are playing the 'Yes, but' game. The friend makes a suggestion and you say, 'Good idea – but ... ' The chances that you will give up smoking on the basis of this conversation are nil.

The reasons are that, first, however well meant the advice may be, being the recipient of it is probably making you feel angry and guilty. No one enjoys being told to change something they already know they should change, so all your energy is going into repelling the advice. When you feel you are being told what to do, your first response is virtually always to defend your existing position. It becomes impossible to listen carefully to what the other person is saying, however sensible it is.

Second, it is most unlikely that you will not have heard this advice before, as the reasons that people continue to smoke have little to do with ignorance of its long-term effects. Third, the tone of the conversation precludes any real honesty on your part. It will guarantee that you withhold the most important aspects of the issue for you. It neither gets to the reasons why you smoke nor taps into any of the reasons that you might want to stop.

Most seriously, the conversation implies that your friend is a well-adjusted human being whereas you are a bit of a sad addict, so, however well meant, the conversation could undermine your confidence.

Furthermore, you have to live with the results of the advice, not your friend. If you do take your friend's advice and it all goes horribly wrong – for instance, days of cold-turkey-hell where your relationships temporarily collapse under the searing anger and misery of withdrawing so suddenly from tobacco, the friend is a handy scapegoat: 'He/she made me do it.' If the advice turns out well, then it reinforces the notion that other people have more willpower, are cleverer, more able and more decisive.

Even at its most apparently straightforward, advice-giving actually runs a significant risk of being ignored. Doctors are respected professionals who complete a long training before being let loose on us, their patients. Their advice carries genuine authority. Yet research has shown that between a quarter and a third of all prescriptions are either never taken to the pharmacy or remain in the patient's bathroom cabinet.

A television documentary sticks in my mind. The subjects were three 17-year-old diabetics with startlingly different lives. One had experienced a severely disrupted childhood involving foster homes and a painfully high level of personal rejection. The programme followed his umpteenth emergency admission to hospital in a coma because he was not taking his medication. His eyes and feet were in a poor way and the sympathetic, remarkably non-judgemental young doctor told him that he would surely die, and soon, if he didn't take his insulin. The lad's shoulder-shrugging grin made it clear that the advice was pointless. The real question was the sadness and meaninglessness of his life and addressing that, unfortunately, seemed beyond the skills of his doctors.

Some advice-giving is about control. Think about the most recent time when you passed on a piece of advice and ask yourself how far it was really an attempt to control the other person through the apparently benign process of giving advice. If you are the parent of a teenager, for instance, this is a particular trap. The wish to save our children from the distressing consequences of their inexperience often leads to a deluge of do-it-my-way counsel. This can be interpreted by its recipient as, quite accurately, an attempt to keep the apron strings tight. This can have two sorts of undesirable consequence: meek, under-confident adults who lack robust assertiveness or, at the other extreme, compulsive rebels, still psychologically fighting their parents even in middle age.

Advice-giving can feel generous. It can come from a warm heart. When a client expresses misery, it can be tempting to take refuge in expressing fellow feeling through describing something similar that happened to you.

Reading your own biography into a client's concerns is dangerous for any number of good reasons. Most obviously, you are not the client. However similar your situations may appear, the client's history, personality and circumstances are totally different so his or her responses and choices will be different. Also, the client may very well have held back the most important aspect of his or her situation. Here is an example:

Penny (coach) and Michael (client)

Penny was coaching Michael, a middle-manager client inside her organization. He came to her for help on how to move his career on. By the end of their second session, Penny was becoming increasingly puzzled about Michael's situation: he said he wanted another job, yet he seemed reluctant to think broadly about the possibilities. Penny knew the organization and the whole sector well. She could see that Michael had considerable ability and was outgrowing his current role. She told him that she sympathized. In her own career she said she had hit a similar plateau, saying that in her case she had made a sideways move. This involved taking a job in the same company but in a different city. This had worked for her, so surely it would work for him?

The coaching ended after its scheduled three sessions with Michael politely thanking her for her help and Penny acutely puzzled. She was aware that the coaching had not really been effective. A year later Penny discovered that Michael's wife, also a manager in the organization, was seriously ill with motor neurone disease. At the time of the coaching the illness had been diagnosed but Michael's wife had asked him not to tell colleagues. Staying put geographically was important to them both because they both felt it guaranteed the continuation of the excellent medical care she was receiving.

In reviewing this work with her supervisor, Penny realized that the turning point in the coaching, guaranteeing its failure, was this apparently bland piece of advice-giving, wrapped up as help. She had not been able to establish sufficient trust with Michael to enable him to tell her of his wife's illness, and was certain that his wife's worries about confidentiality would not have excluded telling his coach – if that coach had acted in a way that had created more trust. And at the point where this might have been possible she, in her own words, 'blew it'.

Saying 'Something just like that happened to me' can seem like a good idea. It is a disclosure and may therefore seem as if it will create trust. Just occasionally it might. But far more often it seems to be saying, 'This worked for me so it will work for you. Do it my way.' It suggests that you are not really listening because you are queuing to speak – telling your story is more important than listening to the client's. My colleague Phil Hayes enjoys recounting an achingly bizarre example of this tendency:

Friend 1:	How are you – haven't seen you for a long time?
Friend 2:	No, I've just recovered from meningitis. It was awful and I've only just come out of hospital. In fact I nearly died.
Non-listening Friend 1:	Oh – I nearly died once.

Less extreme examples of the same behaviour run the risk of appearing to trivialize the client's concerns by not exploring them. Common responses to other people's distress or worry include clichés such as:

Don't worry, time will heal.
There, there ...
Buck up – it's not that bad!
You'll get other chances.
Plenty more pebbles on the beach/fish in the sea.
Least said, soonest mended ... and so on.

Coaching as rescuing

The human impulse to care for the vulnerable has obviously been essential to our survival as a species. Human infants with their prolonged period of defencelessness need the kind and skilled care of adults. Adults are programmed to respond to overt dependency with tenderness.

I still remember the overwhelming emotion of looking at my tiny first-born, seriously ill at ten days old in what looked like a huge cot at University College Hospital in London. His survival was the only thing that could possibly matter, then or ever. Less traumatically, I still remember the fierceness of my response when faced with a tearful 8-year-old saying, 'Mum, Stephen says he'll break my arm if I don't do what he says.' Charities ruthlessly exploit these innate feelings with explicit bids which tap into our urge to rescue. 'Ten pounds will provide clean water/a week's schooling for this appealing child.' 'Twenty pounds will save this donkey/dog/cat from starvation.' Appealing to this instinct is necessary for successful parenting and probably for charity fund-raising, but it is a false trail in coaching.

If you step in as rescuer with clients, you deny them their ownership of the issue. By rescuing, you actively or by implication behave as if you feel they are too frail to solve the problem themselves. This can happen when clients are overwhelmed by their anxiety. They pour out their hearts, telling you how unbearable it is to be burdened by such problems. The pressure to help by finding a solution for them can feel monumental. There are two equally unhelpful ways to respond:

- The client spills out his or her anxiety and the coach simply listens and empathizes, without asking the questions which move the client on. This hand-me-down love results in the client skipping away feeling temporarily lighter, though without having increased his or her capacity to solve such problems in the future. The coach, by contrast, feels unbearably stressed: the client has successfully transferred all the anxiety.
- The client asks the coach to find a solution. The client implements the suggested solution and becomes dependent on the coach for answers to similar questions in the future. The coach quickly gets to be seen as *managing* the client and the client is subtly demeaned in their own and others' eyes.

Sometimes the client will make an overt request for rescuing. Here is an example:

Maria (coach) and Richard (client)

Maria was coaching Richard, a client who was in dispute with his organization. He had applied for a number of jobs unsuccessfully and was now on its At Risk list, meaning that unless he found another job within an agreed length of time, a redundancy process would be triggered. Richard had also fallen out with his boss and had registered a grievance about the boss's behaviour, alleging bullying.

Maria was finding it hard going with Richard. He frequently broke down in their sessions. When asked to name his goals for the coaching sessions, Maria described him as giving vague answers which essentially amounted to 'I need a shoulder to cry on.' Richard also lavished Maria with compliments, for instance about how easy she was to talk to and about how well she understood the organization.

At their third session, Richard made a specific request. He wanted someone to accompany him to the informal meeting which would start the grievance process. 'You understand me so well', he said, 'and I don't trust myself to give a good account of all this stuff at the meeting. Will you come with me?'

Maria is in coaching because she likes people and wants to help. She understood Richard's vulnerability because she had been in an apparently similar situation herself. However, she knew that she had to resist because by accepting she would have been colluding with Richard's belief that he was powerless. Agreeing would have implied 'You really are in a bad way'; 'I can step in and look after you.'

Maria wisely refused Richard's invitation, seeing that her true role as Richard's coach was to tackle his lack of self-belief. One of the ways she was able to do this was to help him prepare so that he could represent himself at the meeting with skill and confidence. If she had fallen into the trap he had laid for her, she would also have been stepping spectacularly outside her coaching role. Appearing as an advocate for Richard would have made it impossible in subsequent coaching sessions for her to have given him the robust feedback, challenge and confrontation that he needed, in addition to the empathetic support that she was already providing.

You are at risk of rescuing when you find yourself thinking or doing any of the following:

> What would he/she do without me?
> I'm not looking forward to this session; it'll be round and round the same loop.
> I don't think he/she is going to get this right – his/her old pattern is going to assert itself yet again.
> Impatience: why can't he/she just do what I say?
> Making harsh judgements about the client's capacity.

Believing that if you were in their shoes you'd do the job better. Toying with the idea of actively intervening in the client's system on their behalf.

Rescuing implies that the client is a victim and if you act on the impulse to do it, it will for certain undermine the client. If you do rescue, you may also find that the 'victim' turns on you: 'You didn't rescue me cleverly enough!'

In general, when you lose faith in the ability of clients to solve their own problems, you are losing faith in the coaching process, thus ensuring that it fails. That is why it is so important to avoid all the many ways in which we can subtly dishearten our clients through giving advice, or through its close cousin, rescuing.

What if clients ask for advice?

Every now and then a client will ask for advice outright:

What do you think?
If you were me, what would you do?

Where you are holding back your advice with extreme difficulty, this can be a seductive invitation. What you do depends on the circumstances because nothing in coaching is an absolute rule.

An experienced client will even challenge you on your home territory:

Come on, I know coaching isn't about advice, but I'm actually begging you to tell me what to do!

There are any number of possible ways you can avoid the advice-giving trap when invited to fall into it by a client.

- Ask the client, respectfully and possibly with gentle humour, what it would do for them to know what you would do. This challenges a client's belief that the answer is 'out there' rather than in themselves.
- Say, 'I could tell you what I would do, but you and I are very different people, so I'm not sure that would help. The answer you come up with yourself is the one that will work for you.'
- Avoid a direct answer and go straight to a dilemma-solving technique such as identifying all the options and then rating them all for pluses and minuses.

Conditions that need to be in place to give advice

A prescriptive style is rarely useful in coaching, but there *are* occasions when it is appropriate. For instance, where I have worked with a client over several years on and off, you would probably hear me offering a good deal more advice, ideas and information than would ever have been the case in the earlier stages of the relationship. This is always because, by that stage, I have absolute trust that the client is fully active in managing the relationship alongside me as a complete equal, seeing any ideas I offer as interesting data to be accepted, rejected or worked on as the client wishes. The client is most definitely the arbiter.

When you do not have this luxury, there are a number of conditions that need to be in place before offering advice:

- There are clear right/wrong answers to a question the client is asking – e.g. on the legal, medical or financial position.
- It is a crisis and needs rapid action.
- The client's physical, financial or mental well-being will be in danger without having the piece of advice.
- The client is not in a position to make his or her own decisions.
- You are offering facts, not opinions.
- The client has specifically asked for information and has made it clear that he or she will make up his/her own mind on how to use it.
- You offer your contribution as *information*, making it clear that the client has to make up his or her mind about using it to make a decision and positively inviting the client to comment: 'These are the facts as I see them, but what do you think?'
- You encourage the client to check it out with other experts.
- The subject is genuinely bewildering and needs expert guidance for the client to be able to understand it. You have unquestionable expertise, rather than just another personal opinion, in the area on which the client is seeking advice.
- Giving the advice is unlikely to create dependency, to humiliate or to encourage unwise optimism.
- Your own motivation does not include any of the following:
  - a wish to impress and show off
  - wanting to control
  - too lazy to use coaching techniques
  - feeling a need to pay the client back for some slight.

In practice, these guidelines can seem fuzzy. Here is an example.

Liz (client) and John (coach)

Liz had lost her local authority Chief Officer job because of a merger. As her coach, John had helped her come to terms with the initial shock and at first she was optimistic about getting another job at the same level. As a single woman with no dependants she felt she could be flexible and she was notably not hung up on titles or status.

However, she had a strong commitment to public sector work and thought initially that she wanted to stay inside local government. John and Liz revamped her CV and also did a fair bit of interview coaching, as both of these were areas she had felt to be weak. When she was turned down for two jobs, she began to look a little more widely, and soon landed an interview for an interesting-sounding change-management job in a profit-making organization allied to her old specialism. This did wonders for her battered self-esteem but she still felt her heart was in the public sector and that perhaps she wanted to be a Chief Officer again after all. She decided to go through the selection process 'for practice'. She did an excellent interview and was offered the job. This was where the problems set in. Did she want it or not? At an emergency coaching session she and John looked at the upsides and downsides of accepting or rejecting the job. She was still no clearer about whether to accept or not. They ended the session with her hope that a good night's sleep might bring more clarity.

Alas, it did not and the next day she was on the phone for perhaps an hour of agonizing. 'I want you to tell me what to do', she begged. True to the principles described above, John said that he could not do that. The core of John's dilemma was that privately he strongly felt that she should accept as it was probably the best offer she was likely to get in her current market.

She turned the job down.

Three months later she still did not have a permanent job and was miserably doing a series of temporary projects. She bitterly regretted having rejected the private sector job.

So should John have 'told' Liz to accept? Of course he, too, agonized about this, but came to the conclusion that he was right to stick to his principles. First, there was no knowing whether she would have taken any notice of his advice. There was a strong chance that if she had accepted the job she would have been as unhappy and regretful about leaving the public sector as about her eventual decision to try to stay in it. As part of the coaching, she and John had examined all the options, including how realistic it was that she would be offered another local government job that she really wanted. It was her gamble, her life, and she made her choice.

In this case, as in all good coaching, John was clear that he was responsible *to* but not *for* the client.

Establishing your life position

To be a successful coach involves an unusual combination of attitudes and attributes. You have to have both a high degree of self-respect and a high degree of respect for others. This position has never been better described than by Thomas Harris in his well-known book, *I'm OK, You're OK* (1973), an early contribution to Transactional Analysis.

In it, he describes four possible life positions based on two axes: 'I'm OK – I'm not OK', and 'You're OK – You're not OK'. I prefer the anglicized version, 'I value me – I don't value me', and 'I value you – I don't value you'. Set out as a matrix, they produce a chart like this:

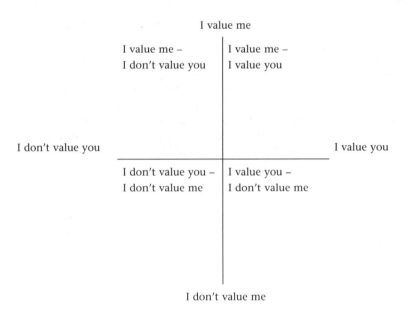

Harris suggests that all of us begin life in the bottom-right quadrant: 'I value you – I don't value me'. This is because, however benign our parents, we are small, weak and dependent. It is inevitable that we get things wrong: our parents always appear to know best. We have a profound need for recognition – what TA adherents call *strokes* – either physical or verbal.

If there is little or no stroking because, for whatever the reason, parenting has been a catastrophic failure, we can descend to the leaden misery of the left bottom quadrant: 'I don't value you – I don't value me'.

In the top left quadrant, the child has learnt that by striking back he or she can survive. Often this is because the child has been at the receiving end of authoritarian parenting so because this child has seen toughness, he or she knows how to be tough, and it becomes a life position to bully and threaten.

Harris describes the top right quadrant as a conscious choice. The other three derive from unconscious processes: raw feeling, but 'I value me – I value you' is made as a result of thinking. He says:

> We do not drift into a new position. It is a decision we make. In this respect it is like a conversion experience … Fortunate are the children who are helped early in life to find that they are OK by repeated exposure to situations in which they can prove, to themselves, their own worth and the worth of others. (original italics)

Life positions and coaching

As a coach, it is difficult to coach well from any but the top right quadrant, but we may all dip into and out of the others from time to time.

I value me – I don't value you

This life position comes out of the energy created by fear. The best form of defence is to attack. Trust is difficult because others could be out to undermine you. You have to prove how good you are all the time because life is a contest for dominance. When this is your position, you secretly believe you are competing with your client because you have something to prove – knowledge, skill, life experience or moral superiority.

There is a benign version of this position where you tell yourself you want to help, or 'give something back'. Alas, this is often a thinly veiled attempt to help by *rescuing* a client – from their incompetence or ignorance. You will experience a lot of frustration, disappointment and possibly even anger because clients will resist you. The client will feel at the very least patronized or judged, and at the very worst rejected and disliked. Coaches who work out of this position all the time are unlikely to get much work because their wish to control is so visible, and in extreme cases because their hostility is palpable. However, you may find yourself falling into this position when you realize you have taken an irrational dislike to a client or are finding it difficult to respect them.

I don't value me – I don't value you

This life position is born out of profound pessimism and fear of conflict. You take a gloomy view of the human race, believing that others are hopeless cases, that our life paths are predetermined and choice impossible. Events have made you their victim. Coaching from such a position of powerlessness is doomed to failure. If you believe that neither you nor your clients can learn then you will be proved right. Coaching is unlikely to be an attractive career for people in this position, but you may find yourself fleetingly visiting it at times of great crisis in your life – for instance if you have major financial worries or a core relationship is at risk.

I value you – I don't value me

In this life position, you believe others are cleverer, more resourceful and more important. You have never grown out of the feeling that most of what you did was wrong as far as one or both parents were concerned, or learning that whatever you did would be ignored.

In this position you are at risk of perpetually playing the 'Mine is better than yours' game: accumulating honours, possessions, money, or, as a coach, distinguished clients who lend you some of their power and glamour. In this case you may be playing the 'I'll be able to value myself *if*...' game. I'll be OK as long as I am successful – through getting massive approval from others. Because this position depends so much on getting approval from others, the underlying feeling has not changed, so no amount of success can alter the underlying feeling, and a lifetime of over-achievement may follow.

As coaches, we probably all need to fight against the underlying pull of this life position. For instance, you may have felt socially disadvantaged if perhaps you come from an underprivileged background. The first time you coach a Chief Executive, you may feel that this is a person of greater importance than you because you may still be affected by the hierarchical attitudes of most organizations, especially if you are still working inside one. If you still have a regional timbre to your voice and are working with clients who speak with public school accents, this may awaken all kinds of early feelings of inferiority. You may feel it if you are conspicuously younger than your client, or have little knowledge of his or her company's business.

If this is your fantasy, then identify and face up to it. It will be challenging to do in-depth work with a client because your self-consciousness will get in the way. It will be difficult to create a genuine partnership of equals with your clients because secretly you see them as the senior partner. You will therefore hesitate to give candid feedback or to confront a client – behaviours all coaches must master. You may end up accommodating your client's needs while ignoring your own and taking far too much responsibility for the relationship, thus ensuring its death.

Realistically, this is often a necessary phase in a coach's development when you are still learning new skills. The challenge is to make this phase as brief as possible.

The ideal: I value me – I value you

If you can sustain this position throughout your professional and personal career, you will be a contented person and in a strong place to coach effectively. In this position you see yourself and your client as equals, regardless of gender, age, hierarchical position, social status or intelligence. You will be able to be honest and so will your client. You will be able to work at an emotional as well as at an intellectual level. You will be able to receive feedback undefensively as well as to give it skilfully. This can be a risky position. To be in it you make yourself vulnerable – but then so does your client.

When you are in this life position you respect the client's core self and professional expertise. The client respects you for your skill as a coach.

Getting into and staying in this quadrant is the only way you can generate the trust that the coaching process needs in order to flourish.

Authentic listening

Genuine listening is about acceptance. Genuine listening is also rare. Mostly what we experience is pretend listening. One of the worst offenders I have known here was a former client of mine, in most other respects an excellent fellow, but who had a phenomenally low tolerance for boredom. He anticipated boredom in most conversations, so his coping tactics included roaming restlessly around his magnificent office, opening his fridge to take out a drink or a bar of chocolate, looking out of the window, or adjusting the volume on his CD player while all the time protesting, 'Go on, I'm listening ... !', often while he had his back to his guest. As a way of ensuring that his visitors never stayed long, it was successful. As a way of communicating acceptance it was disastrous.

Rapport and congruence

One of my colleagues tells the story of a friend who travelled the world for a year with little money and no languages other than English and schoolboy French. He literally never had a problem finding free hospitality and shelter. The reason was that this young man had unforced mastery of the art of creating rapport. How is it done?

We all know the answer because the ability to create and break rapport and understand its consequences is hard-wired into the human brain. Teaching so-called 'body language' has become a cliché of management training courses, often reduced on these events to a trivialized exercise in mimicry of body posture. Rapport, congruence and empathy are not 'techniques'. They are *ways of being* with a client.

Real rapport is more than copying body posture, though two people who are actually in rapport will indeed mirror each other in how they are sitting or standing. When you are in rapport, you will be matching the other person: body, voice volume, breathing, gesture, space, language, pace and energy. You are entering that person's world. To an observer it will look like an elegant dance, first one leading and then the other. In an ideal world this would happen naturally. The coach's world is often not ideal because all kinds of intrusions make it difficult to sustain rapport.

Real rapport comes from unconditional acceptance of the client. This is not the same as liking the client, though in practice you will probably come to like the majority of your clients. When you unconditionally accept a client, warts and all, you will be congruent and when you are congruent you will be in rapport.

Unconditional acceptance means that you are curious about the client. You want to know what it is like to walk in his or her shoes. You accept not just the nice bits – that is, the admirable parts, the behaviours that spring from values just like your own, but the parts that are less admirable and of which they may feel ashamed or worried. Most of us grow up learning that acceptance is conditional. Some examples might be that love and acceptance depend on being

- nice to people all the time: putting their needs first;
- quietly spoken and modest;
- lively and entertaining, always smiling;
- 100 per cent successful 100 per cent of the time.

An important part of the coaching process is to uncover what these inner voices and assumptions are – I describe one approach to this in Chapter 5.

Coaching works when it offers clients the opportunity to discover that they can be valued as a whole – moving past the conditional assumptions that have cramped their growth. The coach will not judge. This is so rare in our society that clients may doubt at first whether they can trust it; hence the cautious feel that many first and second sessions have. It does mean, of course, that as a coach you have to know, deal with and move beyond your own assumptions about what is 'worthy' and what is not. If you cannot, you will find yourself *simulating* congruence instead of *being* congruent – a distinction immediately obvious to any client.

When rapport and congruence break down

These are the six most common reasons for loss of congruence:

Fear
The coach is at the 'I value you – I don't value me' quadrant of the life positions matrix. Fear of not being good enough floods the internal system. Extreme self-consciousness then prevents the coach from managing the rapport at a conscious or unconscious level. There may be some congruence and rapport but unfortunately it will consist of the client leading the coach most of the time, rather than the graceful *pas de deux* that happens when there is genuine rapport.

Overwhelming need for the client to like you
We all need to like and be liked, but if the wish to be liked gets out of hand, it will prevent you challenging appropriately. This feeling again arises from fear and lack of self-confidence. 'If I challenge, this client won't like me.' In ordinary conversation with friends we may have cheerful disputes, but in general we keep profound disagreements to ourselves – or maybe even select our friends because they share our opinions and prejudices. A coach often has to disagree, but the disagreement comes from the security of knowing that when it is done respectfully it will be totally acceptable to the client and you will maintain rapport and congruence.

Judgement
The coach cannot suspend judgement about some perceived aspect of the client – maybe their profession ('I never did like journalists/bankers/estate agents'), their values, their clothing, their nationality or religion or their personality. The sort of disapproval that originates in prejudice will leak out in all kinds of ways and is usually perfectly apparent to the client.

Imposing actual or implied values on to the client
The coach dominates the process with values that overwhelm because they are projected so strongly through their behaviour, normally through showing enhanced or withdrawn attention. This imposes new restrictive conditions on the client so that the client feels, 'I am only valued when I talk about my successes', or 'This coach likes it best when I cry', or 'I feel I have to over-dramatize my problems – that's what he/she seems to respond to.' Forcing the client into incongruity in order to please the coach is one sure way to damage the coaching process.

Preoccupation on the coach's part
The coach has so many issues going on in his/her own life that it is impossible to concentrate on the client.

Unawareness on the part of the coach
The coach does not know that he or she is fixed in particular ways of talking and communicating. For instance, when training coaches, one of the most common ways that we notice an inexperienced coach gets this subtly or dramatically wrong is in mismatching the client's pace. The client is languid in style but the coach is energetic – or vice versa. Another example would be that the client has an unusually quiet voice, but the coach remains loud. Yet another might be that the client's language shows a liking for a particular sort of metaphor but the coach does not spot it and uses his or her own version of the same words instead.

Real congruence starts with a buoyant and sincere wish to understand the other person – to see the world as they see it. At the same time you have to be self-aware and self-accepting, letting your own barriers down, free of the need to defend yourself. When you no longer fear others you will not feel the need to protect yourself from difference. When you are able to do this you will probably find that everything else follows.

Mismatches

When you mismatch someone, you break rapport. Common mismatches include:

- Fiddling with your watch, pen or ring – may convey boredom or impatience.
- Staring unblinkingly at the other person – may suggest aggression.
- Sitting with crossed arms – may look as if you are defending yourself against the other person's ideas.
- Turning your chair slightly away from the other person – may imply lack of interest or (depending on other body language) lack of confidence.
- Touching your face while talking – implies timidity, especially if the hand is actually in front of the mouth.
- Scowling or frowning – suggests disapproval.

- Looking at a clock or watch – implies you want to move on to something else.
- Waggling your foot – may suggest nervousness or impatience.
- Sitting with crossed legs; sitting hunched – may look as if you are trying to make yourself smaller and therefore as if you lack confidence.
- Sitting back in your chair when the other person is sitting forward – may suggest lack of involvement.

- Rubbing your nose, looking away – sometimes suggests lying.

- Avoiding eye contact: suggests lack of interest or lack of confidence.

Constant mismatching will distract and dismay your client. But occasionally a deliberate piece of mismatching is very useful. Here is an example from a colleague:

Jane

I had been asked to coach Jane, a senior television producer whose boss reported that Jane could not manage her team. Allegedly, Jane's influencing tactics could be reduced to one style: tell people what to do and if they don't do it, bawl at them. Jane appeared for an introductory discussion looking distinctly hostile with 'What's all this about?' and 'I don't want to be here' conveyed in every aspect of her appearance. This was scheduled as an introductory conversation, to explore what coaching was and whether she was up for it.

Throughout the meeting, Jane huddled in her chair with her shoulders pointing away from me, avoiding eye contact and radiating anger with an abrupt and loud voice. Feeling uncomfortable, I made a conscious attempt to match her posture and voice volume. She did listen to me and seemed to appreciate the careful listening I applied to her account of how she had been traduced by the organization, but the angry posture remained.

After ten minutes I deliberately broke whatever rapport there was, sat up energetically in my chair, then immediately softened my voice and slowed it down, asking her to tell me about the feelings that this apparent assault on her confidence was creating for her. It was hard to keep doing this conscious mismatching in the face of such resolute resistance. However, after about three minutes, she slowly swivelled around to face me for the first time, her own voice dropped and some angry tears began to fall. We were then in genuine rapport for the first time, and the real conversation could begin.

Mismatching is also useful when you want to punctuate a coaching session by moving from one agenda topic to another, or where the client appears to have got stuck, as Jane did in the account above, in a mood that does not seem helpful. Sometimes this break can be something as obvious as 'Why don't we get up and have another cup of coffee?', or just a more subtle change in your own posture and energy level.

Is this manipulation? No, because to work it depends on your thoroughgoing commitment to 100 per cent respect for and curiosity about your client.

The three levels of listening

It would be rare to confess to being a poor listener – about as rare as owning up to being a bad driver or to having no sense of humour. However, coaches can't afford the luxury of self-delusion. Ruthless honesty against a very high standard is the only possible tactic.

I like the framework proposed by the Coaches Training Institute because it allows for a hierarchy of listening effectiveness, all of which depends on the self-awareness of the coach. It is described in an excellent book by Laura Whitworth, Henry Kimsey-House and Phil Sandahl, *Co-active Coaching* (1998).

Level 1

This is the client's level. As the client you are self-absorbed. You don't have to worry about anything except getting your story out. You have lots of questions, all of which are clustered around one question: what impact is this having on me? So, for instance, if you visit your GP, your concern will be to wonder how long you will have to wait, to try to control any nervousness you may feel, to remember to list all your symptoms, perhaps hope that you don't have to undress – and so on.

As a client this level is fine. As a coach it is disastrous. You will be thinking about you, not the client. Signs that you are at Level 1 include:

- finding yourself asking the client for more facts: 'how many; when; who; what's the structure; what's the history', – when the client hasn't mentioned them;
- noticing that you are getting flustered, that your inner dialogue is about your own anxiety:
  - What can I ask next?
  - Was that a good enough question?
  - Will this last for the whole session?
  - Does the client like me?
- wanting to give advice;
- talking about yourself: lots of *I* and *me*.

Sample level 1 conversation

Client: I need to get better at delegating. I'm working 70 hours a week at the moment.

Coach: Yes, that's really not a good idea; you'll wear yourself out.

Client: But I can't really see what else I can do, we're so busy.

Coach: You'll probably find the whole way you're doing it is a bit wrong. I've got a really good handout I can show you. It's worked for lots of clients so it should work for you.

Client: Mmm, well ...

Coach: It starts from an analysis of how you typically spend your day. I've got a sample here. Shall we work on it now?

In this example, the coach is over-concerned to position herself as the expert. She wants to be helpful, but she is not listening because her own agenda is getting in the way and she has resorted to giving advice before she has established what the client wants.

Level 2

At Level 2, coach and client are seamlessly locked in to an absorbing and intensely concentrated conversation. They are most definitely in rapport, their body posture, voices and energy levels subtly matched. The conversation will flow but the client will be doing most of the talking. The coach's questions are skilful, picking up on the language the client has used, working exclusively from the client's agenda and never giving advice. The questions explore, clarify, summarize and probe, always extending the client's thinking and willingness to learn something new. As the coach you hear what is not being said as well as what is. You are listening for the underlying meanings and are aware of your own impact on the client.

If you can remain at Level 2 for most of a coaching session you are doing well: it is the level at which the majority of effective coaching takes place.

Sample Level 2 conversation

Client: I need to get better at delegating. I'm working 70 hours a week at the moment.

Coach: That sounds tough. How should we work on this?

Client: Well, I think I'm doing it OK, but my staff tell me I'm not. I don't know what they mean really.

Coach: What exactly do they say to you?

Client: An example would be that my assistant tells me I'm constantly checking up on her, but how else am I supposed to find out how things are going?

Coach: Checking up … So that's her feedback. 'Finding out what's going on … ' Sounds like there's lots of anxiety there for you. Do you want to stay with this one as a useful example?

Client: Yes, OK.

Coach: So imagine I'm your assistant, how exactly do you delegate to me?

Here the coach is following the client's agenda scrupulously, using his words, deepening the conversation and generating useful data for the conversation that follows.

Level 3

At Level 3 you are doing what has been described as 'radio-field listening', aware not just of everything required at Level 2, but also of the emotion, of the risks it might be possible to take in the conversation, of the underlying choices and of what could be at stake for the client. You trust your intuition. You feel connected with the client at an emotional as well as at an intellectual level, even if no emotion has been named. You see the whole coaching relationship stretching out behind and in front of you and it feels special. These are moments of real connection – of a kind that few of us ever reach in a 'normal' conversation with a friend.

Sample Level 3 conversation

Client: I need to get better at delegating. I'm working 70 hours a week at the moment.

Coach: That sounds tough. How should we work on this?

Client: (small silence and a laugh)

Coach: (gently) So? (Another pause) That laugh sounds strained.

Client: It is. I can't take this pace. My staff tell me I'm 'interfering', but I don't know how else to keep everything under control. It's ruining my personal life and if I don't watch it my health as well. My wife complains she never sees me and I don't know when I last put our daughter to bed because I'm home so late. I'm awake every morning from 4.00 a.m. and then I can't get back to sleep worrying about work. It's an enormous strain.

Coach: So this is an enormous strain and it feels as if there's a huge amount at stake for you, job and home.

Client: Enormous. It's a burden I don't want.

Coach: Burden is a heavy-sounding word! So I'm also sensing that there's considerable willingness to shed that burden and to try something different?

Client: Yes, though I can't see what it would be. But yes, I'm up for it ...

Coach: So some of this seems as if it's about feeling in control. Shall we start by looking at how that links to the way you delegate?

Through working at Level 3, the coach has established a whole-life perspective and has focused the client's mind on what is at stake through continuing to work so many hours. She has done this through listening for the silences and hesitations, by listening for the metaphor and for the emotion behind the words. She has left spaces inside the conversation which the client can fill if he wishes. By doing this she makes it clear that she neither condones nor condemns the long working week, but is simply accepting and respecting the position the client finds himself in. She has spotted the underlying need that the behaviour serves. By noticing the negative energy that his stress is creating she has also harnessed a willingness to begin the change process.

Working from the client's agenda

Implicit in all of this is the assumption that it is the client's agenda that matters, not the coach's. The minute you stray into Level 1, you will be working from your agenda, not the client's.

Coaching is unlike many other kinds of one-to-one relationships in that the coach has no agenda of his or her own. For instance, a doctor may have a favourite and useful drug that he prescribes for tonsillitis. A teacher may have a curriculum which the pupil must follow, even if both teacher and pupil are uninterested in the topics; a therapist may feel she has to follow the philosophy of the particular 'school' of psychotherapy that trained her – and so on.

Coaching starts and finishes with the client's agenda. This is because coaching is about change. Clients come to coaching because they want to change their lives and get results which show that change has happened. This may be about improving relationships, changing jobs or acquiring new skills. Clients know their lives in a way that the coach never can, so only the client can say what the agenda for change is.

The coach's role is

- to ask the questions which uncover the client's agenda and make it explicit;
- to turn this agenda into the goals which the client can work on;
- to safeguard this as the only agenda for the coaching;
- linking the client's agenda with his/her core values and beliefs;
- to work with the client to identify and then move past the blocks and fears which are holding him/her back;
- to remain eager for the client to do well on progress towards his/her goals while at the same time remaining healthily objective about the whole process;
- to move the client to action towards these goals, reminding the client of his/her original commitment to them;
- to help the client identify the learning associated with meeting the goals on his/her agenda.

That is why the exquisite skill of asking good questions is such a critical one in coaching and forms the subject of the next chapter.

Being worthy of trust: a two-way process

As a coach, I ask my clients to trust me. I am always aware of what a huge assumption this is. Why should they trust me? What can I do to accelerate that trust? Equally, my starting place in the relationship is that I will trust them. Where trust is broken, it can of course be repaired, but as with a piece of shattered china, the repair will always be there, even if apparently invisible, and it will never be so strong as it was when unbroken.

Trust may grow slowly, depending on the skill of the coach and the willingness of the client to be open. This is hard for many clients. They have become accustomed to defensiveness and sometimes to performance. Realizing that they do not have to perform for you is often the turning point in the effectiveness of the coaching: realizing they really can trust you with their failures and uncertainties and that you will not condemn or judge. Equally, they realize that you will acknowledge their honest achievements and their efforts to change. What does trust really involve? The answers must be honesty, predictability, commitment and reliability.

As with so many other issues in coaching, this is a two-way process.

The client's side in creating trust

First, the client is consistent in what he or she says. When the client describes a particular set up, he or she will describe it in the same way each time. If I get to see the client in action with his or her team, I will see the situation they have described – plus a great deal more, but the client's tale will still ring true.

When clients commit to the process of coaching, this means treating the coach as respectfully as they expect to be treated themselves. In a healthy coaching relationship, what the client says and what the client does are one and the same. The commitment to the coaching is more than just words. If we agree 'homework' it is done and, even if it is not done, there will be learning in why it has been put to one side for the moment. When clients say that they will continue to ponder some theme we have discussed, they do. When they say they will give me candid feedback, they do.

What the client says outside the session is also important. What is said inside the sessions should be consistent with what is said outside it. Where this is not the case, trust will be destroyed. An example of this happened to one of my colleagues who had coached an angry senior manager made redundant by his organization and still smarting from the hurt and rejection. My colleague had asked for feedback at the end of each session and it had been agreed between them that this was part of the informal contract they had made. The client said that he had found the sessions 'very useful' and spelt out the usefulness in some detail. Yet two weeks later my colleague heard that the client had described the coaching to a third party known to both of them as 'pointless navel-gazing'. When respectfully challenged about this at their next session, the client blustered and equivocated. Not surprisingly, that was their last session.

Clients gain my trust and respect where they are willing to give the coaching process a go. Signs that they are willing to do this would be, for instance, if they are willing to explore previously forbidden emotional areas or hear tough feedback and to sit out the resulting discomfort without attacking me as the bearer of bad news. Coaching demands an unusual degree of openness from both client and coach. A client who is willing to make himself or herself vulnerable through honest disclosure will earn my confidence.

Lack of commitment is betrayed in many large and small ways. For instance, a client who consistently cancels the date at the last moment for what seem like implausible reasons is indicating for sure that he or she does not give a high priority to the coaching. A client who arrives for the session late and looking ill-prepared and bemused about the agenda tells you that his or her mind is on other things. Such clients could be showing that their interest in learning with you is fragile and may be waning.

The coach's side in creating trust

All of these conditions need to be equally present in the coach.

The first step is to look at your own assumptions about how far you can trust the client. You don't need to like every client in the way that you would like a close friend – in fact it is impossible to do so. You will respect the many aspects of the client which are admirable, but will also be curious and interested in the many self-protective barriers which the client has skilfully erected around him- or herself.

You may disagree strongly with a client's values, political or religious views, for instance, but if you are not coaching them in that arena, their views should be irrelevant. Many clients may present initially as disagreeable people. For instance, a client who bullies or manipulates represents a style of management that I particularly dislike. However, I have worked successfully with many such clients, though I would not have lasted a week with them if they had been my boss. At the other end of the spectrum are the clients who lack assertiveness. They may be condemned by their colleagues as 'weak', or, more kindly, as 'lacking toughness'. With these clients, too, I can usually work well, yet if I worked with them as colleagues they might exasperate me.

What is the difference? As clients I am intrigued by their dilemmas and difficulties. I want to know what self-imposed barriers they have created to success. I accept their plusses, their quirks and failings unconditionally. My role is to release their own talents and resourcefulness. I don't have to like them.

As a coach what you say and what you do have to be consistent. At the simplest level, you must deliver on your promises. If you say you will email an interesting article, you must do it. If you declare enthusiasm for coaching, you must be enthusiastic. You will give the client 100 per cent of your attention in every session, just as you expect 100 per cent attention back. It will be immediately obvious if you are drifting off or coaching on autopilot.

Where you say you believe in not giving advice, you will adhere to that principle in practice and on the occasions where you do offer advice you will draw attention to it through labelling what you say. It may also help in early sessions to draw attention to other coaching behaviour – for instance, when asking for feedback, pointing explicitly to approaches you have taken, or to the types of question you have asked.

You will refer to clients respectfully outside the sessions, never belittling them with other coaches. Where you feel you cannot work respectfully, then the coaching must end. As you expect from your client, you will never cancel or arrive late for a session on spurious or trivial grounds.

Your unbounded curiosity about people will mean that you will not take refuge in the bogus concept of *chemistry*. Clients will often ask for a look–see meeting, explaining that they need to 'check the chemistry'. In a crowded market place this is the client's right, but it is the coach's right too, even though most coaches have yet to get to the stage where, like the most famous and in-demand music teachers, they subject their clients to an audition to see if they are at the required standard. As a coach you will need to remember how easily 'checking the chemistry' is really code for 'Do I like him/her?' This can often in its turn be code for 'Are they just like me?' You do not need clients to be just like you to be able to work with them successfully. My own assumption is that I will be able to work with more or less any client until circumstances prove otherwise.

You will strictly adhere to your promise of confidentiality. Any betrayal here will wing its way back to your client in very short order. A colleague of mine describes the most common approach to confidentiality as 'only telling one other person'. As coaches we need to do better than that. If there are limits to confidentiality, tell the client what they are. Clients need to trust that we will not gossip or betray any of the many secrets we hear in the coaching room. This may range from early knowledge of a company takeover, with its potential to buy shares cheap and sell them dear later, to other kinds of insider knowledge about adulteries or people's sexuality.

The lure of being on the inside track can be a bait to blabbing. Promises of confidentiality slip easily off the tongue. One sign that you are observing such promises is that you may talk to a client about other clients and their issues but never disrespectfully or in a way that could identify that other client. In this way your current client will feel safe to trust his or her secrets with you.

The openness you expect from a client needs to be matched by openness on your side. This might mean *very occasionally* trusting the client with your own vulnerability, but this will always risk the possibility of you and your client changing places (these themes are explored in more detail in Chapter 8). It does mean staying open to the client's views, listening without judging, *walking a mile in the other person's moccasins*, helping the client to voice views that it might otherwise be difficult for him or her to express.

It also means that you are open to any request or challenge from a client. So, for instance, in one session the subject of a client's difficult marriage was on the agenda, and she suddenly stopped in mid-flow to say, abruptly, 'I need to know that your marriage hasn't always been perfect.' There was no way we could continue the conversation until the feeling behind this request had been candidly explored. This turned out to be not so much a request for intimate confessions from me to her, as a sudden feeling on her part that somehow I was judging her. Exploring honestly what that feeling was and staying open to her feedback was essential to re-establishing trust.

Finally, as a coach you will demonstrate willingness to learn from your clients. This is something that is taken for granted by the best coaches in other fields – for instance singing and sport. An outstanding opera singer will usually have a singing coach. The best theatre companies employ voice coaches, even for distinguished actors. These coaches will tell you how much they learn from their coachees. Similarly, as life or executive coaches, when we stay open to influence from our clients in the same way that we expect them to be open to influence from us, the coaching relationship will be infinitely the richer.

3 Simple but not easy: the skilled language of coaching

Asking the right questions, phrasing your comments in just the right way ... this is a prime coaching skill. When done well, it looks effortlessly easy. When not done well, it clouds the potential of both coach and client. If you can learn how to do it well, you will have cracked one of the most challenging barriers to effectiveness as a coach. In this chapter I look at some of the common traps for coaches and describe how to circumvent them.

As with so many other domains in coaching, this skill falls into the category of *simple but not easy*. This is because it is not just a matter of learning some coaching-by-numbers techniques. The techniques are important, but when they work they are underpinned by deeply held values and reinforced by hours of confidence-building practice. This is the area where as a beginner coach you are most likely to struggle. One of our trainee coaches spoke for many others when she said:

> Intellectually I can accept the case for keeping it short and sweet and working from the client's agenda exclusively, but advice giving is so entrenched in my mental concept of *helping*, that it's taken me a long time to see how loaded my questions are. And when I'm there with a real client, I panic and then I fall into my old default mode!

Coaching well involves an intense awareness of the language you use and this does not come naturally to everyone. When coaching well, your language will have a purity and probably also a brevity that your everyday conversation does not normally have or need. Each word will count. There are some paradoxes here. Beginner coaches virtually always try too hard and in trying too hard they make coaching far more difficult than it needs to be. Less is more in coaching, but to get to that point you have to understand which words and interventions count and which simply get in the way.

Knowing the traps

At the risk of appearing to emphasize the negative, I'm going to take some space to describe some of the most common traps, all of which I have seen over and over again in people who are just setting out as coaches.

Here is an example, taken from a recording of a real-life piece of coaching:

Client:	I need to work shorter hours. My life balance is all wrong.
Beginner coach:	Have you tried asking your PA for feedback on where your time is going?

In this example, the client has named the issue on which he wants to work. The coach's mind immediately springs to a possible powerful solution: raising the client's awareness of how he currently spends his time by suggesting he asks his PA for feedback.

This is how the conversation continued:

Client:	I need to work shorter hours. My life balance is all wrong.
Beginner coach:	Have you tried asking your PA for feedback on where your time is going? Her perspective would probably be very useful.
Client:	No, I haven't.
Beginner coach:	That would be really useful – often I find that my clients don't really know where their time is going and the PA is a day-to-day observer. As a starter for change it's really useful.
Client:	Well ...
Beginner coach:	It's something you could do between now and the next session ...
Client:	Well, I don't know ...
Beginner coach:	OK, just a thought ...

As a coaching conversation, this one is going nowhere. If we speculate about what each side was thinking but not saying in this very typical piece of dialogue, it would probably go like this:

Thinks but doesn't say		**Actual dialogue**
This is such a huge issue for me. I've been round and round it so many times. I wonder if she can really help me?	Client	I need to work shorter hours. My life balance is all wrong.
Oh help ... ! This is a biggie. Where on earth	Beginner coach	Have you tried asking your PA for feedback on where

should I start? I know! That exercise where you ask the PA for their feedback. That will help him.		your time is going? Her perspective would probably be very useful
This sounds like a time-management course. I didn't come here for that.	Client	No, I haven't.
He's resisting, so perhaps I'd better push it.	Beginner coach	That would be really useful – often I find that my clients don't really know where their time is going and the PA is a day-to-day observer. As a starter for change it's really useful.
There's no way I'm going to do this. Just because her other clients find it useful doesn't mean that I will.	Client	Well …
Perhaps I'm not being persuasive enough?	Beginner coach	It's something you could do between now and the next session …
Absolutely not!	Client	Well, I don't know …
What on earth do I do now?	Beginner coach	OK, just a thought …

While the speculations about the client's thoughts are just that – speculation – the coach's thoughts are entirely authentic, because she described them to me in technicolour when, as her supervisor, we listened to the recording together.

Trap 1: Advice-in-disguise questions

This coach, like so many other beginners, has fallen into the trap of asking advice-in-disguise questions. These questions come from the coach's wish to be helpful through offering his or her own solutions, dressed up as questions. The give-away is the first word:

Have … ?	Was … ?	Is … ?
Haven't … ?	Wasn't … ?	Isn't … ?

Would ... ?	Has ... ?	Should ... ?
Wouldn't ... ?	Hasn't ... ?	Shouldn't ... ?
Do ... ?	Did ... ?	Were ... ?
Don't ... ?	Didn't ... ?	Weren't ... ?
Does ... ?	Are ... ?	Can ... ?
Doesn't ... ?	Aren't ... ?	Can't ... ?

For instance:

> Have you thought of ... ?
> Would it be a good idea if ... ?
> Should you check that out with someone else?

These questions invariably come from the coach's agenda, not the client's. A sure sign that you are falling into this trap is to notice that your question can be answered yes or no. These questions suggest that there is a right answer and of course that is the one in the coach's mind.

Question: Have you done x or y?
Answer: Yes.

Apart from all the other disadvantages created by offering advice described in Chapter 2 (see pages 30–33), there are two other, equally compelling ones for avoiding these questions. First, as in the example above, they can be readily deflected by a client who has two easy options: mindlessly agreeing immediately or abruptly declining to enter further into the debate. The client's energy is going into the evasion instead of into thoughtfulness and learning.

A sign that this is happening is in the lengthy nature of the coach's questions and the brevity and speed of the client's answer. Second, and more important, this type of question always makes the coaching conversation far longer, more contorted and more difficult than it really needs to be.

The leading question
An even more lethal version of advice-in-disguise is the leading question, as legendarily used by the lawyer who is cross-questioning a hostile witness in court:

> So would you agree that you have been lying, and you did commit
> this crime?

You can hear this sort of question asked every day on current affairs radio and television programmes by journalists whose basic position is that politicians are fibbing until proved otherwise. The tradition is reinforced by the practice of parliamentary debate where differences are artificially emphasized. It is seen at its most exaggerated in Prime Minister's Question Time, the ritual where the Prime Minister is subjected either to exaggeratedly sycophantic questions from his or her own party:

> Would the Prime Minister agree that this has been his wisest act yet?

or to overt attempts at sabotage from the other side:

> Would the Prime Minister not agree that it is time his government resigned?

This type of question has never been better mocked than by Mrs Merton, the 1990s TV chat-show 'host'. 'Mrs Merton' was a convincingly dowdy 50-year-old Northerner with a horrible perm, very unlike her alter ego, the much younger comedienne Caroline Ahearne. Mrs Merton's sly and apparently guileless questions often disarmed her guests, especially at the beginning of the series when the guests were often not in on the joke. One of her best was addressed to the glamorous and much younger wife of the magician and performer Paul Daniels:

> So, Debbie McGee, what was it that first drew you to millionaire Paul Daniels?

Trap 2: The why question

When you ask the question 'why ... ?' it seems at first like a benign, open question. In practice it is another trap. The question 'why ... ?' invites analysis and intellectualizing.

In this example, the client has raised the question of a highly unsatisfactory team meeting. This client already knows she has difficulties in chairing meetings and wants to improve.

> Coach: Why did you decide to hold that team meeting when you did?
> Client: Well, our policy on meetings is that we never let more than ten days go past without a team meeting and it was already nine days since the last one so I thought it was time ... (*ramble, ramble, ramble*)

The coach's real questions were about what was in the client's mind before calling the meeting and what she wanted to get out of the meeting. The coach has not had his real questions answered here because by starting with the word 'why ... ?' he has triggered a cerebral response which gets nowhere near the real issues for this client.

The 'why ... ?' question is also unhelpful because it often focuses on the client's motivation. Nine times out of ten when you ask this question you will get the response 'I don't know', or 'It's just how I am'. If the client already knew what her motivation was, she might not be asking for coaching on the issue.

> Coach: Why did you lose your temper with X?
> Client: I don't know. I just seem to have a short fuse.

Similarly, 'why ... ?' can seem like an interrogation or an accusation. For many people it reminds us of the kinds of questions that we were asked as children by our irritated parents:

> Why did you get your trousers so muddy?
> Why do you fight with your brother?
> Why have you lost your bus pass for the third time this term?

When asked like this, it can easily be interpreted by the client as having the underlying meaning, 'Why were you so stupid?' The reply you get is then likely to be either the blank shrug that goes with 'I don't know' or a long-winded and defensive justification.

Trap 3: Researching the data

This is a more subtle trap but it is a trap nonetheless. Let's suppose that you have a new client from an organization you don't know at all. The client begins his account of a problem concerning a poorly performing member of his team. The temptations might be to:

- ask the client for an organization chart;
- ask the client to explain any unfamiliar acronyms he is using;
- establish how big the team is and how their roles relate to that of the problem member;
- ask how old the team member is and how long he or she has been in the job;
- ask for the actual name of the team member's job ... and so on.

All of this is unnecessary. The client already has this data so it is pointless to ask him or her to give it to you. It will be far more important for you to take the client into areas that he or she has never considered and that means asking a different type of question. The most likely explanation for your behaviour is your own anxiety:

'Do I really understand this client's organization?' (Probably not, but you don't need to)
'How is this team like other teams I know in different organizations?' (Irrelevant – it may be or may not be)

The pertinent data – pertinent to the client, that is – will emerge when you ask the right questions. Anything else is simply postponing the moment when you get to the heart of the client's issues. When you find yourself searching for data, notice it as a sign that you are at Level 1 listening (see page 47), more concerned about whether you are asking the right questions than in truly listening to the client. Extra facts are a distraction and will take you away from the real issues rather than towards them.

On one of our coach training courses, my colleague Jan Campbell was working with Annie, a promising coach who had spent her career up until that point as a distinguished university teacher. Noticing how often Annie spent in a relentless search for facts in her practice coaching, Jan memorably burst out, 'Annie, you are *not* doing a PhD thesis on the client's problem!' I remind myself of this with an inner smile of recognition when I am tempted to start the equivalent type of questioning with a client.

Trap 4: Asking about people who are not present

A client presents you with a puzzle. Let's say it is about how to harness the flagging motivation of his/her PA. The trap here is to ask about the PA's motivation or concerns.

    Coach: What does she feel about it?
    Client: Who can say?

There are useful ways to ask about other people's feelings (see page 70), but this isn't one of them. None of us can ever know for sure what another person's motivation is. Clumsy probing about other people's motivation or feelings may confirm the client's belief that the other person is the problem, rather than looking at his or her own contribution to the problem.

You may encounter another variation of this temptation. Let's say the client is thinking about a radical change of career. You know something of the client's personal circumstances through other questions you have asked. You now ask, 'What would your mother/wife/husband/partner/boss think about this?' Again, it is a distraction from the client's own responsibility to speculate about what the not-present other person might think. Interestingly, I notice that when we are tempted to ask this kind of question, the third party is often an authority figure. Asking about that person's views might therefore seem to be implying that the absent person has the final power to decide, and may have to be placated or manipulated in order for the client to have his or her own way. In this way, old myths and excuses could be unwittingly perpetuated.

Trap 5: Long and double questions

As a coach, when you ask long questions you are at risk of turning the spotlight of the coaching onto yourself. Long questions normally come out of uncertainty. Inside, the coach is thinking: 'What shall I ask next? If I go on talking I'll get to something eventually and it will cover up any pauses which might otherwise embarrass me ... ' As a coach, you cannot afford the luxury of doing all your thinking out loud. Questions with long preambles followed by many dependent clauses will only confuse your client. This coach found himself falling into this trap:

> So when you have this problem with punctuality, and I know you've described it as baffling, and how it really annoys your boss when you're late for her meetings, I wonder what the circumstances are – I mean whether it's when you're really hassled about everything else that's going on in your life?

Not surprisingly, the client's response was: 'Yes – I mean no ... I don't know. Could you repeat the question?' The question the coach was really asking was: 'What are the typical triggers for unpunctuality for you?' If he had asked the question this way, the client would have found it much easier to answer, though possibly also more challenging.

Buried inside the long question there are often two or even three sub-questions. An example would be:

> So tell me how you first came to feel concerned about this. Was it when you first joined the company or did it start later? And has that concern always been as strong as it is now?

This kind of question comes across as a barrage, however gently it is asked. It confuses because, as the client, you don't know on which bit of the barrage to concentrate. I notice that when trainee and beginner coaches ask this kind of question, the client's most frequent response is typically 'Err ... Um ... ', or 'You've lost me there.'

Tactics that work

All these traps, and the types of question that go with them, have one thing in common. They narrow the search for answers, rather than broadening it out. They confuse and distract. They focus attention on one place rather than persuading the client to extend out to many places, including, often, the places he or she might at first rather not look. One way and another, they all lead to dead ends.

So one of the secrets of good coaching is to know how to ask questions that do the opposite: liberate the client by broadening the search for answers, take the client into new pathways and challenge the client's thinking.

The coach's freedom

As a coach, you are in a remarkably free situation. You have the luxury of remaining detached from whatever outcome the client achieves. It really doesn't matter. You want the client to get an outcome which will make a positive difference in his/her life, whether it is greater clarity or a workable solution, but you are not attached to any one path.

You don't need to know the whole story, only the bits of it that matter to the client now.

The past is less important than the present and the future.

You don't need to be right.

You don't need to understand the context in order to be able to coach effectively. I often coach clients whose technical worlds are literally incomprehensible to me. A recent example includes a nuclear engineer who considerately asked me at one point early in our coaching whether it would help me if she briefly outlined the laws of thermo-dynamics. I reassured her that it would be a waste of our time. I might understand the individual words, but it would be unlikely that the whole sentence would mean very much.

Another client managed a complex overseas operation in a country whose political system is as different from the standard western democracy as it is possible to be, with internecine manoeuvrings, widespread corruption and a great deal of physical danger. This client was relieved to discover that he did not need to give me potted histories of the various factions involved. Whether or not I knew about them was irrelevant to the success of the coaching. Similarly, I have coached theologians, doctors, lawyers, interior designers, architects, retailers, pharmacologists, finance directors, actuaries, civil servants, hospital managers, chefs and many others without knowing anything about their professional worlds except perhaps as a consumer.

In fact it is even more liberating than this. It is a positive help to know nothing about the context or the content. The more you know about the content, the more likely you are to be seduced into the role of expert. This case has been supremely well made by Timothy Gallwey in his *Inner Game* books, for instance *The Inner Game of Work* (2000). Gallwey worked for a time as a tennis coach and came to realize that the real opponent for a tennis player was not the person on the other side of the net. Rather it was the mental programming of the player. The real opponent was in the player's own head. A player without bodily self-awareness and further handicapped by lack of self-belief was almost bound to fail. Gallwey began his *Inner Tennis* courses with the explicit aim of coaching participants in the techniques of mental and physical self-awareness rather than in some preordained set of tennis techniques.

The contrast with traditional coaching is instructive. The traditional coach relies on his or her own ideas of what makes, for instance, a good serve: 'Watch me and do it like this', or 'Keep your eye on the ball at this or that point.' This would be followed by feedback from the coach to the player: 'At the crucial minute, you let your arm drop and took your eye off the ball.' In this example, the coach is doing most of the work and the player is robbed of responsibility. The coaching turns into a performance to please the coach rather than the player taking responsibility for his or her own game.

In the *Inner Game* approach, the roles are reversed. The coach asks open questions aimed at raising the player's consciousness of his/her physical and mental states with the aim of the player taking the responsibility and doing the feedback on him- or herself:

> What worked then?
> What didn't work?
> What was in your mind at the start?
> What do you need to do now?
> Where was the ball when you connected with it?

The results were startlingly successful, so successful that an *Inner Ski* school was started too, with coaches trained in the same technique. In his book *Coaching for Performance* (1996), Gallwey's then collaborator, John Whitmore, tells a wonderful tale of how the ski coaches were able to coach people in tennis, in spite of knowing literally nothing about the sport:

> Several of our Inner Tennis courses were so overbooked that we ran out of trained Inner Tennis coaches. We brought in two Inner Ski coaches, dressed them in tennis coach's uniform, put a racket under their arms and let them loose with the promise they would not attempt to use the racket under any circumstances.
>
> Not entirely to our surprise, the coaching job they did was largely indistinguishable from that of their tennis-playing colleagues.

However, on a couple of notable occasions, they actually did better. On reflection the reason became clear. The tennis coaches were seeing the participants in terms of their technical faults: the ski coaches, who could not recognize such faults, saw the participants in terms of the efficiency with which they used their bodies. Body inefficiency stems from self-doubt and inadequate body-awareness. The ski coaches, having to rely on the participants' own self-diagnosis, were therefore tackling problems at cause, whereas the tennis coaches were only tackling the symptom, the technical fault. This obliged us to do more training with the tennis coaches to enable them to detach themselves more effectively from their expertise.

Effective questions in coaching

The most effective questions in coaching have a number of characteristics in common.

- They raise the client's self-awareness by provoking thinking and challenge.
- They demand truthful answers by cutting through obfuscation and waffle.
- They are short.
- They go beyond asking for information by asking for discovery.
- They encourage the client to take responsibility for him- or herself.
- They stick closely to the client's agenda.
- They lead to learning for the client.
- They are more than likely to begin with the words 'what' or 'how'.

See the contrast even in everyday enquiries about another person's health or well-being: 'Are you feeling better?' invites a brief 'yes' as the answer. 'How are you feeling?' opens the way for a longer, fuller answer if the other person wishes to make one. See it even more strongly in questions which seek factual answers from a client and questions that provoke a deeper response:

Fact-seeking questions	Deeper questions
Which topics are you going to include in your presentation?	What will a wonderful presentation look like, sound like and feel like?
How many hours a week do you work now?	What would an ideal work-life balance be for you?
What's so worrying about this situation?	What will this worry look like in five years' time?

Some super-useful questions

The easiest way to understand the difference between effective and less effective questions in coaching is to look at some actual examples. When I was relatively new to coaching, I was fortunate to get sent by my then boss to a course on organizational consulting run by Columbia University. There I encountered a set of questions which were so obviously special in their impact on people that I immediately adapted them to my coaching work. There is an equivalent in therapy – so-called 'magic questions' from which these questions had probably sprung. Whatever their origin, I attached a crib sheet to my diary and shamelessly kept it open during coaching sessions. I would explain that I needed the prompt and that the client would be the beneficiary.

This list, much adapted, has proved its worth time and time again as an outline script, not just to me but to the many hundreds of other coaches we have now trained. It will work in almost any situation, regardless of the setting or the issue. There are several points to note about it:

- The questions are content-free.
- They are short.
- They do not include the word 'I'.
- They work elegantly as a natural progression, starting with asking the client to state the problem, going on to restating the problem as a goal, then to naming options and finally to first steps to action.

Here are the questions:

1 *What's the issue?*
   Asks the client to state the problem. Can often usefully cut through a client's lengthy account by asking him or her to summarize what the problem actually is.
2 *What makes it an issue **now**?*
   Issues that clients bring to coaching have typically been around in the client's life for a long time. But often there is some immediate provocation or development which is providing energy for change, even if this is in the form of anger or worry. Paradoxically, this anger or worry will provide energy for change and resolution. That is why it is worth naming and surfacing it.
3 *Who owns this issue/problem?*
   If the client does not own it, there is no point in discussing it. You can only coach the problem owner. Some clients come to coaching in order to find out how to change someone else whereas the basic assumption of coaching is that you can only change yourself. This

question puts the onus back onto clients to own whichever bit of the issue is theirs.

4   *How important is it on a 1–10 scale?*
If the problem is not important then why are you and the client wasting time discussing it? Importance captures the idea of issues with potential for major impact on a client's life. Anything the client scores at less than 5 should be set aside.

5   *How much energy do you have for a solution on a 1–10 scale?*
This question often draws an interesting response. The client may have told you the problem has an importance of 9, but then tells you that his/her energy for a solution is only 3 or 4. If so, you will want to ask a follow-up question such as 'What would need to happen to increase the energy to 8 or 9?'

6   *What have you already tried?*
This question stops you offering pointless advice which the client has already tried or considered and it also lets you in early on the client's thinking. Most coaching problems have already been the focus of a great deal of energy and thought on the client's part. You need to know what this energy and thought has produced. If the client has not tried anything yet, that will also provoke an interesting discussion.

7   *Imagine this problem's been solved. What would you see, hear and feel?*
Up until now, the client has been deep in the problem. You will typically see this reflected in the way the client has been sitting and talking – often slumped or despairing. By asking this question you tap into his or her resourcefulness. Clients will sit up straighter, stop frowning and will look generally lighter.

8   *What's standing in the way of that ideal outcome?*
This question broadens out the client's thinking. Expect new insights to occur from this point on.

9   *What's your own responsibility for what's been happening?*
An essential question. The client is always part of the problem as well as part of the solution. This question makes that assumption explicit and encourages clients to see how they have, maybe at an unconscious level, been sustaining the problem through their own behaviour.

10 *What early signs are there that things might be getting better/going all right?*
However dreadful the situation, there is always something that is working. Identifying and building on it is part of the process of change and improvement.

11 *Imagine you're at your most resourceful. What do you say to yourself about this issue?*
This question assumes that underneath all our typical confusion, at

some level we do know what we should do. Another version of this question: 'If I could give you a pill which contained all the courage and insight you needed, what would you do?' I have yet to find a client who could not find an instant reply to this one.

12 *What are the options for action here?*
Now that the question has been looked at from several angles, the client can begin to consider the options for change.

13 *What criteria will you use to judge the options?*
Options are even more useful when you have criteria against which to judge them. Typical criteria might be: practicality, cost, fit with the client's values, time – and so on.

14 *Which option seems the best one against those criteria?*
At this point you are narrowing down again towards action – including, of course, just pondering.

15 *So what's the next/first step?*
The answer may be to do some more research, to have a conversation, or to make a big life decision.

16 *When will you take it?*
Asking for a commitment to *when* makes it more likely that the client will actually do something different as a result of the coaching.

I have seen this format, adapted of course to individual vocabulary and preferences, work time and time again. Not only does the format work; it also works at speed because there are few diversions.

If you are new to coaching, I recommend a practice with a willing guinea pig to see how it goes. On our training courses, we ask participants to coach each other using this list, asking these questions and no others. Both coach and client are usually amazed at how well the format works.

Sticking to the client's language

The effective coach notices and picks up on the client's language. When clients are talking about issues that really touch them their language changes: it becomes more vivid, sometimes more direct, sometimes more metaphorical. It gives you clues to what really matters to the client and this is virtually always worth exploring.

Sean
Sean, one of my BBC clients, constantly used metaphors that were virtually all military. His *troops* were going to *go over the top* in their *battle* with the *enemy*.

This *battle* might be an enjoyable *joust* or it might *go nuclear*. When I pointed out this pattern to him, he was amazed and thoughtful. 'Well, yes', he said, 'I see my department as being engaged in a life or death struggle for survival. We're fighting the independent production companies and our BBC bosses for commissions and if we don't win it will be the sack for all my producers.'

I asked him what implications he thought there might be to seeing his task as a *battle*. 'Ah', he said, suddenly thoughtful, 'you mean I might be seeing enemies where there aren't any?' This conversation was a turning point: the beginning of devising a new and successful strategy for the department. The new strategy was backed up by coaching in which Sean developed and practised the influencing and negotiating skills he had neglected for so long in his thirst for a fight.

Sometimes it is enough just to pick up on one word. Here is an example:

Philip

Philip is running a major building project. The project has been the focus of adverse publicity about its environmental impact and, as its public face, Philip has had to appear at open forum meetings where he has faced hostile questioning. He describes feeling *devastated* by some of the questions from the audience, so devastated that he feels he gave lame answers and lost face.

Non-helpful responses from the coach might include: 'There there ... don't worry, everyone feels devastated at some point'; 'Toughen yourself up, mate; if you can't stand the heat, stay out of the kitchen', and so on. Instead, Philip's coach notices and stays with the most vivid word in his description and says: 'Devastated? That's a strong word.' There is a brief moment of silence and Philip says 'Yes, devastated.'

Coach: ... by?

Philip: By their rudeness and aggression.

Coach: And that was devastating because ... ?

Philip: [fervently] Because it implied that I had no integrity but, actually, my whole reason for working on this project is because I strongly believe it is the right path to take – it's the least bad option for the community and will have many positive benefits. I would never *ever* ally myself with something that was going to be damaging environmentally.

Coach: Powerful stuff! What would you say to yourself now about dealing with those hostile questions differently?

Philip: (Short silence) Well it's obvious isn't it? I never said to them what I've just said to you!

Coach: So – in the next meeting?

Philip: I tell them what my fundamental beliefs and values are around this project. And I tell it with passion! And if they still criticize – and they may – so be it. I don't think it can hurt me.

Exploring feelings

This core coaching skill has the simplicity of the obvious, and, along with that, the risk of it being constantly ignored.

Virtually all clients already know what the 'solutions' are to their problems. Examples might be:

Problem	Solution
I can't manage my time	Prioritize
I don't know what to do about my career	Take logical stock of your career and follow the rational path
My boss is difficult	Give your boss some feedback

The reason clients find it difficult to follow the apparently obvious path is that feelings are getting in the way. Many of us, but particularly people with a strong preference for logic and rationality, act as if we believe that logic will solve the problem. Logical methods of problem solving are even taught on management development courses.

Unfortunately, the logical solution may be obvious, but remain unimplemented. For the problems above, for instance, why can't the client take his or her own advice?

I could prioritize	But I am driven by assumptions from my early life about hard work and my identity is bound up in work
I could follow the logic of career choice	But I am terrified of novelty and change
I could give my boss feedback	But he frightens me, as all male authority figures do

This is why, along with looking at issues rationally, it is important to enquire into the feelings. No client issue worth the focus of a coaching session will ever be without a feeling aspect. As coaches our role is often to help clients articulate feelings that have been there but unrecognized or to help them say out loud what they have kept inside.

Warning

When you ask a client about feelings, you will often get a thought. The symptoms of thoughts are clients who say, 'I feel that ... this is exciting/interesting/worrying.' As soon as you hear the word *that*, you are getting a thought.

You are getting a feeling when a client says 'I feel excited/worried.' Point this difference out to the client and press for the feeling.

How to ask for feelings:

A client describes an issue.

Coach: How does that feel?
Client: It feels X.
Coach: And how does that feel?
Client: It feels like [gives a metaphor or simile].
Coach: That sounds [difficult, or striking] – say some more about that?
Client: [Describes what the metaphor feels like.]

Clive

Clive is a senior civil servant and is working for an exacting Cabinet Minister. It is his second coaching session and he has said he wants to explore the whole issue of how he manages his time.

Coach: So you're finding it difficult to manage your time?

Clive: Yes, I did the time management course years ago and I know I should have A, B and C lists and all that stuff, but I still can't stick to it, which is stupid. I'm working really long hours and getting stressed.

Coach: So how does this pattern of long hours and stress feel?

Clive: It feels out of control, mad ...

Coach: out of control ... mad ... what does it feel like, being out of control and mad?

Clive: Like being in a whirlwind, a tornado, stressed to death, prone to jumping down people's throats but of course it would be death to do that with my current Minister. He works on such a short fuse himself!

Coach: Death – that sounds extreme – say more?

Clive: Yeah, death, the end. Driven, helpless, high speed, dangerous, destructive.

Coach: Death, driven, helpless ... What would you like instead?

Clive: I'd like to be a more steady cardiograph, calm, peaceful.

Coach: And how would that feel?

Clive: Wonderful. Peaceful, in control. Able to do my job properly.

This kind of dialogue, including its typically peculiar leaps from one metaphor to another, gives both coach and client a vocabulary for exploration. It surfaces the issues that are getting in the way of the logical solution and leads to a solution which is more likely to stick.

There are two natural places to ask for feelings. The first is at the beginning of exploring the issue. The second is at the end when the decision has been made by the client about what to do.

David

After a lengthy discussion with his coach, David has concluded that he needs to leave his current job.

Coach: So just one final check, David. What would need to happen to persuade you to stay?

David: Nothing. I've got to leave! I must move on.

Coach: That sounds really final. How does it feel, knowing you must move on?

David: Scary but exciting.

Coach: Say more about scary and exciting?

David: Scary because I've got so comfortable and it will force me to check out that I'm as good as I think I am and that's frightening. Exciting because I know I will grow in a new job and that's what always motivates me. In fact just contemplating it now makes me feel – whoopee!

Coach: So?

David: Let's get down to working on how I'm going to do it!

Note: there are only a few questions in this area that the coach needs to ask and they can be asked constantly:

> How does that feel?
> Tell me about that feeling ...
> Say more ... ?

Brevity

The most powerful coaching questions are often extremely short because they cut to the heart of the issue. The ideal question is between seven and twelve words long. I believe the most powerful question of all is this one: 'What do you want?' Although another strong candidate is: 'What needs to happen to ... ?'

Ros

Ros is a new Chief Executive who has inherited a less than ideal team. She expresses lack of confidence about her own ability to cope and also a rising level of concern about her Finance Director, Isobel. The coach encourages her to let off steam for a few moments.

Ros: ... and then Isobel made it much much worse by once again correcting me in a meeting and telling me that as I'm not a finance specialist, I had no idea what I was talking about and she couldn't really understand what on earth I was going to do about interpreting the accounts – on and on and on. I was so annoyed. And her manner with her team is awful – she's rude and she consistently loses her best people. We really can't have senior people behaving like she does.

Coach: What do you want?

Ros: I want her to go!

Coach: So what needs to happen to make that happen?

Ros: I've got to talk to my Chair and get him on side and then find a civilized way for her to leave as soon as possible.

At last – clarity. Once these words 'I want her to go' have been spoken, the question then becomes how it can happen, not whether or not it is a good idea.

Sometimes the most effective question is a single word: 'So ... ?'; 'And ... ?'; 'Because ... ?' Or even a questioning silence.

You could even say that any coaching conversation reduces itself essentially to three ultra-short questions: 'What?' (Identifying the issue); 'So what?' (Implications); 'What next?' (Action).

Summarizing

Summarizing is important. First, it shows that you are listening because you cannot summarize accurately unless you have been listening. Second, it reassures clients that you are keeping track of things. This is particularly important where there has been a period of intense and discursive conversation. Equally important, it keeps you in the frame and emphasizes your role. Also, it gives you a check that you really are understanding what the client is saying.

Summarizing provides punctuation in the coaching conversation. The coach's summary – perhaps every five minutes or so (patterns vary, of course) – makes it a two-way and not a one-way conversation.

When you feel you are getting confused by the twists and turns of a client's story, that is probably a reliable sign that you need to summarize. I now actually say to clients 'I'm getting a bit lost here – can I try a summary?'

Beginner coaches often need to rely on summarizing to get them beyond the panic of Level 1 listening. If you know you can always summarize, you know you will always have something to say which is respectful to the client and helps you get back on track.

Genuine summarizing has these features:

- It does not contain any judgement of your own.
- It does not interpret.
- It uses the client's language.
- It ends with a question – 'Have I got that right?', or 'Is that a fair summary of where we seem to have got to?'
- It is genuinely a summary and therefore brief rather than a polly-parrot rendering at the same length as the client's own account.

Some useful summarizing phrases are

> I think it would be useful to summarize where we've got to here ...
> There seem to be three or four main views that you have been put-ting forward ...
> Can I check that I've really understood the points you're making here? What you feel is that ...
> So, to summarize so far ...
> Or even the very brief, So you feel angry/sad/happy/confused about this?

Getting to the crux

This describes the skill of forcing a client to name what is ultimately at stake in whatever the issue is. The relief of being able to talk to another person who listens non-judgementally is such that clients will often begin to ramble. Signs of this are:

- the client tells you the same thing in several different ways;
- you begin to feel bored because you've already heard what the issue is;
- an instinct that the long story is a way of avoiding the main issues;
- the client starts way back in the distant past history of whatever he or she is describing;
- the client gets lost in all the detail: 'Where was I – I'm losing my thread here!'

As a coach, it is not a good use of the coaching session to let the client rove about in all the detail of a story. Getting to the crux is about pinning down what the real issue is – for you and the client. An example might be a client who has spent a long time describing her anger at what she feels was manipulative behaviour on the part of a team member. The team member has ended up making her feel stupid in front of others. This is not the first time this team member has done this. The conversation between you and the client has begun to take on a circular flavour. As the coach you intervene to say: 'So Barbara, the crux of it is that you're angry and fed up with this behaviour and want to do something about it?' Naming the real issue allows clients to address the nub and decide what to do about it.

Useful phrases

> So what's the crux here for you?
> So the crux of it here is . . .
> Listening to you describing this, what you're saying is that this is really about . . .
> Can we cut to the chase? What's really bugging you here – is it x or y?
> So the nub of all this is that the real issue here is . . .

Getting to the crux is a sophisticated form of summarizing. Like summarizing, it is often best put as a question. That way clients can disagree and in disagreeing come to their own understanding of what the real bottom line is for them.

Example

Coach: So the crux here for you is that you need to join a health club and get your exercise programme going?

Client: Mmm . . . No, it's more that I should start walking more – for instance to the station every day. I don't think I'd stick to a health club routine.

Interrupting

Interrupting people is generally thought rude in our society. As children we learn that you never or rarely interrupt – it is part of being socialized. Hence, for instance, the mixture of horror, awe and amusement that the tougher journalist-presenters evoke: they break the taboo.

In coaching we also have to break the taboo. The client is paying us to get to the heart of things and coaching time is limited. Also, clients have already probably gone round and round the loop several times with friends. For many clients, there will be a well-rehearsed drone to the story. You will get to recognize the signs of this.

Interrupting needs to be done with discretion. There are always caveats to consider:

Potential for interrupting	But ...
A client is going on and on, giving enormous amounts of detail which seems irrelevant.	The client may need to do this in order to get the story straight in his or her own mind.
The client is talking continuously about the past. Coaching is not psychotherapy where the purpose may be to reinterpret the past. It is about the future.	The client may need the catharsis of talking about the past.
The client gives the full script of every conversation. The give-away is lots of 'So he said ... and then I said ... '	This may be one of the client's ways of storytelling. The client may need feedback on how to be more succinct. If clients do this with you they are probably doing it with everyone and potentially getting the reputation of being a bore.

Why interrupt?

Clients often go on too long as a way of avoiding getting to the real point. Talking at length may be a conscious or unconscious tactic – a way of keeping the coach at bay. These clients may tempt you with distractions they know you will find alluring. This is nearly always because you are on the track of some nodal point for change. One British politician owned up to this tactic with his personal trainer:

> When I am under the cosh being pushed to my personal limit I might suddenly reveal a fascinating piece of low-level gossip to distract him or show intense interest in his life and welfare.

Sometimes, the same clients who play on your politeness may be the first to say later that the coaching was just a lot of pointless talking.

Not interrupting may mean that you are colluding with a client that the problems all lie with someone or something else. Other clients may not know how long is *too long* for talking about an issue and will need your help in establishing it. Some people talk a lot when they are nervous. Interrupting them will reassure them. Clients may know well enough that they are going on too long but may still have got into the habit of doing it. You do not need to know all the background in order to be able to coach effectively – in fact often you need to know remarkably little, but clients may assume that you do need to know a lot of background.

If they go on too long as a matter of routine, both they and you will become dissatisfied because you will never get to the nub.

How to interrupt

- Negotiate the expectation that you will interrupt in your first session with the client.
- Trust your intuition that it is time to do it.
- Set aside your worries about whether the client will dislike you for doing it – the chances are that they will respect you more. Coaching is definitely not like a polite conversation with a friend.
- Ask permission – 'May I interrupt you here?'
- Use body language to help – e.g. a hand held palm up (traffic cop style) to the client.
- Say, 'I'm getting lost here – do I really need to know all the detail? What do you think?'

This skill also links to being able to give clients robust feedback. Point out their patterns, for example:

Coach: I notice that whenever we start talking about x, you seem to change the subject. Is this just me or is my suspicion right that this is a difficult topic for you?

Client: Oh crumbs, yes, you're right. Let's talk about it now!

Example

Coach: So how did you get on with the idea we talked about last time – of joining a dining club as a way of meeting some potential partners?

Client: Oh well, I met my friend Patty and I was talking it through with her and she said she'd known of someone who had gone to one of those clubs and she'd had quite a nice time but she said she wouldn't necessarily want to do it herself because –

Coach: [interrupting] I'm more interested in what you're going to do!

Client: Oh yes, well actually Patty said she might come with me but I'm not sure about that because she can look a bit vulgar and as I said to her, we might look a bit of a right pair if you know what I mean. People often think we're sisters but I don't know why they –

Coach: [interrupting)] So you and Patty might go together?
Client: Yes, that's the idea.
Coach: When might you do that?
Client: Why not strike while the iron is hot – next week!

Encouraging clients to be specific

When a client is bewildered, angry or concerned about an issue, he or she may begin by explaining it through extravagant generalizations, assertions or comparisons. This is a sign that feeling has taken over from logic and also a signal to you that the issue is important to the client. Encouraging the client to be specific is often the swiftest way to begin unpacking what is really at stake.

Here are some examples of how to use the technique:

The client makes a comparison:	This is the worst boss I've ever had.
The coach surfaces the comparison:	Worst in what way? Or, Worse than what specifically?
The client makes a generalization:	She's always late.
The coach challenges the generalization:	Always? No exceptions?
The client makes a bald assertion:	I don't like the way this organization is going.
The coach asks for a specific example:	What specifically don't you like about the way the organization is going?
Alternatively, the coach asks for the opposite:	So if everything were going well in the organization, what specifically would be happening for you?
The client states implied rules which indicate firmly held beliefs:	We should know exactly how this recruitment programme is going to be organized.
The coach surfaces the implied rule and asks what the result would be of changing the belief:	What would happen if you didn't know exactly how the recruitment programme was going to be organized?

Look out here for *must* and *should*. For instance, if a client says 'I must have advance warning of changes in plans', the coach might reply, 'What does having advance warning of changes do for you?'

Can'ts may represent particularly strongly held self-limiting beliefs:

The client says:	I can't hope to change the way I work.
The coach replies:	What's stopping you?

Moving the discussion on

Closed questions have their place in coaching.

> 'Have we exhausted that topic?'

This implies that the answer is yes and will allow you to move on quickly to the next part of the session.

Linking questions or statements are also useful here. Links combine a brief summary of the discussion that has just happened with a look forward to the next section. Here's an example:

> So in this part of the discussion we've looked at how the pressures on the business are affecting it in a number of ways (you then briefly enumerate them) and our plan now is to look in more detail at each of these. Is that OK?

For daily examples of how to do this elegantly, examine any live discussion programme on television or radio. Broadcasters call these links *segues*, meaning a technique of sliding seamlessly from one topic to another by making a link between them.

The simplicity that counts

The kind of language I have described in this chapter goes beyond technique, though technique is important.

Language in successful coaching is the disciplined simplicity that comes from trusting clients to tap into their own resources. It is about paring down to the essence – having the questions but understanding that you don't need to have the answers.

4 Taking stock: the learning client

The process of coaching begins with an assessment of where the client is now. Our prime task as coaches is to facilitate learning for the client and that is impossible unless you and the client have a shared understanding of where you both currently stand. In this chapter, I look at a range of techniques for making this initial assessment.

Clients bring a whole range of issues to coaching. These may show as urgent dilemmas or as nagging background puzzles. It would be quite usual to find that in any one client several major work and life issues present simultaneously. This should not be surprising because in coaching you are working with the whole person, not some subset – even if that is what the client initially assumes. Clients have many times assured me that they are completely different people at home from how they are at work. This, in itself, should set alarm bells ringing, for both coach and client.

This client, for instance, vividly described himself thus:

> **Evan**
> I say goodbye to my wife and son, heartily kissing them both, and set out on the walk to the station. I always feel melancholy leaving them. As I'm doing it, I feel a bit like a cartoon character. In the cartoon, I start as Domestic Man, a nice, mildish, smiley pussycat. Domestic Man is blinking slightly helplessly through his glasses then he gradually transmogrifies into the dark and frightening Work Person who gets off the train in London. The briefcase, which would look a bit of an affectation for Domestic Man, has become a weapon of mass destruction. The glasses magnify the piercing eyes. The suit, which would look like an Oxfam donation on Domestic Man suddenly fits in all the right places. Instead of an amiable slouch, Work Person seems about seven feet tall, has a towering stride, and a don't-mess-with-me scowl to match.

Evan ran a Directorate in a large public sector organization where his reputation was for intimidating and demanding leadership. In requesting executive coaching, Evan knew that something was wrong somewhere and saw coaching as a way to find out what it was. Initially he imagined that we would be looking exclusively at his work world. But part of the secret of finding the answers he needed was in looking at the connections and indeed disconnections between the two selves he so powerfully described when given the opportunity to talk about his whole life.

Whatever the issues a client brings to the coach, there will be a sequence of necessary stages through which coach and client must pass:

1   Where, who and what am I now – in my life, my work, my relationships, my skills?
2   Where, who and what would I like to be ideally?
3   Given those answers, what goals do I need to set for myself?
4   How can I achieve and sustain those goals?

The process is iterative and dynamic. When one set of goals is achieved there will be new challenges and tasks ahead. How to answer the first of these questions is what this chapter is about.

A feedback-exclusion zone?

So beginning the self-discovery journey starts with a well-rounded scrutiny of where the client is now. This is tough for many clients whether they are executive coaching clients or have signed up for life coaching. Most of us live in a feedback–exclusion zone and the Scottish poet's well-known plea remains an impossible dream

> Wud that God the gift wud gie us
> To see oursels as others see us.
> (Robert Burns)

Few of us really see ourselves as others see us. In the corporate world it is striking how isolated senior people can be and what a high cost both they and the organization can pay for this isolation. In her riveting account of the late 1990s crisis at Marks and Spencer, Judi Bevan lays it out with stark clarity. She compares Sir Richard Greenbury, the Chief Executive who led Marks and Spencer to the brink of complete collapse, with Margaret Thatcher, who did the same for the Conservative Party:

> Like Margaret Thatcher, Greenbury was an example of the classic leader who hung on too long. Surrounded by weak people who pretended at all times to agree with him, he was eventually pushed out by those he believed were his loyal lieutenants. The parallels with him and Thatcher were clear. Both possessed of towering egos, they had rallied the troops in times of crisis and then allowed themselves

to be diverted, seduced by the perfume of power. They both failed to nurture a worthy successor, or to bring in new blood. Their increasingly irrational behaviour was tolerated by their acolytes, who found them inspiring on the way up, as long as the formula produced success. For Thatcher, the catalyst for her removal was the poll tax, for Greenbury it was the profits collapse and the attempted coup by Keith Oates. Both were great leaders whose tragedy was that *they failed entirely to appreciate the impact of their personalities on those around them.* They both tended to shoot messengers bearing bad news and so the bad news ceased to reach them – until it was too late.

(Bevan 2002, my emphasis)

This reminds me of being a participant on a BBC management development course in the 1980s when the then reigning Director General was invited to come and hear our possibly somewhat naïve proposals about how to solve the BBC's organizational problems. Most of the time he remained affable and politely interested. However, he suddenly flipped into glacial overdrive at the notion that there was anything wrong with the morale of the BBC's staff, then generally accepted as a major problem, snapping pettishly, 'Don't tell me staff morale has never been lower. Morale has *always never been lower.* Let's get on to the positive, shall we?' Needless to say, with self-preservation sensibly to the fore, our suggestions were made in a noticeably more timid way after that.

In general, the people around us don't tell us the truth. Leaders don't get told the truth by those around them. They don't get told the truth by their bosses and are even less likely to get told the truth by those they manage. They don't get told the truth about the organization and they don't get told the truth about their own leadership styles. There is no mystery about why.

First is the shoot-the-messenger tendency as described by Judi Bevan in her blow by blow account of what happened at Marks and Spencer. People who challenged Rick Greenbury would be treated to terrifying red-faced blasts. A respected journalist on the *Investors Chronicle* wrote what turned out to be a balanced and highly accurate forecast of troubles to come. She was treated to a 'Rickogram': a rude and ill-considered diatribe which the Editor must have enjoyed publishing under the headline 'Fierce riposte from M&S's Mr Grumpy'. While a journalist can wriggle free from such attacks, it is much more difficult for colleagues who feel, rightly or wrongly, that their futures depend on the patronage of the leader. It is easier to buy time and whimper in corridors with fellow sufferers than to confront.

The fear of ejection is very real. We can see what happens to the majority of whistleblowers, large or small: they find it difficult initially to get taken seriously and when they do, many seem to end up leaving the organization. Most of us fear separation and do not want to be outside the herd.

This has never been more compellingly described than in Jerry Harvey's controversial essay 'Eichmann in the organization' (1988). Here he argues the probability that no one ever told Adolph Eichmann, the notorious Nazi who implemented the policies of the Holocaust, that what he was doing was morally wrong. Harvey quotes the case of the Danish King during the Second World War who, with his government, told the occupying Germans that if Danish Jews were to be forced to wear a yellow star as a preliminary to deportation, then the King would be the first to wear one too. Danish Jews remained in Denmark. But such courage is rare, not just in times of war and life or death emergency but in the mundane exchanges of corporate life.

Fundamentally, many of us are profoundly afraid of genuine feedback. One large study of US managers showed that only half of the sample had ever asked for feedback (Jackman and Strober 2003). Among the many reasons cited were a number of familiar avoidance patterns. These included:

> *Reawakened childish dependence*: being given feedback potentially awakens the feelings of being a child upbraided by more powerful parents. The feedback receiver dreads being chided for behaviour that falls short of the parental ideal.
> *Procrastination*: the subject of the feedback knows something is wrong but cannot bear the idea of exploring it.
> *Denial*: it might get better if just ignored.
> *Brooding*: the person has a morbid preoccupation with the negative and an overwhelming sense of foreboding. Dread of what they might discover becomes magnified.
> *Jealousy* in relation to others: the potential feedback subject fantasizes that others will emerge more positively from the exercise and hates the idea of being benchmarked in case this turns out to be true.
> *Self-sabotage*: the subject looks for ways to make the expected negatives real.

Giving feedback is a high-level art and in spite of the fact that it is a skill taught on more or less any management development course in the western world, it is still more honoured in the breach than in the observance. Giving honest feedback will name the pluses as much as it identifies the minuses, but it can still feel like making criticisms, and to do that face to face is uncomfortable. It can feel like attacking the person, and therefore be potentially hurtful to the recipient. So for this reason, too, colleagues may hang back. I find that when my clients do get feedback through some of the mechanisms I discuss in this chapter, they will often say, 'Well, I've heard some of this before, but I never knew people cared that much.' In other words they have been given hints, but too opaquely, or possibly too unskilfully, for them to hear.

Breaking through the feedback-exclusion zone

You could describe almost the whole process of coaching as being about breaking through the feedback-exclusion zone because an essential preliminary of any successful coaching is increased self-awareness. However, for the purposes of this chapter I want to concentrate on some particular tactics and approaches that coaches can use to help the client with the very first stages of the coaching process. You will have your favourites and the ones that you can make sing for you. These ideas are meant as a menu of options – you will never have time to use them all.

The core questions at this stage are:

Who are you as you see yourself now?
How much do you know about your impact on others?
What are the pressing issues for you?

Autobiography: how did you get from there to here?

I have always regretted it when I have not asked clients for a brief account of their lives so far. If you are going to do it, the first session is your best chance. It builds intimacy and rapport and also establishes that you are interested in the whole person, not just the work person. The whole person has evolved from life experience, so hearing a client tell his or her life story is one way you begin to understand the client's world.

There are a number of other compelling reasons for doing it:

- For all of us our relationships with authority figures evolved from our relationships with our parents and parent figures such as teachers. Our relationships with peers will have been affected by how we got on with siblings and early friends. These influences on relationships at work will have important effects on approaches to leadership and to being a follower. You need to have some glimmering of understanding about this as the client sees it.
- What clients emphasize and what they leave out is always interesting and relevant to their view of themselves.
- Most clients have never told a complete life story to anyone previously and most enjoy the experience.

Some warnings

- You are not doing psychotherapy or psychoanalysis in coaching. For this reason I encourage clients to take no more than thirty minutes to tell their story.
- If clients resist, do not press.
- Explain why you are asking, using the explanation above.
- Reassure of confidentiality.
- Be prepared for cathartic reactions in clients who have had a childhood trauma such as child abuse, the death of a sibling or parent.
- It is not your role to make interpretations: leave that to the client.
- Do not expect to get 'the whole truth' from this session – it is usually too early. For instance, a gay client may not tell you about his or her sexuality because they may not feel they can trust you at this stage.
- You will want to develop different emphases depending on the expected nature of the coaching. For instance, clients whose expected focus is career coaching can usefully be asked more questions about their career choices to date.

A useful framework

You will not need to ask all these questions. Pick what appeals and develop your own versions of them, as you see fit.

Suggest that the client tells you his or her life history – 'It will help us both if you tell me a bit about yourself – your parents, your place in the family and so on and other aspects of your early life as well as a brief career history – is that OK?'

- Where were you born?
- What was your place in the family – birth order?
- What were your parents' occupations?
- What effect has your birth order had on you – e.g. the experience of being an only child/the youngest of four?
- How did you feel about school?
- What were you rewarded for as a child? What were you punished for?
- If you had to point to one outstanding experience in your childhood – one that had a really major impact on you, what would that be?
- Which of your parents were you closer to?
- Which parent has had more effect on who you are now?
- How did you get on with your siblings?
- What about early personal friendships and romantic entanglements?
- What effects have marriage/partner relationships had on your life?
- (For clients with children) What has the experience of being a parent done?

- What did the experience of higher education do for you?
- How did you make your career choices?
- What helped you decide to move on from earlier jobs?
- What have been the highs and lows?
- What themes and patterns do you see emerging in the story as you have told it?
- What are the links to the coaching we will be doing? (Not all clients see any links. If so, that's fine; just move on.)

Annette

Annette was Chief Executive of a consultancy, a firm of which she was a founding director. The firm operated in the not-for-profit sector, drawing its clients from major charities and public sector organizations. She described herself as having had a lonely childhood with little overt affection. She was the daughter of two famous theatrical people, both of whom married several times before and after being married to each other. At the last count, she told me, she had three living step-parents, many step and half-siblings, but no full siblings. Early recollections were of being *prinked up* as she put it, *to appear as a fashion accessory at glamorous parties*, followed by many bleak moments, including being sent to boarding school at the age of 5. Her own marriage and children were important to her but she had chosen to work in London during the week while her husband worked on his own business from home, forty miles away.

What patterns emerged for her in telling this story? She said that for the first time she understood how pervasive had been her lifelong feeling of being alone in a crowd, and that this had been a protective mechanism. It had toughened her up and she felt she could deal with any challenges in her professional life, including dealing with uncompromising and troublesome client organizations. Also, she felt that in telling her life story, she had had a moment of insight into the performance aspect of her job: 'I enjoy making pitches for work. I enjoy preparing, I enjoy dressing well for it and I do it well. I've suddenly thought this might be something I've inherited from my parents, though I hate to say it! In fact even the rackety nature of my job could be a bit like theirs.'

And the links with the coaching on which we were just embarking? This was a moment of *aha* for Annette. 'The main reason I'm here', she said, 'is that I need to understand more about my style with my staff.' The firm was beginning to struggle in its ultra-competitive market place and Annette had had hints from her team that part of the reason was that, as the founder, Annette hugged too much work to herself and was a charming but remote presence. 'They tell me they don't know what I feel about them', she said. 'Mm ... I wonder why I've never realized this before, that it's got a lot to do with protecting that little girl I used to be in those early days ... ?'

Understanding the pattern also creates a moment of potential choice for the future. *This is how I've been up until now. That was then, this is now. I can choose to be different.*

Just occasionally it can feel as if the telling of the story is almost all that needs to happen. The most dramatic example I have ever encountered was this one:

Michael

Michael came to his first session with one burning issue. His boss, Felix, had decided to expand his team from four to eight as part of planned growth in the firm. Michael was deeply uncomfortable about this change, feeling that it was a strategic mistake and that it would make decision making far more complex than it needed to be. Felix and Michael had a close relationship – in fact they had worked together for ten years and Felix had brought Michael into their present company with him. Michael's role in effect was to be special adviser to Felix and had helped him do what he described as 'keeping the stupidities of the organization at bay'. They socialized outside work and their families got on well together.

In describing his early life, Michael painted an unusual picture. He was one of eight children in a tightly knit fundamentalist Christian household which held severe and uncompromising views about mixing outside the exclusive society created within the tiny church community. He was one of a pair of fraternal twins right in the middle of the family. His father was a lay preacher. He and his brother – at first subtly and then overtly – rebelled against what they saw as the strictures of the family's way of life, its religiosity, its harsh rules and its stifling lack of privacy. They even developed a special twins' language which their parents could not understand. As adults they had broken away, completely rejecting their faith. This had included 'marrying out' and being cut off from the family as a consequence.

As he was telling me this, Michael suddenly broke off, stared at me wildly, smote his forehead melodramatically and said, 'Oh my God, I've just realized –'

'You've realized ... ?'

'Eight children ... eight as the size of the new team! Felix is not my brother is he! The team is not my family!'

Michael's realization that he had unconsciously brought a deeply shaping childhood experience into his work was a profound and liberating moment for him. He realized that he had been making false assumptions about the changes ahead and was thus able to think completely differently about the work situation.

Alternative approaches to autobiography

A Life in the Day

When the *Sunday Times* newspaper began its colour supplement in the early 1970s, its then editor, Hunter Davies, devised a brilliantly simple but endlessly fascinating back page feature called *A Life in the Day*, often mistakenly described as *A Day in the Life*. At the time of writing, this feature is still going strong over 30 years later. The person who is the focus of the article is asked to describe a typical apparently humdrum day: what time they get up, what they eat and drink throughout the day, how they get to and from work – all the way through until bedtime. Asking clients to give me *a life in the day* is a wonderfully revealing and mutually useful exercise, especially where I know I have the luxury of working with clients over a longer period, so there is less time pressure.

The activity unearths a different quality of data from anything else I have tried. For instance, I discovered the following with these clients:

> *Clive* feels so pressured by his job as a Finance Director that he unwinds by staying up every night long after his family have gone to bed. He surfs the Internet for hours. Only then can he relax. His sexual life is suffering as a result and so is his energy, as he still has to get up at 7.00 a.m., regardless of whatever time he has gone to sleep.
>
> *Man Weh* feels the pressure of being the only son and a second-generation immigrant from Hong Kong. His elderly parents speak little or no English and he visits them every day. He also feels obliged to devote a good deal of volunteer time to various support groups working for the London Chinese community.
>
> *Diane* has six cats, four dogs, a guinea pig and two rabbits whose comfort she puts before her own. Her anthropomorphized relationships with them are probably preventing her putting energy into the more demanding area of human relationships.
>
> *Colin* loves the rough and tumble of the undemanding male company that he finds in his local pub. This is refreshingly different from the competitive relationships he has at work. This also leads him to drink more beer than is good for his liver or his waistline. Divulging this aspect of his life allows him to speak out loud a worry that he might have an alcohol problem.

Lifelines

It is often a good idea to get clients thinking ahead of your session. An alternative approach to autobiography from simply asking clients to tell you their life story is to brief them to draw it as a graph, bringing the result to the session. The horizontal axis represents years and the vertical axis represents the peaks and troughs of experience. This approach has the benefit of concentrating on the most important moments of the client's life, whether they are the moments of sadness and disappointment or of triumphant success and happiness. Also, as with any technique that avoids verbal analysis, you may get to the core issues more quickly.

What size are my windows?

In the 1950s, two researchers at the University of California devised a simple way of understanding how personality is expressed. In a cute imitation of naming a suburban house, they called their model after a combination of their own names, Joe Luft and Harry Ingram = Johari. The model is probably one of the best known in management development: the Johari Window (Luft 1970). Executive clients will probably already have come across it; clients from other fields may not be familiar with it.

I like to use this 50-year-old model with clients because there is nothing else quite like it for discussing how far what you and others see is the same.

I have set out the model slightly differently from its usual format for ease of understanding (Figure 4.1).

Seen very clearly	**My blind spot**: I don't see these pluses and minuses about myself but others do	**The arena**: I see these pluses and minuses about myself clearly and so do others
What others see		
	The unknown: buried to both myself and others	**The façade**: I see these things about myself but keep them hidden
Not seen clearly		Seen very clearly

What I see

Figure 4.1 The Johari Window

The ideal Johari Window is one where the arena at the top right is much bigger than all the other panes, the principle being that change in the size of one window will affect each of the others. The arena represents the self we share with others. When it is the biggest single pane it means that your view of your strengths and weaknesses will be similar to the views of others. People will know that what they see and the real you are one and the same. Where the façade is the biggest pane, your life could be spent defending what you believe are your secrets. Fear of exposure as an impostor may be a motivator. You may strike others as mysterious or cool or possibly they may pick up a feeling that there is something inauthentic about you. Life behind the façade is exhausting – it takes a lot of energy to hide.

Where the blind spot pane dominates, this could also be bad news. It suggests that you may be blundering through your life with little idea of the way others see your strengths and weaknesses. The phrase 'Bull in a china shop' is sometimes used to describe this kind of person.

A large unknown pane will mean that you are likely to be both a mystery to yourself and to others.

There are two ways to grow the arena. One is by asking people for feedback. When you do this you reduce the size of the blind spot pane because you ask people to share the views they have of you. The second way to increase the size of the arena is through disclosure: telling people about your feelings and thoughts.

Using the Johari Window in coaching

- Draw the model for clients, explaining it as you go.
- Ask clients to draw their own Johari Window, explaining why they have decided on the size of each pane.
- Discuss what changes, if any, they would like to make.

Annette, continued

Annette drew her Johari Window with the arena as the smallest area and the façade as the biggest. She put a question mark against the blind spot: 'I don't know – perhaps that's interesting in itself!'

At first Annette saw her success as being due to the effort she had put into maintaining her façade: the expensive designer labels, the immaculate make up, the glossy office, the fifteenth-century country home and the carefully cultivated professional persona.

Coach: 'Who is the real Annette?'
Annette: 'I'm not sure, and I'm a bit afraid of finding out. Maybe I could get hurt.'

Linking the future of her firm with the hints she had had about her own over-controlling behaviour to colleagues, Annette decided that there was an information gap: what did they really feel about her? She decided to find out.

360-degree feedback

I suggest this process to perhaps a third of my coaching clients. When done well, there are few other ways as reliable of pinpointing a learning programme for a client. Mostly in coaching we are dependent on *storytelling* from the client as the main source of data. When you commission a 360° process you are bringing the *observation* of others into play – hence its value.

360° feedback is a planned process of soliciting comment from a selection of people in a range of relationships all around you (hence the label 360°). These people will typically come from whatever significant constituencies there are in the client's work life, for instance, peers, boss or other seniors, customers/clients, and people who are direct reports.

Where you are doing executive coaching, it is critical to make the compelling business case to the client for the self-awareness that 360° feedback can bring. 360° is not just another nice-to-have. It can also be critical to the success of the business. In his book *The New Leaders* (Goleman *et al.* 2002), Daniel Goleman quotes research into what distinguished the leadership of a number of highly successful US healthcare companies from the least successful ones. Positive performance was measured by return on equity, share price and so on over a ten-year period. He says:

> Tellingly, the CEOs from the poorest performing companies gave themselves the highest ratings on seven of the ten leadership abilities. But the pattern reversed when it came to how their subordinates rated them: they gave these CEOs low ratings on the very same abilities. On the other hand, subordinates saw the CEOs of the best performing companies as demonstrating all ten of these leadership abilities most often.

So self-delusion was associated with poor company performance and a high level of self-awareness with company success. In one of Goleman's own parallel studies he also found that the more senior the managers, the more they were likely to inflate their own ratings. 'Those at the highest levels had the least accurate view of how they acted with others.'

There are a number of different ways 360° can be done:

By the client

This is the simplest and most direct method. Ask the client to pick eight people and to contract with them for some private time and for honest answers to the following questions:

> In what ways do you think I am already effective?
> In what ways do you think I am less effective?
> What could I do to improve my relationship with you?
> What would be the one piece of advice you would give me about how to improve my effectiveness?

Prime the client on how to stay non-defensive and to encourage honest responses, pressing for examples and further clarity, and writing down everything their feedback givers say without editing. This method has the tremendous advantage of people owning their opinions directly to the client and the client hearing them without any intermediary. However, it does depend on clients being able to stay in non-defensive mode when they hear things they don't like, and it also depends on the ability and willingness of the feedback givers to be straightforward.

Questionnaires

There are hundreds of commercially available questionnaires, most of which can now be delivered to respondents via the Internet. The questionnaire should be based on unambiguous behavioural descriptions. An early version of a 360° questionnaire in one organization was widely greeted with snorts of derision because one of the items was 'behaves in a way that leads others to trust him/her'. To the sceptical audience at whom it was aimed, the phrasing was clear evidence of management gobbledegook. Actually, as a description of behaviour it was simply too broad for anyone to answer easily. The questionnaire should always be tailored for the organization, using its own language and linked to its particular organizational development needs to get around this kind of problem.

About 60 items is the right number with a five-point scale for rating effectiveness. Fewer than that number of items and it is unlikely you will be capturing the complexity of individual behaviour. More, and respondents will tend to tick any old answer just to hurry through the boredom of the process. It's vital to have free-flow open questions at the end where people can write in their comments. This helps give the messages clearly and also explains why people have scored the client the way they have.

The client should always be free to choose the respondents. This guards against any tendency to hide behind the idea that the feedback is something that is being done to the client. You need at least eight and ideally twelve respondents to achieve a valid result, including the client's self-perception. Confidentiality is vital. This is why it is always better to have the collating process handled outside the organization.

Telephone interviews

This is the Rolls Royce version of 360°. Again the client nominates and prepares the respondents. You telephone them under conditions of non-attributable confidentiality, conducting the same structured interview with each, exploring areas such as creating direction, leadership style, performance management, influencing style, communication, and so on. You then write a report for your client based on what you have heard. My reports typically run to seven or eight pages. The advantage of this method is that you can probe for examples and for clarification. You can also explore any interesting inconsistencies – for instance that the client's impact on more junior people is different from their impact on seniors. The disadvantage of this method is that it depends critically on your ability to ask good questions, to stay objective, to avoid convergent thinking at the same time as not missing the important themes, and to write the report in a way that your client can hear. For added objectivity you might want to commission a colleague who has never met the client to undertake this process for you or to partner you in it.

The debrief is the place where the learning begins. Your role here is to:

- help the client look unblinkingly at the messages, positive, negative and middling;
- steady and reassure clients who only see the negative;
- challenge the clients who are unduly complacent;
- remind clients that feedback is not an instruction to change: they can choose what they take notice of and what they ignore;
- help the client make links to how they see themselves and to other feedback they have received over the years;
- help clients make links to their own perceptions of their learning agenda.

I sometimes give clients a blank grid to take away, ponder and complete to bring back with them for the next session (Figure 4.2).

Use this grid to fill in what the main messages are for you:

		Good news		
Not aware already	*Pleasant surprise: over-modesty?*		*Affirmation: how can I carry on with the good work?*	Already aware
	Shock/denial: how true is this really?		*Challenge to action: how can I change and do the new behaviour consistently – if I want to?*	
		Bad news		

Figure 4.2   Responding to 360° feedback

The impact of 360° feedback is usually considerable.

Annette, continued

Annette's feedback confirmed many of her own insights into how others saw her, but it also surprised her. People in her team saw her as calm, composed, stylish and very cool. The firm had grown on the basis of her personal reputation, and people acknowledged the sheer depth of her knowledge and expertise. Her team saw that her ability to make shrewd judgements about the future market and its trends was an important contribution to the firm's success – 'a natural strategist' summed up many similar comments.

Her composure even in a crisis, which both she and others saw as one of her greatest assets, was also perceived to be a weakness. 'Does she actually have feelings?' asked one person exasperatedly. Similarly, her drive, another considerable plus, also had the power to alienate. 'I think she just sees us as invoicing machines' was how one person put it. Many people spotted her failure to grow a successor, pointing out that this was putting the firm at risk.

Similarly, they spelt out in painful detail how undermining they found her difficulty in delegating. By not delegating she was implying that she lacked trust in the talent and ability of her senior team. The extent of their annoyance and frustration came as a shock to Annette. But perhaps the biggest shock of all was that when asked about what they perceived her values to be, the majority of the people filling in the questionnaire said they did not know. Others assumed that Annette's core motivation was money making, a big turn-off for the majority of her staff. They had joined the company because they were attracted by the idea of working in the non-profit sector and shared many of that sector's values. While it was true that Annette was a natural entrepreneur, she had also chosen to build her firm aiming at non-profit organizations because she too shared these values. 'Surely they can see', she asked mournfully, 'that I'd make so much more money if I'd decided to go for other sectors!' But alas, it was clear that people did not see this!

In discussing these results with Annette, we agreed that the agenda for coaching was:

- building on her strategic ability to reposition the firm against its competitors and to do this through involving her staff;
- rebooting her leadership style by learning how to describe her values far more clearly;
- learning to disclose her feelings, including talking more about her family and asking other people about theirs;
- adopting a coaching approach with the seniors in her team and then delegating a significant amount of work to them.

Getting 360° feedback was supremely useful for Annette. It allowed her to test her own ideas about what she needed to develop against what other people saw. It gave her considerable insight into her Johari blind spot. Like many other clients, the majority of the content in her blind spot was about the overuse of her strengths. The process allowed her to make informed decisions about which parts of the feedback to pay attention to and which she could downplay. Ultimately, it gave her the tools she needed to start the process of rebuilding her firm.

Annette was a steady and focused client, already halfway there in terms of self-awareness. Sometimes you will coach people for whom this is not true. Here the 360° process has the potential for enormous shock because how the client sees him- or herself is so much at odds with the perceptions of others. In this case, the Johari blind spot is far bigger than either the arena or the façade.

Malcolm

Malcolm was poised to leap to the most senior tier in his organization and initially asked for help in dealing with the selection process. In discussing his agenda, it emerged that he had a number of pressing issues with his current job and we agreed to extend the remit of the coaching to include these issues. It was clear that 360° would help. The dismally negative messages in the report alerted me to the need for extra care in the debrief. People saw Malcolm as an angry bully, impatient, prone to inexplicable rages, impossible to please and unable to develop any but the most able of his team. His saving graces were grudgingly seen as his intelligence and his expert knowledge. I emailed Malcolm a copy of the report a carefully calculated 24 hours ahead of our meeting, asking him to mark anything he thought would deserve special attention and suggesting he did not overreact to the contents because we would be talking them through together and putting them in context.

For someone others saw as a bully, Malcolm looked white-faced, shaky and shockingly upset when we met for our session. He was soon in tears. I asked what the tears were about. 'Shame', he said. 'I've had an insight into what it must be like to be managed by me. I'd hate to be managed by me. They don't even like me do they? How could I have got to this?'

My role was to stay steady, calm, compassionate and focused. I am always aware with a report like this of the danger of colluding. This could include some or all of the following:

It's not true.
It's their fault that they don't see your virtues.
It was a bad day for them when they filled it in.
These must be someone else's results.
You used to be like that but of course you've changed ...
and so on.

Most of that session was spent in constructing exactly what behaviour Malcolm's colleagues saw and why it had the impact it did. We got down to micro-behaviours: the way he sometimes darted forward in his chair; his piercing stare when puzzled; the jabbing finger when explaining his point of view; the way he raised his voice when confronted.

We also looked hard at the fear of failure that lay beneath all of this and how this fear drowned out perspective. I explained the 'I value me – I value you' grid (see Chapter 2). Malcolm bravely placed himself firmly in the top left quadrant – 'I value me – I don't value you'. In looping back to his autobiographical account, Malcolm made the clearest possible links to a childhood with a bullying and alcoholic father. 'I learnt to fight back then, but what I've got to learn now is that I'm not fighting him – he's been dead many years in any case. I despised him but I'm doing the same kind of behaviour. It's urgent for me to learn to like myself and then to start liking others, rather than fearing how they might damage me unless I get in first!'

The next major question for Malcolm was his fear: fear that his behaviour was so ingrained that he might not be able to change. It was easy for me to answer this question with a vigorous yes and I have rarely seen a client so motivated and committed to a learning programme.

Several years later, I met Malcolm in another context. He told me that he had never been so frightened in his life as he had been at the moment of receiving that report and that the jolting shock had been the painful but necessary beginning of a new life.

Psychometrics

As part of the 'know thyself' theme for clients, it is useful to be able to offer them a suite of psychometric questionnaires. Psychometrics means, literally, measuring human personality and as a science it has been around for many decades. What is measured and how you measure it and which method is best will continue to be the focus of fierce debate. There are thousands of questionnaires available, many of dubious merit. I prefer to rely on the few tried and tested instruments which are backed by convincing research, are easy to understand and have proved genuinely enlightening to clients time and time again.

The case for psychometrics

Many of us assume that the way we approach the world is, plus or minus a few unimportant details, just like the way others approach it. Psychometrics offers a useful way to demonstrate in just what ways we are like and unlike others.

Psychometrics offers a short cut through what might otherwise take many hours of further discussion and the language of psychometrics can become a useful shared vocabulary not just between coach and client but between client and other clients.

Using two or three such instruments gives several different methods of approach because the starting point of each will be contrasting but valuable.

Popular choices for coaches are:

> *The Myers Briggs Type Indicator^{TM}* (MBTI),[1] first developed by Isabel Myers and her mother Katharine Briggs in the middle years of the twentieth century and constantly updated ever since. The underlying framework is Jungian. Clients emerge as having a preference for one of 16 different personality types. The Indicator highlights preferred thinking style and offers hypotheses about the behaviour likely to be associated with each style.
>
> *The FIRO-B^{TM}* (Fundamental Interpersonal Relationships Orientation – Behaviour), first developed by the US psychologist Will Schutz for the US Navy during the Korean War. The questionnaire produces scores against six possible dimensions of need and style in terms of how we typically behave with others.
>
> *The 16 PF* (Sixteen Personality Factors), first developed by the British psychologist Ray Catell.
>
> *Big Five personality questionnaires*: these are based on research combining results and thinking from many earlier questionnaires and identifying five overarching factors in human personality. Suites of questionnaires include the *NEO* and the *Hogan*.
>
> *The Belbin team roles questionnaire.* This well-known questionnaire identifies which of nine possible informal roles in a team the client will typically prefer to play.
>
> *The OPQ* (Occupational Personality Questionnaire), developed and distributed by the British company Saville and Holdsworth, recognizably in the same genre as the 16 PF.
>
> *Career Anchors*: Edgar Schein's approach to uncovering career motivators. (This is available to order at any bookshop as a booklet which includes a questionnaire.) The basic proposition is that in every life there is one driving motivator. The questionnaire and booklet suggests a format for uncovering what this is. Especially useful for clients where career is the focus.

---

[1] This questionnaire, the FIRO-B, the 16 PF and the Strong Interest Inventory are distributed in the UK through Oxford Psychologists Press, who also run accredited training courses.

The Strong Interest Inventory. This is a vocational interests questionnaire, useful for people with career dilemmas. The Strong also has a long and distinguished history and has been updated many times since its first appearance in the 1920s.

The Thomas-Kilmann Conflict Mode Instrument, first developed in the 1970s. The underlying framework is similar to Thomas Harris's grid, described on page 39. Five typical conflict-management styles are identified, giving clients the opportunity to see which they tend to prefer and which they tend to avoid.

The Ennegram has until recently been an orally taught approach to personality, said to be based on Sufi thinking. There are now questionnaires available which help identify which of the nine personality types represents your typical style.

Using psychometrics skilfully

The most important question to ask is why you are using a psychometric questionnaire at all. Working with new coaches, I often observe undue interest in questionnaires such as the MBTI. We can all be attracted to these and other tools and techniques out of anxiety. The thinking goes something like this:

> If I have a questionnaire to administer and interpret, at least I will be on safe ground. I won't have to worry so much about what question to ask next. I'll have a structure to help me.

When this is your motive, recognize it for what it is: a way of exerting control over the client and over your own fear of incompetence. Using a questionnaire or any other coaching tool for this reason only postpones the moment of coming face to face with the fear and, paradoxically, ensures that you will stay at Level 1 listening (page 47). You could also be tempted to use questionnaires indiscriminately, blind to whether or not the client really needs them. As the old joke has it, 'Give a boy a hammer and he'll discover that everything needs hammering.' Work on your listening skills and questioning technique first.

Don't meddle in this area without training. Licensing training is necessary for most tests: you can't buy them unless you are a registered user. Training prevents disrespectful misuse of such instruments, on the basis that they could come to seem like an interesting but essentially trivial exercise of about as much importance as a magazine quiz.

Also it is easy to assume that you understand a questionnaire because you have been on the receiving end of an interpretation as a user or seen a colleague introduce it to clients, but my observation here is that it is easy to underestimate the extent of what you don't know. Training may seem like an expensive and time-intrusive exercise, but repays the investment you have made, many times over.

The best place to use psychometrics is probably somewhere near the beginning of a coaching programme. Some coaches plan a half-day meeting for the second session where they debrief a number of instruments together. If you have the qualifications and experience, this is probably the ideal way to do it.

However wonderful a psychometric questionnaire is, and many are wonderful, it is never the whole truth about a person. First, the questionnaires are self-report instruments, so they are always potentially open to being filled in as we would hope to be seen rather than as we really are. High-quality questionnaires have safeguards against this tendency, but none is completely foolproof, so all questionnaires depend to some extent on the subject's willingness to take the risk of being candid. Results can also be affected by mood or by particular periods of stress or crisis.

Carl Jung, on whose thinking the MBTI is based, described his typology as 'compass points in the wilderness of human personality'. Those are wise words. Similarly, it can be tempting to assume that questionnaire results represent some kind of final judgement on a person, regardless of that person's own view of themselves. One of the most important questions in the debriefing discussion is, 'How does this seem to you?', or 'How does this tally with how you see yourself?' The client's answer here has to be the best and last word on the topic.

The feedback discussion is at the heart of the process. It involves

- allowing enough time for a full exploration;
- asking how the client felt answering the questions;
- reassuring the client that you will be keeping his/her results confidential;
- acknowledging any scepticism or irritation as healthy;
- briefly explaining the underlying theory behind the questionnaire;
- asking the client to make an estimate of how he/she is likely to emerge against the various dimensions or factors;
- comparing this with the questionnaire results;
- establishing how far the results match self-perception and any other sources of feedback such as 360°;
- looking at examples of behaviour which match reported results;
- seeking examples of behaviour which do *not* match the reported results;
- looking at strengths and development areas and agreeing how to take these forward.

In using psychometric questionnaires you are potentially disturbing the balance of power in the client–coaching relationship. In the normal run of a coaching conversation, the client has the information and you have the questions – in pursuit of a shared understanding. With psychometrics, you have expert information about the questionnaire. This could disadvantage the client and probably explains why many clients will express nervousness about completing a questionnaire with whose purpose they are unfamiliar: 'Will it tell you something about me that could be uncomfortably revealing?'

Poor use of debriefing techniques can include what one of my colleagues dubs *psychological rape*: telling the client that he/she is something devastatingly unpleasant from the lofty pinnacle of your expertise:

> The questionnaire tells me that you are undemocratic in the way you run your team.
> You are at risk of imploding if you don't manage your stress better.
> You don't delegate very well do you?

This is why the principles of creating trust through respect must prevail here as elsewhere in coaching. If the client does not want to take a 'test' even after you have given him or her your best shot at reassurance, then don't press it. Taking any psychometric questionnaire should be voluntary. Watch out for any tendency in yourself to make arbitrary assertions about what a client can or can't do (jobs, skills, relationships) on the basis of the results of the questionnaire. No test has sufficient predictive validity to do this, but in any case such an assertion would be an abuse. Equally importantly, it's essential to resist the temptation to over-interpret. Your role is to explain. The questionnaire results are hypotheses only. Any interpretation should be left to the client. Finally, be alert to your own results on the same tests, sharing them with clients in the interests of equality and keeping constantly alert for the biases and blind spots which might influence how you work with your client on these same issues.

5 Choosing the future: creating goals for coaching

Once clients have taken stock of their present, they – and you – will want to think about their future. This chapter gives you a range of options for helping clients to establish their goals.

Goals for the future are best created through identifying what we have and comparing it with what we want. If the gap is tiny then it is unlikely that we will have any appetite for change, and without this appetite there can be no coaching agenda. Even anger is better than apathy. The awareness of dissatisfaction is what creates our energy for transformation and improvement.

•

The Wheel of Life

This simple, powerful and well-known exercise is rightly a favourite for coaches. Sometimes known as the Balance Wheel, or the Fulfilment Wheel, it asks you to assess your satisfaction with your life as it is now, comparing it with how you would like it to be. The centre of the Wheel represents zero fulfilment or satisfaction and the outer edge of each wedge represents total fulfilment (see Figure 5.1).

The case for using this tool is that it encourages clients to see their lives as a whole – often for the first time. It conveys the expectation that, as a coach, you are as interested in the personal aspects of their lives as in the work aspects. Also, it is another way for clients to tell you about what is currently going on in their lives.

For many clients this is a relatively painless way to pass on important data to you. Here are two examples, both from clients whose presenting issues were career change:

> **Hannah**
>
> Hannah: I've filled in the health wedge at 5. That's because I'm waiting for my histology results next week, and that will tell me whether or not I've got cancer. If I have, I expect the work I do with you to take a different slant from the result I'm hoping for – that I haven't got cancer.

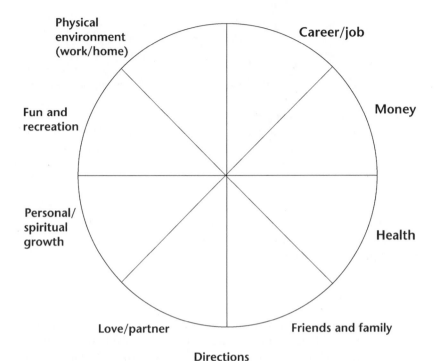

Directions

This exercise asks you to assess your satisfaction with your life as it is now. The centre represents zero satisfaction. The outer edge represents 10: total satisfaction. Rate each wedge on this 0–10 scale, then draw a line connecting each one. What kind of a wheel emerges? What kind of a ride is it giving you?

Figure 5.1 Balance Wheel exercise

Coach:	That must be a huge concern for you. Do you want to say more about that now?
Hannah:	No – Well, yes. I'm having to be so brave with everyone and really I'm scared out of my wits. I'm putting on this Brave Hannah face.
Coach:	[Nods]
Hannah:	Actually, I wouldn't mind just talking it all through with you just to get it into perspective. I'm normally a very optimistic person, but bottling it up hasn't been good for me.
Coach:	OK Brave Hannah – let's unbottle and see what other Hannahs there are and how they feel!

Richard

Richard: I'm really proud of my relationship with my partner, Bernardo. We've been together for 15 years. I'm also keen to be seen as a good example of an 'out' gay man in a powerful position, but this also poses me a problem.

Coach: How is this a problem?

Richard: Because my company wants to move me to a country where Bernardo would not be able to get a visa and we refuse to be separated!

In both these cases, the Wheel allowed these clients to declare important issues in a swift and legitimate way, rather than having to find some other means of giving the coach such vital data.

How to use the Wheel

- Send it to clients in advance of the first session, explaining how to fill it in and asking them to bring it with them, explaining that most clients find this a valuable exercise, as a way of starting them thinking about changes they may want to make in their lives.
- At the session, ask clients to talk you through the thinking behind the way they have scored each wedge.
- Ask follow-up questions to clarify.
- Don't press clients who either say directly or indicate indirectly that they do not want to talk about any particular area, but log it for future exploration, perhaps when trust between you has grown.
- Ask clients what links they see between the way they have scored the different wedges. An example might be that a client who has scored his satisfaction with work at 8 or 9 has also scored his partner relationship at 1 or 2. Sometimes when a client Wheel looks like this, the client has poured everything into work at the expense of a marriage. It has become a negatively fulfilling cycle: work is enjoyable and rewarding so the client puts love and energy into it; the marriage is unfulfilling and unrewarding so the client dodges putting love and energy into it, thus ensuring that it becomes even less fulfilling and rewarding. This may seem like a simple and stunningly obvious connection, but it is often a point that the client has avoided seeing until that moment.
- Ask how clients would prefer their Wheel to look, then follow this with a question about how much energy they have for change in any

areas that show low satisfaction. Don't assume that a low score means a willingness to change, or even that your role should be to challenge reluctance to change a low score. If the client has no energy for change in this area, then log this information as useful, but also log it as a no-go area for now. An example would be a client whose score in the health wedge is 4, but who tells you firmly that she has no current energy to tackle this dissatisfaction.

- Ask which particular areas the client wants to concentrate on for the coaching and note between you that these are potentially powerful areas for turning into goals.
- Ask how the areas of satisfaction and dissatisfaction link to the client's initial ideas on goals for the coaching.

This method of asking clients to think about what they want is the classic way of using the Wheel. However, there are others. Here is an example:

Dan

I have worked with many clients like Dan. Ambitious, smart and worldly, Dan rarely worked less than a 70-hour week. He had been in his organization's fast-lane promotion scheme since joining it as a young graduate. Dan was deeply driven by the need for external recognition and by an insatiable wish to prove himself competent. He wanted the prizes of promotion, bigger cars, better pay, but they were being achieved at a high cost. At the age of 40 his health was suffering: he was seriously overweight and had recently been diagnosed with high blood pressure during his annual health check with the company doctor.

There were also hints that his insistence on ever higher standards was having a negative impact on the team he managed. Two highly valued members of his team had recently resigned, citing the difficulties of working with Dan as their main reason. Deep down, Dan could not trust anyone. One of his fundamental beliefs was that 'If you want a job done well, you had better do it yourself'. He couldn't delegate, nor could he slacken his own pace.

Dan was politely scornful about what 360° feedback could reveal to him: this was not an objective measure, so why should he trust it? Using the Balance Wheel in its traditional form was not likely to be useful either. I guessed that Dan would have told himself he was perfectly happy to be doing so well on the physical environment, career and money wedges, and to hell with the rest.

Instead, I presented Dan with a different version of the Wheel, labelled the Skills Wheel, with spokes for Spiritual, Family, Friends, Fun, Health, Community, Business and Emotional. I asked Dan to rate his skills on a 1–10 scale on each wedge.

Part of the reason that Dan presented for coaching was that he had the inestimable benefit of a newly appointed Chief Executive who was leading a drive to shorter hours with family-friendly policies while also increasing the company's commitment to high performance in its market. This had suddenly changed the cosy familiarity of the criteria Dan had been using to judge his own competence. Now there was the strong suggestion that a manager without skills in whole-life areas was unlikely to maintain his success at work and that what team members respond to is a well-rounded human being. Paradoxically, devoting more time to skills in these other areas was also likely to bring more success at work.

Dan gave himself full marks on the business wedge, but rated himself at below 4 on all the others, including giving himself zero on several. His marriage had been sacrificed for work, he had missed the greater part of his children's upbringing, had lost all but notional contact with his parents and brothers and certainly had no time for fun or looking after his health. 'Feelings' he regarded as a no-go area. The spiritual had been sacrificed for the material and, needless to say, he had no spare energy for his community.

Realizing that he was going to be judged on his competence in the scarily unfamiliar areas on the Skills Wheel was just the kick-start Dan needed. The coaching concentrated first on how to learn to trust and coach his team so that he could detach himself from the grind of trying to do their jobs as well as his own. Then we tackled what he dubbed his 'Dan Leading a Better Life Project'. Here his competence-driver could kick in, but for the first time it was applied to his whole life rather than to a narrow definition of work.

Alternatives to the Wheel

There are many alternative approaches which you might prefer. Another one I like invites the client to name and develop the categories. For this you need a large sheet of paper – a flip chart page is ideal.

- Hand the client a set of felt-tip pens and ask him or her to draw a pie chart in the centre of the page, leaving plenty of space to add further rings. This inner circle should represent how the client spends his or her time now.
- Add a second circle outside the first, allocating different proportions representing how the client would ideally like to spend his/her time, listing the benefits this would bring.
- Add a third circle, writing in each category what will need to change in order to bring these changes about.

Kevin

Kevin was a 53-year-old senior manager in an oil company. He was a 'lifer' – someone who had spent his entire working life in one organization. He had lost his zest for work yet with a recent promotion was finding himself spending more and more of his time at work. Work also felt increasingly meaningless. Kevin felt he wanted to contribute something to people less fortunate than himself and was frustrated by his inability to devote time to the third world charity which reflected his strong religious beliefs. In his inner circle he drew a number of compartments for work, indicating 'organizational politicking', managing his team, visiting chemical plants, going to conferences and travel.

Kevin's job involved at least 80 days a year of international travel, and Kevin had increasing distaste for the stresses this created. His marriage was a long-standing, loving relationship and his wife had recently retired. They had no children and she felt they could be spending more time together, especially on their joint love of golf, eating out, visiting friends and on holidays in Spain – another passion. A generous salary was matched by a generous company pension scheme, so money was not an issue.

His second circle shows a dramatic contrast: work reduced to a small proportion of how it is shown in the inner circle and the leisure pursuits much enlarged. Benefits include better health, increased time for relaxation, learning Spanish and enjoyment of his marriage. In the third circle, Kevin described what needs to happen to bring about the ideal. Essentially this boiled down to talking to his employer about voluntary redundancy and moving to a consultancy role, beefing up his consultancy skills, learning Spanish 'properly' and concentrating on the work he really enjoyed.

Two years later, all of this had happened. Kevin and his wife had sold their large house and bought an inner city pied-à-terre. With the profits they bought a pleasant house in Spain near a splendid golf course and now spend seven months of the year there. In the remaining five months, Kevin freelances for his old company and several others, and also gives free consultancy to his favourite charity, where his hard-won worldly wisdom is much valued.

Drawing your life

Many clients have endlessly analysed their situations. They can articulate exactly what is wrong yet somehow things still stay the same. For these clients, a so-called 'right-brain' approach can really help. This means moving away from the comfort of words and analysis and using the playful, creative, less structured part of the brain.

- Hand the client a large piece of paper and a clutch of nice juicy felt-tip pens in a range of colours.

- Ask him or her to draw two pictures. The first: how your life is now. The second: how you would like your life to be.
- Reassure the client that no artistic ability is required and let him or her loose with the paper and pens.
- Talk through the resulting drawing, asking the client what needs to happen to move from the present to the desired future.

Bernard[1]

Bernard, a former colleague of mine, did this exercise on a career development workshop. His drawing showed a thatched roof house with the name *Bernard's Consultancy Ltd* over the door, his new wife, Penny, waving cheerfully from an upstairs window. A van with 'Wine' on it was by the gate and also a signpost pointing towards London. At the time, Bernard was in a salaried post and I had just offered him another steady and relatively well-paid job in London, working as a training consultant in the department of which I was then head.

Bernard had had a turbulent time prior to this, both personally and professionally, but he had little hesitation in turning down my offer of a safe haven. He told me then, and has reiterated several times since, that his drawing was so vivid and so compelling that, in spite of all the apparent risks and uncertainties, he just had to leave the organization and start up his own training consultancy, something he did with great success.

A final twist to this story is that twelve years later he also moved away from Greater London to buy a Devonshire vineyard, thatched house attached, with the wonderful name, Down St Mary. He and Penny are now that comparative rarity, English winegrowers. He is happily mixing this business with his continuing interest in training, so the vineyard van was also a forecast of things to come.

An ideal day

Invite clients to tell you the story of their ideal day from the time they get up in the morning to the time they go to bed. What would be happening? What, specifically, would they be doing? Ask clients to use the present tense, describing the day as if it is actually happening.

An alternative which is especially useful for clients with life-balance issues is to hand the client a blank diary representing a complete week. Say:

> Imagine you have given up your present job. Fill in this diary with an ideal week of activities which do not include paid work.

---

[1] Unlike all the other names in this book, this, with his permission, is his real name.

Most clients find this an absorbing exercise – I usually ask them to complete it between sessions. The follow-up discussion will include topics such as:

> How difficult was it to fill all the time? (Usually it is impossible)
> What would it be like to live this life?
> What would it be like to live your life with this as the yardstick rather than fitting your private life around your work?

Identifying life purpose

Sooner or later in any substantial piece of coaching, one core question appears: 'What's my life purpose?' Underneath this question is the one virtually all of us must ask ourselves at some point: what meaning does life have anyway? A sense of pointlessness is often behind the initial request for coaching. It is why, even in the real and apparent trauma of sudden redundancy or sacking, clients can feel energized and optimistic. It is another opportunity to find out what this core purpose might be.

In Alexander Payne's brilliant and fiercely unsentimental film *About Schmidt* (2003), the 66-year-old American Warren Schmidt (Jack Nicholson) discovers that virtually everything he had taken for granted has been a disappointment, worthless or a lie. After the sudden death of his wife, his life unravels. He discovers that the wife he never loved enough had had an affair with his colleague. His daughter demands regular remittances but prefers her lover's family to her own because she finds acceptance there. The work he laboured over for so long is heartlessly and casually destroyed the moment he retires. He has no skill or emotional vocabulary to manage new relationships or to revisit old ones.

The film charts with perfect elegance the shock of finding out that we have somehow missed the point and squandered the talents we have. In another dazzling and slyly funny touch, there is a reminder that such musing is only possible in rich first-world societies. Schmidt's inner narrative voice in the film is conveyed through the inappropriately candid letters he writes to the 'poorest of the poor' child he sponsors through a charity – a 6-year-old African boy who speaks no English and can neither read nor write.

As coaches, we would hope to meet and work with Warren Schmidt many years before things get to such a hopeless stage. If you never answer the question about life purpose then you will potentially feel a perpetual sense of something lacking. It will be more difficult to make either career or life decisions confidently and without 'buyer's remorse' if you make what turns out to be the wrong decision. By contrast, once you are clear about life purpose, such decisions are much easier. Any major turning point can be held up against the life-purpose benchmark.

Don't pussyfoot with clients about life purpose. It sounds a bit of a portentous phrase – and perhaps it is. But introduce it confidently.

Some approaches to identifying life purpose

The simplest is to ask a series of straightforward questions. Where you have already done an autobiography session with a client, these questions may usefully build on to the answers the client gave you then.

> What's unique about you?
> What do other people constantly say that they value about you?
> If you are a fly on the wall hearing some of your greatest admirers talking about you, what do you hear?
> What do you enjoy most about your current job?
> What skill or task do you perform so easily that you don't need to think about it?
> What do you enjoy most about your non-work life?
> What secret dreams do you have about things you would really love to do or try?
> What unrealized goals are there for you?
> What themes or threads run through your life?
> What quality or experience in your current life/job would you sacrifice last?
> What do you want to leave behind you as a legacy
> – in your current job?
> – in your life?

A personal mission statement

In the organizational world, clients are familiar with the idea of a mission statement – a pithy and memorable summary of that organization's reason-for-being. Many such statements are meaningless gobbledegook, so general that they could apply to any organization – for instance 'To be the best in our field.' At their finest, mission statements are motivating and memorable. One of the greatest ever was NASA's in the early 1960s: 'To put a man on the moon by the end of the decade.' Ask clients to give a two-sentence summary of what their unique mission is, and then to write it down, using it as the benchmark for all later decisions.

Clients with formal religious beliefs may find it easier to answer the question in the quasi-spiritual way in which it has been framed because they are unembarrassed by reference to non-material domains. But even avowed atheists rarely jib at the question. If they do, I ask: 'So if you did believe in there being a purpose to our lives, what would your purpose be?'

A postcard from the future

I did this exercise myself on a course thirteen years ago. The instruction was simple. Imagine it's some time in the future: choose your own time frame. Now write yourself a postcard from that time, reminding yourself what you are now doing, saying what you love about it and describing what you did to get there. Exactly as my clients do now, I felt the thrill of realizing that the ideal was indeed within my grasp, and seeing it written down made the ideal tangible.

Writing your own obituary

In the late nineteenth century the Swedish armaments manufacturer Alfred Nobel opened a newspaper and had a moment of terrible shock: he read his own obituary. In fact the newspaper had confused him with his brother Ludvig, who had just died.

Nobel had spent his career up until that moment as a resplendently successful entrepreneur. He had discovered and patented dynamite and had built a massive fortune on the proceeds. Expecting to read praise of his verve and cleverness, instead Nobel read that people saw him as a 'merchant of death', someone who had spent his life making money out of the wickedness of war. From that moment on he decided to devote his life and his enormous wealth to the arts, to science and above all to peace. The Nobel Prize is still the world's most respected award and a tribute to one man's discovery of his true life purpose.

As a coach you can draw on the moral of this tale. Asking clients to write their own obituary is a powerful exercise indeed. Most clients quickly realize that true life purpose is as much about what they want to give as it is about what they want to take. It is the giving that bestows significance, not the taking. When you are focused on taking, you can never have enough of whatever it is you want to take, whether it be money, fame, power, glamorous possessions, houses, the thrills of chasing sex or of outwitting competitors. When taking is the concern you have to be constantly on your guard because others might steal or damage what you have, whether these are cheeky younger colleagues after your job, a rival for your love or feckless burglars after your possessions.

All of this is immeasurably bolstered by the myths and fantasies with which we surround ourselves. The most popular include:

I'll be able to slow down tomorrow.	Reality: unlikely. Working with manic energy becomes a habit.
Working long hours now will clear time for me later.	Reality: the longer the hours you work, the more you train others to expect those hours as your norm and they will obligingly fill up your in tray for you.

Buying my children nice things will make up for the time I can't spend with them.	Reality: nice things can never replace parental time.
I am my job – they couldn't manage without me.	Reality: they forget you more or less as soon as you have gone.

Asking about core life purpose cuts through all of this, and often comes as a shock.

Sometimes a simple reframing is all that needs to happen. The client is already in the right arena, doing the right sort of job and leading the right sort of life. What is missing is seeing the significance of the choices he or she has made. A well-known tale describes the work of three men laying bricks on the same project. Asked what he is doing, the first replies, 'Laying bricks.' The second man replies, 'Building a wall.' The third man replies, 'Building a cathedral.' It is not difficult to imagine whose work gave him most satisfaction. People's choices of life path, of partner, of job, of work sector and so on are rarely accidental. Part of our work as coaches is to make explicit what has always been present but partially hidden.

Mark

Mark was running a voluntary sector organization. In previous years, before Mark's time in the job, the organization had found to their dismay that money from grants and bequests was diminishing, so, to fund their campaigning arm, they had established a trading company. This had become very successful – so successful that it was in danger of dwarfing their other activities. There was a split in the organization between people who saw themselves as tough, commercially focused operators and the people who had joined because they believed in the original mission and purpose. The commercially focused people saw the campaigners as 'fluffy' and the campaigners saw the marketers and finance specialists as cynical and opportunistic.

Mark straddled the two uneasily. He had been appointed because of his skill as a campaigner but now found himself running a business. Initially, Mark came for coaching to explore the organizational dynamics involved in these dilemmas, but the focus quickly turned to what these apparent splits meant for him personally.

A combination of the autobiography exercise (see page 84) and looking at life purpose provided some interesting insights. Mark had grown up in a big Catholic family in West Belfast and as a boy had naively joined in riots and fighting 'because it was fun and exciting'. It had given him insights into what it was like to feel beleaguered and disadvantaged. 'It was a paranoid community' was how he described it.

Early on in life, Mark had discovered that he had a gift for advocacy. He had used it at university in the Student Union and it took him seamlessly into a series of what he called 'sub-political' roles – for instance working for an English MP as a researcher.

It was easy for Mark to answer questions about his life purpose. 'Righting wrongs' summed up his answers. He was never happier than when fearlessly acting as David to the Goliath of an apparently more powerful adversary. The stress for him was that his role increasingly seemed to be constraining him from drawing on his strengths.

The choices seemed simple: change jobs or refocus the job he had. He chose to refocus the job he had, feeling that the core purpose of his organization was indeed close to his heart and that he could easily reposition the role by creating a new role as Director of Operations, reporting to him, to manage the commercial parts of the business. This would leave him to focus on the external, ambassadorial role while also directly heading up the campaigning function inside the organization.

The impact of this choice was considerable. Flexing his Chief Executive muscles in a different way meant that the commercial activities of the organization became focused on how they could support campaigning, rather than the other way around. Mark described himself as 'springing out of bed each morning, knowing I'm doing what I was born to do!'

Identifying values and drivers

Asking about life purpose takes you into the core territory of the being self rather than the doing self. It is saying to the client, 'What really matters to you?' You may get answers to this question through exploring life purpose, or you may prefer to look at it through activities explicitly designed to flush out the client's values and drivers. I have two approaches, both of which I like and find useful, depending on the client and the circumstances. Both are particularly useful with clients facing career dilemmas because they start by identifying answers to the questions 'What do you really want?'; 'What's important to you?' rather than where so many clients believe they have to start, which is with 'Who will hire me?'

The Fantasy Figures conversation

I learnt this protocol from my colleague Phil Hayes. Its apparent simplicity is in the art that conceals art. You ask the client a series of questions, including enjoyable and revealing questions about people they most admire.

1   What's important to you about what you do professionally?
2   What would you rather be doing professionally?

3   What's important to you about what you'd rather be doing?
4   Who are the one or two people you most admire, contemporary, historical, real or fictional?
5   What's important to you about these people?

Where the answers to questions 1, 3 and 5 reveal significant differences in core values, ask: 'How could you get more of what's important to you in what you're currently doing?', or 'In what other contexts could you get more?'

This activity works best when you give clients the questions and invite them to think about them for a few moments, or even to write down the answers, before discussing them.

Bella

Bella was working in a high-tech company on a project to develop new software for websites. Before that she had worked in television as a producer of documentary programmes. The company was in difficulty and Bella came for coaching knowing that redundancy was likely. She expressed a high degree of dissatisfaction with her current work environment, saying that she found it stifling. She wanted to be ahead of the game with a plan for doing what she called 'springing myself from this prison' as soon as the situation was clearer. She told me that the core question she wanted the coaching to answer was, 'How can I discover what I really want to do and then do more of it?'

In answering the *Fantasy Figures* questions, the opportunity to do creative work was what Bella valued about her professional work. What would she rather be doing? She looked back to her time as a television producer when the programmes she made all had social conscience at their core. They combined documentary with drama and had been both enjoyable and demanding to make. The reason this was important was that several of these programmes had had considerable impact, influencing opinion formers and ultimately social policy.

Her heroes? Nelson Mandela, the former South African President, and George Eliot, English novelist of the nineteenth century. What was important about these two people? Mandela she had chosen for his unaffected grace and simplicity, some forgivable vanity, the toughness of his commitment to social justice and truth, his ability to inspire and ultimately to build a nation, despite decades of imprisonment. George Eliot she admired for the ambitious sweep of her imagination, her creative genius as a storyteller and for defying opinion by living with a man to whom she was not married, at a time when this was the focus of powerful social disapproval.

As she answered these questions, Bella became thoughtful and then began to smile. 'I've answered my own question, haven't I?' she said. Her core drivers and motivators emerged clearly. They were about unashamedly big themes:

equality, social inclusion, and a relish for the political fight it took to get there. The route to getting there was all about using her core gifts for storytelling, working with young or inexperienced actors and scriptwriters, directing and editing. Once this was clear, how to get all of these things back into her life became the focus of our work together.

Being 'In the Zone'

Sports people describe moments of maximum performance as being 'In the Zone': a time when you just know that you are going to win, play or perform well, doing as well or better than you ever have before. And the wonderful thing is, it feels effortless. The same phenomenon has been called 'Being in Flow'. These moments are characterized by:

- time passing quickly;
- a feeling of exhilaration;
- mind and body seamlessly joined;
- conscious happiness;
- a sense of playfulness;
- energy;
- awareness of skill or ability being effortlessly at your service.

I have yet to work with a client who cannot identify such moments. They may select a specific day or few hours, a whole project or an even longer period in a job role which was particularly satisfying. Knowing what these moments are is an immensely powerful lever for coach and client. They are, like identifying life purpose, the benchmark for decision making and for planning the future.

To call on this approach, you will need to allow at least half an hour. Some clients may prefer to prepare for this session in advance.

- Introduce the idea of being 'in flow' to clients and ask them to identify up to four such moments in their lives – more if you have the time and inclination. Encourage them to think about moments from their personal as well as professional lives and also moments that cover different phases or decades. By asking for several peak moments you will be creating a richer picture.
- Give clients enough time to think it through, perhaps while you refresh the drinks or both have a loo break.
- Write down all the key words as they talk. You could use a flip chart for this: it makes the themes easier for clients to see later. Most clients talk fluently about these moments. If they are struggling to

describe them, ask:

- – What made this moment or time special?
- – Who else was present or involved? What were they doing?
- – What was it that you specifically did that made it so important?
- – What were your feelings then?
- – What was achieved, done or learnt?
- – How did you feel about that achievement or learning?
- – What values and beliefs were you calling on?
- – What need was it serving?

- When clients have finished, hand them a highlighter, asking them to mark the words that jump out for them.
- Suggest possible links, if they are struggling – sometimes such links may be easier for you to see than for them.
- List the values and drivers that emerge.
- Invite them to ponder the implications. Some possible questions here might be:
  - – Having listed these values and drivers, how do they seem to you?
  - – What is so important about them for you?
  - – What surprises are there for you in what is not on your list?
  - – What is it like for you when you are honouring these values?
  - – What is it like for you when you are not honouring them?
  - – What needs to happen to make these values real drivers in your life now?
  - – How prepared are you to make those changes?

This is a hugely enjoyable exercise. It focuses only on the positive and virtually always tells clients more than they first realize. Examples would be a client one of whose peak moments was being godmother to her closest friend's first baby and realizing that uniting family interests, friendships and spiritual beliefs was not only a prime need but also something for which she had a talent. Another was the participant on one of our coach-training courses whose peak moment was at last getting the opportunity to sing the part of the Angel in Edward Elgar's popular and moving oratorio *The Dream of Gerontius* in her local cathedral. The Angel guides Gerontius from this world to the next. Singing this role encapsulated her love of and talent for singing, her need for performance and limelight and also the need to do something for others that had profound meaning for them.

Here is another example:

Vivienne

Vivienne described herself as being in a poor state when she first came to me. She had failed to get a new job in a reorganization and was angry, disappointed and frankly feeling that the world was against her. She was doing a series of temporary project roles and accepted that another permanent role in her current organization was unlikely. She was angry with the organization and angry with herself, and deeply disliked her current boss, feeling that he was manipulative and dishonest. At 49 she knew that very early retirement was a possibility and that as a single woman with no dependants she could live on a modest pension if necessary. This is her account of the impact of looking at peak moments:

> This was a transforming activity for me: it really zapped me, but in the best possible way. My peak moments were all about working with individuals on their development or about working on my own development – these were the things that had given me real satisfaction. The focus in these develop-ment conversations was also about feelings and emotional wholeness. Another of my 'moments' was about my painting hobby and yet another about cooking for friends. There was nothing in my peak moments or list about management or leadership – that really startled me because I had spent 20 years as a manager!
>
> Other values were about creativity and autonomy, very very important. When I was living these values I was a different person, energized, happy and content. How had I managed to survive so long in an organization that was about the opposites – bureaucracy, money making and control?
>
> It felt like blindfolds falling off – it was so easy! I knew I had to leave and soon. I knew the organization saw me as a nuisance and also felt guilty about me. As part of my leaving settlement, I negotiated the first two years of my fees for the psychotherapy qualification I now knew I was going to do – and got a good deal on the pension too. I sold my big house to move into a smaller one to create some more funds while I was in training: I realized I didn't really care about status or impressing others with my worldly wealth – just as well because I haven't got much money now. But I am dead happy. I go on painting holidays; I have reconnected with my friends through loads of regular supper parties. I'm launching myself as a psychotherapist very soon and I may also do an acupuncture training.

The future self: guided meditation

All approaches to life purpose and direction focus in one way or another on the future. You can encourage clients to do this even more explicitly through a guided meditation. If you are attracted to this approach, you will want to develop your own script, but all of the many variants of such scripts have the same core elements:

- Ask for permission and briefly explain the benefits. If clients are dubious, don't press it: it's not right for everyone. Most people have experienced a guided relaxation – for instance on courses – so you could explain that it is just one version of this with an added element. My colleague Tony Betts calls his version 'Theatre of the Mind' – an attractively client-in-control variant.

- You ask clients to enter a light trance state. Some coaches prefer not to name it as such because of the poor reputation of stage hypnotists and other dubiously motivated practitioners. If you believe a client will resist if you name it as *trance*, then don't. I do because in fact trance is a totally commonplace human experience. We can all enter it at will and often enter it involuntarily – for instance when driving on a monotonous motorway or going for a lengthy jog. The state is characterized by unawareness of time passing or of the intrusive effects of the physical environment. Churchgoers will enter it through prayer or meditation and you could well experience the same state at a concert. It is not the same as sleep or a deep hypnotic state. The theory is that when you are in a light trance, your mind is more open to suggestion.

- You reassure clients that they are in control at all times.

- You invite clients to enter the trance state through physical relaxation and closed eyes. This leads to a matching mental quieting.

- Your voice remains quiet, gentle and monotonous. You are aiming for a pleasant drone. You speak very slowly, using linking words like and ... or so ...

- You use only positive suggestion, so, for instance, you would say 'you feel calm' rather than 'you don't feel tense'. Saying the word 'tense' invites tension because what the mind focuses on is what expands.

- Clients imagine themselves at some point in their future where they meet a positive and happy version of themselves. They ask this future self to pass on its wisdom to their present self.

- You then discuss with the client the implications for where they are currently and for what they need to do next.

A sample script

Get yourself comfortable in your chair. Sit without anything crossed – no crossed legs, feet or arms. If you'd like a cushion to support your neck, that's fine.

First let's establish some relaxed, steady breathing. Take a deep breath in from below your waist and feel your lungs filling and expanding and pushing outwards. Hold for a few moments; now let the breath out and feel your chest going in again. The outbreath is going to be much longer than the in-breath. Take the in-breath with your mouth closed and breathe the out-breath out slowly and steadily through an open mouth. [Do several such breaths with the client, counting slowly with each breath.]

Close your eyes and let your body relax.

First let your feet go floppy – let them feel as if they are completely free. Unclench any muscles that may have tightened in your toes. Wiggle the toes and let them relax.

Now do the same with your legs. Let the knees flop and now your thighs. Let your legs feel loose and very relaxed. They may start to feel heavy – if they do, that's fine. They may tingle a little and feel warm.

Now let your hands go loose. Shake out the fingers a little and let them relax so that they feel floppy. And now feel them getting heavy. And now the same with your arms. Let them get heavy and feel very, very relaxed. They may feel warm and tingly. If they do, that's fine.

Keep the breathing slow and steady, breathing in . . . and then out . . . in and then out. [Time this with the client's breathing, matching it with your own.]

And now your shoulders. Let them drop so that the muscles are soft and floppy. And now your neck. Let go of any tension in it. Now the same with your chest and stomach. And let the centre of your body relax. Feel a soft, warm feeling creeping through your whole body.

And now your face. Feel the facial muscles relaxing so that your skin is smooth. Let the muscles around your mouth go soft and floppy. And do the same with the muscles in your forehead.

Feel your circulation relaxing and your heartbeat steadying to a quiet, steady, relaxed beat. And feel whole, feel well, feel relaxed.

And now I'm going to ask you to imagine yourself in a pleasant place. It could be a real place that's special to you or an imaginary one. Call up how this place feels to you and the sensations it creates in your body to know that you're there . . . remember or imagine the sounds you can hear . . . and the views you can see. Enjoy all these sensations . . . Relax even more deeply and let go while you experience yourself in this place . . .

You're lying there now, relaxed and comfortable, feeling happy and open to whatever will happen. In the distance I'd like you to see a figure coming towards you. This person is yourself in the future [you may like to name a time – two years, five years, ten years] as you'd like to be. This person has all the bravery and resourcefulness that you will ever need.

See yourself clearly as you approach. What are you wearing? How do you conduct yourself? You look happy and contented. You're smiling and relaxed and fulfilled. How are you leading your life? What are you doing? Ask your future self these questions and listen carefully to what you see and to the replies to these questions.

There are other happy people in this vision of your future self. Who are they? What are they doing in relation to you? What do they mean to you?

Now you and your future self are going to have a conversation. And first your future self is going to tell what the essence of their being is – what is it that makes this future self so happy and fulfilled? Listen carefully again to the replies. [Long pause]

And now ask your future self what message it has for you. What is the prime message that you must have? [Leave a generous pause here.]

Now ask your future self this question – what do I need to do to get from where I am now to where I want to be in the future? [Pause again.] Listen carefully to the answer.

And now ask your future self, 'What else do I need to know from you?' Again, listen carefully to the reply.

What other questions would you like to ask your future self? [Pause]

Now see yourself and this future self, standing closely side by side in a companionable way. Merge these two selves so that they become one. See yourself having all the wisdom that your future self can offer.

And now thank your future self for the help.

Now see yourself gently leaving this quiet special place and coming back to the present. Take a few moments to remember the messages that your future self has given you. Wait a few moments. Take a deep steady breath.

Gently open your eyes. Stretch, feel alert and refreshed.

After this exercise, invite clients to write down the insights they have received. It would be a rare client indeed who has not received any.

> **Stephen**
>
> I came for coaching with what now seems like a laughably mundane request: I wanted to know how to influence my boss and how to get a better grip on my job which was specifically like a sort of bag-carrier role for him. He was senior enough in the organization to need someone like me to smooth his path, write his speeches, make sure his flights were booked, deal with the press – and so on. When I did this visualization, I saw myself very clearly five years ahead. The other people with me were my wife and young children.
>
> At the time of doing the exercise, I didn't have a wife, only a girlfriend and I definitely didn't have any children! I was also aware in the visualization of how I was earning a living. I saw myself directly running a major part of the organization and running it in a particular way – very differently from the bullying standard leadership style I saw around me every day. It was a complete wake-up call. I suddenly felt I had been wasting my time in a highly paid but totally pointless backroom job, frittering away my energy in a playboy bachelor life and this wasn't what I wanted at all. The advice from my future self was: 'Get real mate!'

The coaching took a completely different slant as a result of that activity. Five years later I am on my way to that senior job. I realized how much I loved my then girlfriend and how mad I would be to lose her. We married within a year and have one and a half of the two children I saw in that meditation. I refuse to do the 12-hour days I see my colleagues working – getting a proper life balance is important and I'm not going to put any of that at risk again.

Fiona

This was a turning point for me. One of the most important things was that I *didn't* see my then current partner in the visualization. I knew really that the relationship was totally flawed, but I felt stuck in it. I saw a different lifestyle and a different partner – a vague image as I hadn't actually got anyone in mind. Eighteen months later, the former relationship is cleanly over, I went flat out to meet new people, I've met the love of my life, I'm getting married and I've got 90 per cent of what I imagined that day.

Setting goals

All the techniques I have described so far in this chapter are the fertile soil for identifying the direction of the coaching because they encourage clients to assess where they want to go in their lives and to compare this with where they currently are. But if this awareness stays at the level of vague generalities, the coaching cannot go very far. A coaching conversation is unlike other kinds of friendly discussion in many ways, not least in the emphasis it puts on change. Where a client believes that nothing needs to change then there can be no coaching. Without goal setting it is unlikely that there will be any significant change.

A famous piece of research at Harvard in the early 1960s by David McClelland demonstrated the importance of formally setting goals. The entrepreneurs in his study who set goals and then developed a plan for achieving them were strikingly more successful than those who did not. Much other research since then has demonstrated essentially the same result: the more specific and measurable a goal is, the more it fits with your personal values, the more you really want it to happen, the more public your commitment, the more likely it is that it will be achieved. For an early review of the research, see McLelland (1985).

If you have no goal you cannot measure success. Possibly the most frequently asked question about coaching is 'does it work?' If your client does not have a set of goals, you will never know because you will have nothing against which you can measure.

Getting stuck on 'problems'

Now that I have worked with so many new or inexperienced coaches and listened to their early attempts at coaching, I have come to see that many coaches find the whole area of goal setting pretty challenging. Typically what happens is this. The client presents his/her issue as a problem:

> I can't manage my time.
> I've got this poor performer in my team.
> I feel stressed all the time.

The coach's sympathy is aroused – she wants to help. She then dives into the many dimensions of the problem: how much, how many, how awful ... quickly feeling as hopeless as the client. Where you have the benefit of videotape or actual observation you can see both client and coach literally sinking deeper into their chairs with the misery of it all. By this stage the coach is feeling desperate: she has to find a solution for the poor client. She's right back to Level 1 listening and her mental dialogue is panic: 'I'm a terrible coach. This client is probably feeling worse by the minute' (she's right, he is). It's so terrible that, sooner rather than later, advice-giving kicks in and, subtly or overtly, the coach gives the client suggestions about what to do. Sympathetic chat, yes, but coaching, no.

Turning problems into goals: a protocol

- The client presents the problem. You briefly establish how important the problem is.
- You turn the complaint into a how-to statement, in effect flipping it round into a positive. For instance, the client says, 'I can't talk to my sister without there being a row.' You respond, 'So you'd like to be able to learn how to talk to your sister with calm on both sides?' Or, for example, the client says, 'I don't know whether to stay in my present job or look for a managerial role.' You respond, 'So you'd like to use this session to get clarity about which path to take?'
- You ask what the client has already tried.
- You then ask the client to imagine the problem has been solved. What would be happening?
- Clients sometimes present their answer as a series of things that would *not* be happening. Such phrases do not make good goals. For instance, a goal for a tennis player might be 'to stop losing matches'. This goal contains the sense of defeat that goes with failure. It cannot therefore be a motivating goal. A far better goal would be 'to win my next six games'. Where clients present their issues as a negative, you

need to invite them to turn it into a positive. Here is a sample piece of dialogue for this part of the goal-setting conversation:

Angela

Angela manages an overseas operation for her employer. She tells her coach in the first session that one of her issues is that she gets far too emotional when faced with confrontation or challenge. The coach establishes that this typically happens in the context of the executive team meetings where she is a member, and that even more typically it is challenges from senior men that she finds most difficult to handle. The coach already knows from autobiographical work with Angela that her own father was a bully, so it is not difficult for Angela to make the connection with a long-held fear that confrontation from a male colleague is in exactly the same genre as the response she learnt as a child when to confront a male authority figure led to punishment and disgrace.

Angela: So when senior men confront or challenge me hard, I get far too emotional. I know I do and I'd like to stop.

Coach: So if this issue were resolved – if I could wave a magic wand – what would be happening for you?

Angela: I wouldn't feel tearful and silly in our exec. team meetings.

Coach: Can we turn that around? Let's put it in the positive. What would be positively happening?

Angela: I would be able to deal with that team meeting and the men in it and be very calm throughout.

Coach: So in this session we should look at how to deal calmly with the meeting and the men at it?

Transactional and transformational goals

In coaching we are working with two different kinds of goals, often simultaneously. *Transactional* goals are specific tasks that a client wants to achieve. These are often externally imposed and have an emphasis on short-term performance. Examples would be:

- Enrol for the gym and make sure I visit it twice a week for an hour's workout.
- Recruit a new marketing manager.
- Deliver an effective presentation to the Board next week.
- Carry out appraisals with all of my staff by the end of February.

There is nothing wrong with such goals: I work on goals like these with clients all the time.

However, *transformational* goals have much more power. These are the goals that are about learning. They are internally focused and are about increasing capacity to deal with similar situations and dilemmas whenever they arise, rather than with achieving a short-term task. The irony about the transactional goals is that they can actually interfere with performance: anxiety narrows the view. Energy becomes concentrated on the goal without seeing the wider picture.

Remember that coaching is about learning and the learning ideally is about long-term sustainable improvement. So, as a coach, I consciously work with clients to turn their perfectly reasonable transactional goals into transformational goals that are about learning. It really only needs a moment or two of reframing to help the client see the difference:

Transactional goal	A transformational equivalent
Enrol for the gym and make sure I visit it twice a week for an hour's workout.	Discover what I enjoy and can sustain to improve my physical fitness.
Deliver an effective presentation to the Board next week.	Increase my awareness of what constitutes effectiveness in presentations.
Carry out appraisals with all of my staff by the end of February.	Develop my understanding of how to manage performance well.
Convince my team that my strategy is the right one.	Influencing with integrity: know how it works and be able to do it.

Establishing the benefits of change

Angela, continued

So, in the example above, Angela has established that she wants to stay calm, but her attention is still focused on the transactional goal of getting through a particular meeting without becoming emotional. The coach now works on elevating that goal to something of longer-term value by positioning it as a learning goal:

Coach: Staying calm at that one meeting sounds like a very useful first step. If you did that, what would it do for you?

Angela: Increase my self-respect, improve my standing with my colleagues.

Coach: Those sound to me like even more important goals because they're about the core you. If you did increase your self-respect and improve your standing with your colleagues, what would that do for you?

Angela: There'd be no stopping me. I'd show that I could be trusted with an

> even bigger operation than I currently have – and I'd love that because I know I could do more than I currently am.
>
> Coach: So what's the core task that goes with this goal?
>
> Angela: Controlling the little girl impulse, being a grown-up.
>
> Coach: And being a grown-up means ... ?
>
> Angela: Staying calm even in a provocative situation.
>
> Coach: So the goal is to learn how to stay calm and grown-up in these provocative situations and the gain will be that you'll greatly increase your satisfaction from work?
>
> Angela: Yes – that's it.

So, in this example, the coach has elicited the presenting issue which the client frames as a problem. The coach asks the client to leave the problem focus and invites her to reframe it as a solution. He then presses for the longer-term learning or transformational goal – a goal which has whole-life implications, further driving the point home by asking what benefits this solution would have for the client: 'What would that do for you?'

Making goals specific

The more specific a goal is, the more likely it is that it will be achieved. Some useful additional questions to put to clients will include the SMART formula that most organizational clients will have met before:

Specific	Is it clear?
Measurable	How will you know you're making progress? If things are going to be 'better', how much better? If you're going to do something faster, how much faster is faster?
Achievable	Is it realistic? Can you genuinely fit it in with everything else you've got to do? What might you have to give up in order to achieve this goal?
Resourced	What will it cost in time or money? Who else will be helping you?
Timed	What's the timescale? By when do you intend to have achieved it?

To these well-known checks of robustness, you might like to add a few more:

Values: where does this sit with your core values? A goal that sits uneasily with core values will rarely be achieved because of the discomfort that it will cause. A goal that lies fair and square with what a client really cares about at a fundamental level is highly likely to be achieved.

What secondary gains or losses might there be? One of the reasons that we can stay stuck in a problem is that there is some kind of pay-off from the stuckness. It is worth exploring this as well as looking at how to change a dull, transactional goal into something more exciting.

Matt

Matt came to me for emergency help over a job application. He was one of two well-qualified candidates for a Chief Executive role. He knew the other candidate and felt strongly disadvantaged in relation to her. She had been acting in the role already, knew the organization inside out and was well respected by colleagues.

What specific help did he need? 'Just tell me what to do to get me this job' he pleaded. Matt's view of the coaching process was that I would be teaching him some 'tricks' that would fool the interview panel. After I had explained that we didn't do 'tricks', we got down to the blocks that Matt felt were stopping him from approaching the interview confidently.

These amounted to one experience where Matt, although well qualified for the role, had felt that an aggressive interviewer had subjected him to an unfair grilling. He knew he had not coped well with this crude attempt to assess him, reacting by concealing his indignation under a parade of indifference and poorly focused answers. He had not got the job and this failure had been followed by clumsily given feedback that had felt equally devastating. 'You lack interview presence' was the crushing verdict. 'You talk too much and you just don't look the part.'

From this experience, Matt had generalized wildly to, 'I'm hopeless at interviews and maybe I'd better just not bother.' The secondary benefit from this belief was that he was protecting himself from failure. As long as he didn't try then he couldn't really fail and could always blame 'the system' for having such inefficient and unfair selection methods.

Matt's transactional goal was 'get a new job'. The transformational goal I put to him as running in parallel was 'Learn how to present yourself confidently and authentically in any situation where you are under scrutiny.' I suggested that any Chief Executive must be ready, for instance, to be interviewed by the media, by staff, or sometimes in the public sector by a formal inquiry. In these situations, the mental preparation and skills needed to give a good account of yourself are extremely close to the preparation and skills needed to do well at a job interview.

Matt readily agreed. This gave a different slant to our work. Instead of merely looking at standard answers to standard interview questions, we worked on his core attitudes and beliefs: for instance about his own power, his achievements and values. Matt learnt how to access a resourceful state instantly, how to envisage success, how to be his most confident self as well as acquiring some useful transactional approaches to answering typical job interview questions, for instance by giving evidence and keeping the answers pithy.

Matt's goal-setting conversation also included a challenging discussion on facing up to the perverse rewards for failure and an agreement about the amount of time and effort he was prepared to put into the preparation with me in the coaching sessions and outside them between sessions. We also set the target of getting the job on which he had set his heart.

Matt got the job – but he also learnt much more than he had expected. His initial approach had the flavour of learning how to fake in order to achieve a short-term external goal. Instead he learnt something much more valuable: how to be authentic and confident in stressful situations.

Concentrating on strengths, not weaknesses

In some organizations, coaching is still seen as a corrective process. It's something reserved for people who are failing. Even where this is not the case, clients may insist that they want coaching which ruthlessly targets their weaknesses. While clients clearly need to know what their weaknesses are, there is some evidence that goals are more powerful when there is a different question:

What better ways might there be of working with my strengths?

For instance, Mark, whose issue I described on page 112, might have been tempted to set 'boost my commercial thinking' as part of his coaching. His colleagues were also critical of the way he ran meetings, saying that he stifled discussion and came down too heavily on people who rambled. Instead of addressing these weaknesses, we concentrated on a different question: how could he make better use of his strengths as a campaigner and advocate? By applying his strengths to both his organization and his team meetings he was able to make significant improvements to both.

Similarly, with Angela, her great strengths were her bubbly personality, her sense of fun and her optimism. These had been severely repressed in the tension of worrying about whether she was going to be 'attacked' at meetings. Instead of working on how to avoid being attacked, Angela's coach asked: 'How could your sense of fun be brought to the meetings?' He also asked her to monitor when she was consciously enjoying the meetings and to log those moments. Much to Angela's surprise and delight, bringing fun and optimism to the meetings resolved the problem of staying calm.

Business and organizational goals

The organizational context provides yet another source of significant pressure for change. It is easy to forget that a senior client for coaching does not come simply as an individual. He or she is also part of an organization. The organization is part of its environment where there will be pressures from customers or users, competitors, regulators, or from technological advance. Virtually all pressure for change originates outside the organization. So in working with senior executives, it is vital to link these pressures with the personal work that you will be doing with the individual.

So, yet another important conversation that you need to have with the client is to establish just what these pressures are, and what business or organizational goals they are creating. Equally, that client is connected to the prevailing culture of the organization and to his or her team. It is improbable that any individual can be successful acting alone, so the behaviour and attitudes of the client's team are also an important part of the picture. All of these will then have an impact on the performance of the organization.

Alastair

Alastair is running a hospital, taking over after the previous Chief Executive was dismissed. He has inherited a large deficit and a highly demoralized staff, mortified that their hospital has been in the headlines for such negative reasons. However, Alastair also knows from his initial few weeks in the hospital that it has an inward-looking culture with doctors who are hostile to the managers they see, rightly or wrongly, as their 'enemies'. Alastair's organizational goals are to

- reduce deficit to zero within 18 months;
- rebuild the confidence and competence of the executive team;
- reorganize the clinical structures through 're-engineering' based on 'patient journeys' rather than on the old functional structures; this project to be led by senior doctors;
- hit all the government-imposed targets;
- achieve the highest possible ratings by government auditors.

This is a formidable list. After working with Alastair using several of the techniques described earlier in this chapter, there were also a number of personal goals, which included:

- finding a permanently sustainable way to reduce his weight;
- increasing his physical fitness, increase his energy;
- improving his ability to influence his peers so that he obtains commitment, not the compliance which had been a feature of the previous regime;
- delegating more effectively;

- establishing strong relationships of trust with his Chair, the Department of Health and the Health Authority.

In working with Alastair at his initial session, the coach's questions were

What organizational targets do you need to meet?
How do your personal target areas link with the organizational ones?
How should this affect our agenda for coaching?

The answers to the last two questions were, of course, that the personal and the organizational were tightly intertwined. Alastair knew he was not, and never could be, the *rescuer* of his hospital. The conversation with his coach demonstrated very clearly that inspirational leadership was fundamental to the organization's recovery and that staying physically fit and energetic was a vital foundation to all the other work.

He could only deliver on the organizational agenda through addressing his personal needs: developing his team through skilled performance management including delegating appropriately and learning how to coach them, and using positive influencing techniques to nurture the upward relationships, as well as building strong relationships with the doctors in the hospital.

Out of this conversation a further need emerged: to develop and implement a communication and 'customer care' strategy which Alastair would also lead. And he could only do this if he used the leverage of his already impressive communication skills both to inspire and to speak hard truths at large meetings of his staff. This created a rich and challenging canvas for the ensuing coaching.

One way of representing this approach to goal setting for executive clients is to see it diagrammatically like this:

Blocks and barriers

Setting goals is a critically important part of the coaching process, but goals alone will not be enough. When clients come for coaching, they do it because they want their lives to change. At the same time, change is scary. Part of the client wants the status quo because even if there is something that is 'wrong', there is comfort in the familiarity of the discomfort. This is why we all cling to self-limiting beliefs, even while we are proclaiming our wish to transform ourselves. An example would be, 'I'm very overweight but it's difficult for someone like me to take exercise and keep to a diet.'

The sabotaging inner voice

This kind of self-limiting belief has been given many different names. Timothy Gallwey (2000) (see page 64) calls it Self 1 to distinguish it from Self 2: the confident human being full of potential and capacity. Self 1 is the know-it-all who doesn't trust Self 2. Self 1's voice is always ready with self-condemnation, predictions of failure and gloomy comparisons of self with others. When Self 2 can silence Self 1, potential can turn into achievement and growth. Richard Carson (1987) coined the term *Gremlin* for the same phenomenon: a nagging critical inner voice always ready to sabotage success.

We all have these voices; they are part of growing up and they cannot be coached, dismissed or killed off. They cannot be coached because they are not rational. They cannot be dismissed or killed off because they are inalienably a part of who we are. The challenge is to unmask, name and manage them, particularly with humour. This way they become less powerful.

The essential things to remember about the sabotaging inner voice is that

- it wants to preserve the status quo;
- it is scared all the time;
- its function is to hold you back through fear;
- it does not like publicity or humour, so exposing it to view and to laughter immediately reduces its authority.

I find that explaining this concept to clients is enlightening, enjoyable and useful. It is an essential working tool in my coaching because it allows me to discuss and alert clients to their typically self-sabotaging behaviour.

Self-sabotaging statements

Here are some sample statements made by the sabotaging inner voice:

I'm only (able to do a little ...)
I'm no good at ... other people are cleverer ...
Don't stick your head above the parapet ...
A person like me could never ...
I'll wait until the time is right before I ...
What would they think if I ... It's stupid to ...
I'd look silly if I ...
I should be ... (better, stronger, nicer ...)
I shouldn't be so ... (silly, needy ...)
This is too ... (risky, big for me ... frightening ...)
I mustn't because (I might be successful; people might laugh; that's for other people, not for people like me ...)
I'm not ready ...
Who do you think you are?
This will go wrong

Appropriate responses could be:

Client	*Coach*
I couldn't do ... or	What would happen if you did?
I'll wait till the time is right before I ... or	What is that waiting doing for you?
I'd look really silly if I applied for that job.	Who is saying you'd look silly? Is that your voice?

You can help clients to identify their typical voice by asking,

What does your voice like saying to you?
When does it typically appear?
What are typical sabotaging phrases you use in your family, organization or life?
Whose voice does it have? (Often a parent or teacher)
How has this voice kept you stuck?

Part of the coach's art will, of course, also be to distinguish the sabotaging voice from occasions when the client is making a sound judgement about what he or she is actually ready to do at a given moment. When clients are genuinely out of their depth, the sabotaging voice is not at work.

I find this concept hugely useful – in my own life and with my clients. I now routinely ask clients to identify the sabotaging voice and what it typically says, to track the voice back to particular incidents or phases in life and then to give it a suitably ridiculous name.

Ultimately, we are held back by fear. Fear is the real opponent in coaching. Fear ruthlessly targets the most fragile spot, starting as faint doubt and, in the right conditions, growing quickly to terrifying proportions. Logic will not help because fear crowds it out, reducing it to a parody of rationality, becoming in quick order anxiety and panic. Yann Martel's character puts it wonderfully in his Booker prize-winning novel, *Life of Pi* (2002), a profound, surreal, audacious and funny novel about a man who survives a shipwreck in a lifeboat with a Bengal tiger for company:

> Fear ... nestles in your memory like a gangrene: it seeks to rot everything, even the words with which to speak it. So you must fight hard to express it. You must fight hard to shine the light of words upon it. Because if you don't, if your fear becomes a wordless darkness that you will avoid, perhaps even manage to forget, you open yourself to further attacks of fear because you never truly fought the opponent who defeated you.

So, naming is a particularly satisfying way of reducing the volume of the voice which counsels fear. One of my own chief sabotaging voices I call *Willie Wasp*. This is the voice that buzzes round in my head when I am already tired and overworked. It tells me that I must say yes to every work invitation that comes my way because, if I don't, I will never work again and after all, 'hard work is its own reward'. Willie Wasp has a kind of Welsh Methodist preacher's accent and the bombastic, pleased-with-itself timbre that I remember from the churches and chapels of my childhood. Naming Willie Wasp has definitely kept him under control. I can still find it difficult to turn work away, but I no longer work six-day weeks or twelve-hour days. Here are some other examples:

Sylvia

I chose the name *Nigel for* my voice. Nigel was, I now realize, a particularly unpleasant and sadistic, possibly jealous, music master at my school who told me at the age of 13 that a piece of music I'd composed was rubbish and that I had no talent. I allowed Nigel to suppress my musical talent – and other talents too – for many years. I chose a non-musical career, though all my relaxation was about writing and playing music. Naming it has significantly reduced its power. Along with the coaching about my current professional role, we also looked hard at my musical aspirations and how I could extend my range of options here.

Jan

My sabotaging Gremlin is called *Gooseberry*. It goes back to a time at school when I was on a cross-country run, fell into a ditch which had some kind of prickly shrub in it and got hideously laughed at by the other girls on the run. It gave me a deep hatred of sports and got in the way of committing to physical fitness as an adult. I've also always hated gooseberries as a fruit. Naming Gooseberry was a powerful way of reducing its impact and within a few weeks of doing this naming, I'd hired myself a personal trainer to teach me Pilates – something I'm now totally committed to and as far from cross-country running as it's possible to be!

Mike

I called mine *Shush* – the name just popped up at me. Shush is female and more than a bit shrill. Throughout my childhood that was the message I got. Shush ... be seen and not heard ... who'd be interested in what you've got to say? One of the main things I got out of the coaching was learning to be more assertive and control Shush's volume. I'm pretty sure that I wouldn't have got my promotion without this having happened. I realized that this inner voice was literally stopping me speaking up at meetings, and after a bit I'd get ignored. People assumed I didn't have anything to say. I did of course, but I was letting Shush stop me. I found my own voice because I learnt how to turn the volume down on Shush!

Other approaches to self-limiting beliefs

Other self-limiting beliefs might be even more profound in their impact. These might be beliefs such as

> I am not lovable
> I am a failure
> I have no power
> Others are not to be trusted
> Other people are to blame for my bad feelings
> I/You/Others can never really change
> I need the approval of others before I can act
> Make one mistake at work and the gutter beckons

Typically these beliefs are formed in early life, often as the result of a single high-impact event or because of the behaviour of a significant adult. These early beliefs are powerful and remain deeply embedded in adult life. Despite our intellectual maturation as adults we often behave and act according to this early 'scripting'. Often these beliefs relate to our deepest fears about our ability to survive emotionally, socially and even physically. As a consequence we can often unconsciously sabotage ourselves, both in terms of managing our relationships and of getting what we want out of life.

If talk of *inner voices, alternative selves* and *gremlins* is too spooky for you, you may prefer other ways of flushing out whatever self-limiting beliefs the client has.

A client states a goal: 'I want to know how to do or be something different.'

When probed, there is virtually always some self-limiting assumption behind whatever is stopping the client from achieving his or her goal. Here is an example:

> Client: I know swimming is good exercise and I'd love to do it because it would be a brilliant way to get fitter.
> Coach: So what's stopping you?
> Client: I can't swim!

At this point the inexperienced coach might ask what could feel like very good questions, questions that meet the criteria for avoiding advice and that work respectfully with the client. These might include:

> So how could you learn?
> What have you already tried in the way of learning?
> What would an easy first step be to getting into the pool?

When I was an inexperienced coach myself, I've asked this type of question with this type of client many times. However, for some clients, unless you have flushed out the underlying self-limiting belief, your coaching will take longer to be successful and in more extreme cases may not be successful at all.

That's why it's always worth seeking or spotting the self-limiting belief that could be holding the client back. Beliefs affect behaviour. For instance, if you are a woman in an organization and believe that there is a glass ceiling on promotion for women, you probably won't bother to apply for jobs at the next level up. If you believe that you are bound to fail at sport because you 'failed' at sport when a child, you will be unlikely to test that assumption as an adult. If you believe that you are less clever than the majority of people you may hesitate to speak in public – and so on. As the old saying has it, 'If you think you can, you can, if you think you can't, you're right'. So, in the sample dialogue above, an excellent next question is:

> Coach: So what might you be assuming that's preventing you learning?
> Client: [long pause] I'm crap at sports and also I got thrown into a pool when I was a toddler by my older brother as a 'joke'. I had to be pulled out by my parents. I'm terrified of water. I believe I'm bound to drown.

Note the form of the question: not 'What's stopping you?' but 'What might you be *assuming* that's preventing you learning?' So this dialogue quickly reveals the self-limiting belief. While this client believes that he is doomed to fail at sport of any kind and bound to drown if he enters the water, he will not be able to learn to swim, even though he knows that if he could learn to swim he would enjoy it as an activity.

As in the example I described above with Matt (page 126), there will always be a perverse reward to staying stuck, and it's worth finding out what that is. In the case of the non-swimming client, the dialogue went like this:

Coach: So, very often when we say we want to do something but in practice don't do it, there's often some kind of spin-off from staying stuck. For instance, a naughty child might get a smack from her parents, but she still gets noticed and that might be better than being ignored if she's 'good'. I'm wondering what sort of benefit there might be for you in staying stuck as a non-swimmer ...

Client: [thoughtful pause] Probably it's a way of protecting myself from danger and also I suppose I dine out a bit on the story of getting thrown in the pool and it still gives me a nice handle to tap into my brother's guilt. I'm not sure how much real danger I was in.

Nancy Kline recommends a method of getting at underlying limiting assumptions in her enjoyable book, *Time to Think* (1999). She recommends asking the client to identify the opposite of the limiting belief – note that the client does the actual identifying of the opposite, not the coach. This is then followed by asking the client what it would be like to know (note the present tense) that the opposite is true:

Coach: So what would the opposite be of believing you're bound to drown?

Client: [laughs] That I'd be a confident swimmer.

Coach: So if you know that you are a confident swimmer, how would that feel?

Client: Absolutely brilliant!

Coach: So stay with absolutely brilliant – how does it feel to be absolutely brilliant as a swimmer and getting fitter?

Client: I can flip up and down the pool, I can do free style, I can swim 1000 metres without getting puffed, I have total confidence that I'm as good as anyone in that pool.

Coach: So, holding on to that belief and that wonderful set of feelings, how could you get there as a confident swimmer?

Client: I noticed an Adult Groundhogs Special at my health club the

Coach: other day – very small classes for non-swimmers. I could enrol
for that.
Coach: Will you?
Client: Yes!

Sometimes, as Nancy says, people will offer what she calls a 'possible fact' as the limiting factor. For instance, in the example above, the answer might have been, 'I did try once and all the children in the pool laughed at me.' This reply, although possibly true and a fact, still hides the limiting assumption. Nancy's comment is that this makes a further question essential: 'That's possible, but what are you assuming that lets that stop you?' This, as she comments triumphantly, will always slide beneath the possible fact and will capture the bedrock culprit: the ultimately limiting assumption.

Accountability

Accountability is about how the client will account during the coaching for changes in his or her life that he or she has agreed to make. The changes will happen outside the coaching session so that is why 'homework' is important. Sometimes thinking and pondering will be enough. Often it is not, and action will be required.

Accountability is a tricky concept. It can seem too much like teacher–pupil or boss–subordinate if it is done in the wrong way. It does not mean finger-wagging if the client fails to carry out their commitment.

Differences from ordinary usage

Accountability in coaching is very different from boss–subordinate or parent–child accountability.

- It does mean that you, the coach, *hold clients to account for what they have said they wish to do to make changes*. It is their agenda and their ideas of where they want to change that is at the core.
- The clients design the items for accountability, not the coach.
- Clients also design *how* they want to be held accountable.
- As a coach you have no attachment to whether clients have carried out their tasks/homework or not. You want them to grow but you have no stake in their doing things to please *you*.
- There is no place for value judgements or blame.
- Whatever has happened there will be learning in it.

The accountability part of the process usually happens at or near the end of the chunk of coaching that is around a particular goal and then again, as a summary, at the end of the session. You, the coach, ask the client:

So what are you going to do to make these changes happen?

- In hearing the client's reply, you press again for SMART criteria.
- Make a note of these objectives, even if you make very few other notes.

Challenging and requesting

This technique is a further variant on goal setting. It is usually light-hearted and enjoyable for both sides. How it goes is like this. Clients suggest a goal and the steps they are going to take. Sometimes these will strike you as vague – maybe a bit fluffy. You challenge the client to make them even more specific – or more challenging. The giveaway is when clients tell you they will 'try' to do something. 'Trying' is a cop-out and hardly ever results in action. You say:

> I challenge you to do x, y times between now and when we next meet.
> I'm going to make a request here ...

The client can say yes, no or maybe. The client may agree to the task but not to the frequency, or may like the idea of the challenge but not the specific form it is taking. If so, that's fine.

Examples
- A client wanted more fun and exercise in her life and had already identified her trampoline as one easy way she could get it. The trampoline was attractive to her children and they tended to colonize it. Coach's challenge: use the trampoline for 30 minutes every day without her children also joining in. Accepted, but with proviso that children may find it too hard to resist on at least one day in two. Client volunteered running as a once-weekly alternative.

- The client found it difficult to confront a mediocre performer in his team. Challenge: do it, using techniques practised in coaching session, and do it tomorrow. Challenge accepted, but timescale negotiated.

- The client had identified finding a new partner as an urgent priority in her life and various methods for doing so were discussed in the session. Coach's request: approach the five friends we talked about, telling them you want them to set up supper-party blind dates for you and do it within the next four days. Challenge accepted, but number of friends reduced from five to four.

Follow-up

You may want to suggest that the client emails you with the results of his/her action plan. This is also an easy way to keep the contact going between sessions. If you and the client prefer not to do this, in the next session, ask: 'How did it go on those action points we agreed last time?' When the client has achieved them all, congratulate him or her warmly and acknowledge whatever effort it will have taken to do it.

When the client has not achieved them, ask:

> What got in the way?
> What would you do in a different way another time?
> What did you learn from not doing them?
> What could help achieve them in the future?

It is normal for clients to explore how you will respond on accountability because many of them will have the idea that it is just like delivering a piece of homework, especially if they have not carried out what was agreed. Explore this in the initial session and also when the client falters.

Ask:

> How would you like me to work with you here? Does it help if we keep strictly to what you have suggested or should I be more relaxed?

This way you put the responsibility right back where it belongs – with the client.

While goals are important to client and to coach, there is also potentially a toxic trap awaiting those who take them as the be-all and end-all. Eckhart Tolle makes the case potently in his book *The Power of Now* (2001). Commenting that our whole lives can be about waiting for the future, the book celebrates the liberating energy of living in the present. Eckhart Tolle contrasts 'small-scale waiting' (in bus queues, in a traffic jam) with 'large-scale waiting' – for a better job or more prosperity. Large-scale waiting, especially without any of the action that will make the goal real, reduces the quality of your life now. The goals he associates with such pointless waiting he calls 'outer goals', all of which eventually end in failure. This is because outer goal achievements are subject to the impermanence of all things. He warns against waiting as a state of mind because it could mean that you only want the future while rejecting the present. Setting goals is important, but not at the expense of feeling alive now. In terms of the model of coaching I put forward in this book, he is warning against the doing self taking over from the being self:

Your life's journey has an outer purpose and an inner purpose. The outer purpose is to arrive at your goal or destination, to accomplish what you set out to do, to achieve this or that, which, of course, implies future. But if your destination, or the steps you are going to take in the future, take up so much of your attention that they become more important to you than the step you are taking now, then you completely miss the journey's inner purpose, which has nothing to do with where you are going, or what you are doing, but everything to do with how.

6 Bringing pace and interest to the session

Work in progress

Making a realistic appraisal of gaps between present and desired future, then setting goals, leaves client and coach with the task of working on reaching those goals. In this chapter I look at some useful approaches to keeping a coaching session pacey, lively and interesting – to both coach and client.

Typically a session will have a simple framework:

5 minutes	What has happened between the time we last met and now?
10–15 minutes	How did you get on with the action points we agreed last time? What have you tried? What have you learnt?
5 minutes	What items do you have for our agenda this time?
	• What priority do those items have in terms of their potential for impact on your life?
	• How much time would you like to devote to each during this session?
	• How does each of these items link to the overall goals we set for the coaching?
90 minutes	Coaching on the agenda items
5 minutes	What 'homework' will you be doing between this session and our next?
5 minutes	What feedback do you have for me on this session?

While skilled questioning is undoubtedly the coach's number one useful tool in having these conversations, there are a number of others that I want to describe in this chapter for making each of those 100 minutes of core coaching add value.

Breaking the trance

As what our Examinations Board dubs the 'Internal Verifier' for our Coaching Diploma, I now watch and listen to recordings of other people's coaching sessions. Of course, I am an eavesdropper after the event in a different role and for a different purpose from either of the two players. I am eavesdropping as part of the coach's training in order to give the coach feedback. Even so, with some beginner coaches, I find that my attention can drift off with the soporific drone of the conversation. Perhaps it is my early training as a TV producer, but I long for some action, some change of pace and, yes, some drama. Everything in my experience tells me that this will make for better learning – as it does when someone is telling you a good story, as it does in a good training event, as I believe it also does in coaching. Sitting still for two hours of the same kind of question and answer can be deeply dull. When appropriate, there are a number of techniques that can accelerate learning as well as providing a change of pace.

Changing the physical pace

Sometimes the simplest interventions are the best. Stopping halfway through a session and suggesting another cup of tea will often revitalize a flagging session. Similarly, suggesting a quick stand-up and physical stretch can be useful.

Drawing is useful because it bypasses the tendency of highly articulate people to intellectualize their problems, so activities like the Balance Wheel or drawing pictures of your life as it is and as you would like it to be also have this extra value (see page 107). Card sorts can also be useful: these are either home-made or commercially available packs of special cards with a variety of labels. For instance, you might offer a client a set of 40 cards where each one had a named motivational driver or value on it such as 'home and family' or 'serving society'. You then ask them to pick their top twenty and then finally to reduce them to their top five.

Depending on the weather and the location of your coaching room, a walk can also be a wonderful way of adding pace and variety to the session. I was working with a client on a longer-term programme whose aim was to establish him as a self-employed consultant in his field. At the time of the session he had just returned from America. It was a luminously sunny, fiery July day. About ten minutes in, he suddenly said, 'Jenny, I just can't concentrate – it's no good, I'm hot, jet-lagged and distracted.' Within moments we were out of the office and had set off on a walk around the attractive buildings and surrounding gardens of one of the ancient Inns of Court, a few minutes away from our offices in central London. We kept going on a circular route for the best part of ninety minutes. The walk even included an unauthorized meander around the magnificent ground floor hall of one building. Was this coaching? Yes. Indeed, there is often something to be said for a conversation where you are side by side instead of face to face – there may be more candour on both sides because you are released from the relentlessness of the eye contact involved in a conventional conversation.

We keep a flip chart in our coaching rooms. Getting up to draw, write, explain useful 'models' and theories and standing side by side while you do it is another way to introduce variety and pace. For instance, I might draw some kind of four-box matrix such as the Johari Window (page 89) on the flip chart and then invite clients to fill it in for themselves.

'Stepping stones'

This activity asks the client to walk through an issue instead of just talking about it. This approach is particularly useful for clients who want to change a repetitive pattern of behaviour, asking them what they would rather have as a benchmark at the outset. Standing up, walking it through and experiencing the feelings and sensations at each stage typically gives clients powerful insights into why they behave the way they do and also gives them a highly motivating experience of a positive opposite.

There are many variations, but one that works well is to set out a series of sheets of A4 paper in a line on the floor of the room, labelled in this order: Environment, Behaviour, Capability, Beliefs, Identity and Wider Implications. The framework comes from the work of Robert Dilts, a well-known NLP practitioner (for NLP see page 3).

Explain the purpose of the activity and ask if the client is up for it. Assuming the answer is yes, ask the client to stand on each sheet in turn, answering a series of questions around each 'stepping stone':

> *Environment*: Where are you when this happens? Who else is with you? What's it like being there?
> *Behaviour*: What's your usual response? What do you typically do? How does it feel?
> *Capability*: What skills and abilities are you using in this situation?
> *Beliefs*: What beliefs do you hold around this behaviour? What's driving it?
> *Identity*: Who is this person, e.g. [client name] the Perfectionist, The Saint, The Rescuer?
> *Wider implications*: Knowing what you know now, what are the wider implications of this?

Now work your way back down the line on the other side, asking at each stepping stone a series of questions based on more resourceful thinking:

Identity: Who could you be?

Beliefs: What could you believe about yourself and the situation that would be more positive and hopeful?

Capability: What skills and abilities do you have that you could use here?

Behaviour: How then could you respond?

Environment: Imagine yourself fast-forwarding to the next time you're in this situation. How will the outcome change?

Brainstorming

At some point in the coaching programme, virtually all clients describe feeling stuck. The stuckness will be around finding a more satisfactory solution to a long-standing problem than the ones the client has already thought of. The client is clear about the goal, maybe thanks to your expert clarification and questioning, but cannot identify how to get there. Typically, the client has gone round and round the same thought processes without coming up with an answer that feels right:

> I don't know how to tackle an under-performing member of my team – he seems immune to all my feedback.

> My weight gain has got out of hand but I hate exercise and I know that diets just make you fatter in the long term.

> We can't afford to move out of our company's premises but they're so shabby and unsatisfactory and in completely the wrong location.

> I want a holiday but my husband wants to buy a car instead.

Brainstorming works well as a technique with this kind of dilemma. (I was once reproached by a participant on one of our coach training courses who told me that the word 'brainstorm' was disrespectful to people with epilepsy, but I continue to risk political incorrectness here for lack of any satisfactory alternative word to this useful process. 'Thought shower', for instance, seems like a clumsy substitute.) So it works as a possible answer to the 'What … ' questions. It also works well as a way of finding answers to the 'How … ' questions.

Brainstorming is a simple but powerful approach to generating ideas, and the great thing is that as a coach you can join in. So where you have been longing to offer ideas, this is one legitimate place where you can do it. However, you have to stick to the rules, the most important of which is that while you are in the idea-generating stage, no evaluation of any kind is permitted: no raised eyebrows, sighs, self-censoring of the 'Oh, that's a stupid idea so I'm not going to say it' sort. This rule applies equally to you and to the client. Brainstorming only works if you say whatever comes into your head without editing.

How to do it
First you ask the client's permission:

> I feel that it would be useful to brainstorm some ideas here. Is that OK?

If the client says it isn't OK, then of course you drop it. However, it would be rare indeed for a client to say no – anything that would break the deadlock is probably welcomed.

Next, get clarity around the question. It needs to be reduced to something simple and straightforward, normally a question beginning 'How can I ... ?', or 'What ways could there be of ... ?'

Now you explain the rules. A lot of people think they know what brainstorming is but in practice they often start evaluating the ideas as soon as they have been uttered – the self-defeating habit that brainstorming is designed to prevent. Explain that at this stage any idea, however silly, outrageous or off-the-wall, is welcome. All ideas will be written down: ideally on a flip chart. Standing up while you do this seems to help because, again, it breaks the trance of the seated conversation. Encourage humour, wildness and silliness. You explain that you will be giving yourself permission to join in because this is not advice, only idea-generation.

When the ideas have clearly been exhausted, turn to a fresh sheet of paper and ask the client what criteria he/she will use to evaluate the ideas. Now you are back in strictly coach-mode. The criteria will normally cover areas such as practicality, cost, fit with the client's core values, time, realism, likely impact on relationships – and so on.

Now put the two sheets of paper side by side, hand the client a pen in a different colour and ask him or her to highlight any of the brainstormed ideas that look interesting enough to explore further. Review these ideas against the list of criteria and move to action in the usual way.

Alan
Alan enjoys good food and wine. He hates exercise because he says he was 'the class fat boy' at school and fended off jibes from other boys by clowning about being fat. He also loathes being fat and has recently become even fatter: 'I went to Marks and Spencer to buy a suit and found that they didn't do Size Huge.' Along with a number of goals relating to his leadership style, one of Alan's performance goals for his coaching is to lose three stone. He frequently has to

represent his organization on television and he describes himself as acutely embarrassed to be so obviously overweight: 'I'm not a good advertisement for us looking the way I do.' Additionally, he has some underlying anxiety about health. His father died young of heart disease and Alan has a nagging fear that he might also suffer premature death.

His learning goal in this area is to find a way of permanently sustaining increased fitness and weight loss by making changes in his lifestyle. He knows every diet: Atkins, Rosemary Conley, Slimfast, Weightwatchers, Slimming World, detox, low fat, high fat – 'You name it, I've tried it.' He also knows that long-term successful weight loss is about steady, undramatic shedding of pounds and that this comes from eating less and exercising more.

In an earlier part of the coaching conversation, Alan's coach concentrates on his motivation: what would be the rewards of achieving and sustaining this weight loss? Alan has no difficulty in describing looking and feeling more attractive, recapturing the sexual interest of his wife, regaining self-respect and losing the vivid sense of shame that he has about his battles with food and drink.

Alan's coach also helps him understand what his overeating might really be about: 'What are you actually hungry for?'

Alan finds the answer to that one easily: reward for himself, and a substitute for affection. As a child, hugs and kisses had been accompanied by biscuits and sweets. He associates sweet things, in particular, with love. His coach knows that his marriage is going through a rough patch where there is little sexual contact. Part of this is because Alan feels he is repellent to his wife through being so overweight and so has avoided approaching her, fearing rejection. Additionally, in this earlier phase of the coaching conversation, Alan and his coach consider how he could give love as well as receive it, on the principle that giving it makes it more likely that you will also receive it.

Alan has highlighted a powerful need to get fitter through exercise, recognizing, too, that exercise is an excellent way of shedding the stress of his high-profile job. This is where the coach uses brainstorming. The question is, 'What exercise could I do that will help me lose weight, get and stay fit?'

The brainstorm goes on for about six minutes. Ideas generated by both Alan and his coach include: scuba-diving, jazz dancing, entering for the London Marathon, walking to work every day, cycling, swimming, taking the stairs instead of the lift to his apartment, joining a gym, getting a personal trainer, learning Pilates, buying a home treadmill – and many more. And what were the criteria he would use to judge any of these ideas? Alan is clear: it has to be something that involves other people, probably something 'blokeish'. It probably has to be competitive, he has to be in charge of it and, strange as it may seem for a self-labelled 'lazy' person, it has to involve the major effort of running because cross-country running was the only sport he ever enjoyed at school. A moment later Alan makes a hurrumphing noise. None of the brainstormed ideas is quite right on its own. However, he has had a moment of epiphany. He now knows exactly what he is going to do.

This is because he starts and then organizes the 'Big Bellies Running Club' for other 'blokes' at his workplace. Soon this is the club everyone wants to join, regardless of whether they are overweight or not. Running a total of twenty miles a week in a London park at lunchtime with a pack of other beefy men suited him just fine. Perhaps he could have got there with another sort of discussion, but there was something about the pace and fun of the brainstorm, that for him, as with so many other clients, freed up his thinking.

Empty chair techniques

These approaches appear in a number of different therapeutic traditions, but most particularly from Fritz Perls of the Gestalt school, and are also invaluable for coaching.

Essentially they all work on the same principle: physically altering your point of view and seeing things from, again, a literally different angle can bring useful insights and can lead to changed behaviour.

The first time I experienced this as a client was with my colleague Phil Hayes, who talked me through one such exercise when my elder son, Luke, was a 17-year-old coming up to important exams. Luke's approach to homework was to postpone the moment of torture when he had to begin the wretched task for as long as possible, to do the homework or exam revision with both his CD player and the television on and maybe a girlfriend in the room as well, and to do what appeared to be the absolute minimum. This contrasted with my own experience of being a girlie swot at the same age, obediently pleasing my parents by putting in many hours of nun-like undistracted hard work in order to pass my A levels. I found it unbearable to watch Luke apparently frittering away his talent and risking his university place, and maybe there was a touch of envy in there too. The result was a great deal of well-intentioned maternal nagging. Phil talked me through a version of the *meta-mirror*, a classic empty chair technique. Within twenty minutes, I had seen how my behaviour looked to Luke. I had experienced the futility of my tactics, indeed seen how counterproductive they were, and had decided how to approach him differently. It's possible that Luke would give a different version of events, but from that day on I stopped nagging. He got excellent A levels and duly went to university. Whether these two phenomena are connected, I don't know, but I do know that my relationship with him, already good, was immeasurably improved from that time on.

Essentially all empty chair exercises work on the same principle. You set up an empty chair identical to the one the client is sitting in. You ask the client to move, to sit in the empty chair and to imagine that they are looking at themselves from another viewpoint. There are many variants of the viewpoint. Here are some examples:

> **Sonia**
> Sonia feels puzzled about how to speak up sooner at meetings. Her coach sets up the two chairs, explains the protocol and says, 'In the other chair I want you to imagine the part of you that wants to be confident and extroverted at meetings versus the more restrained person you feel you normally are . . . Get up from your own chair and sit in the more confident Sonia's chair. Now tell me how you feel. [later] 'What advice would you give the more restrained Sonia about what she could do differently?'

> **Brian**
> Brian is in a dilemma about which career path to choose. He has two good offers and feels paralysed by the responsibility of making the decision. His coach explains the exercise and invites Brian to sit in one chair at a time, imagining he is in each of the jobs, exploring how it feels.

Probably the most useful versions of empty chair work involve a relationship that is problematical in some way. It need not be a relationship that is in crisis; it could be one that is already pretty good but could be even better. A more important criterion is that the present and future health of the relationship should matter. Typically the coach will then ask the client to be the other person, to imagine his/her feelings as the other person, and to look through the other person's eyes at him- or herself.

It is probably easier to see how the technique works through a detailed example. The one I describe here comes from Neuro-Linguistic Programming (NLP), an approach to communication which also has many applications for training, coaching and therapy. The NLP approach has refined the 'empty chair' technique and turned it into something both elegant and powerful.

The meta-mirror
Essentially, the meta-mirror asks a client to enter into a state of maximum empathy with another person and then to identify and draw on his/her own inner resourcefulness.

By physically moving around, the client 'breaks state' – that is, changes both the physical and mental dynamic – and gains new insights and energy. The physical movement of the exercise also enables the client to see significant relationships from different perspectives – literally looking at relationships from another point of view.

When to use it
- There is an important relationship that could be better.
- The client feels fixed in one view or tactic yet knows this is not working – has tried talking it through but has not yet achieved a breakthrough.
- When you have plenty of time – it cannot be rushed.

How to use it
- Explain the approach without going into vast detail.
- Ask the client's permission to try it.
- Where a client expresses extreme distaste, don't insist, but do explore the distaste – it will be valuable material for discussion.
- Respect and rapport are essential throughout.
- To maintain rapport, you should keep yourself at the physical level of clients – i.e. crouch at their chair while they are sitting down – otherwise you will be looming over them: not a good idea.
- Keep your own contributions limited to the sorts of words and phrases suggested here.
- Allow plenty of pauses between your questions and the client's answers.
- Insist on *feeling* answers, not *thinking* answers.

For the purposes of this explanation, I will name the two people.

The client for coaching: Chris; the person with whom Chris has the relationship: Alex.

The steps

Chair and client position	Suggested 'script'
You already have two identical chairs in the room	Explain the technique to the client and ask for his/her permission.
	Invite the client to set the chairs at the angle and distance that feel right for the relationship as it currently is, e.g. How far away would you like the chairs to be?
Position 1 The client is in his or her own chair looking at the empty chair that represents the other person in the relationship	'Chris, I'd like you to imagine that Alex is sitting in the other chair. What do you feel as you look at Alex? What else do you feel?' (You can expect about six descriptive words which will identify the feelings.)
	Invite the client to stand up, loosen up

physically a little, breathe. Then say, 'Now I'd
like you to sit in Alex's chair.'

Position 2
Client moves to the other
chair and looks at his or her
own, now empty, chair.

'Now you're Alex, when you look at Chris, how
do you feel?
And what does that feel like?'

Position 3

Now invite the client to stand up, have another
shake and move to a place where he or she can
see both chairs.
'So, we've got Chris there and Alex there, when
you look at them, what strikes you?
And what else?
What is likely to happen to the relationship if
things stay as they are?
What do you want to happen in future?
What advice might you offer Chris?'
Normally clients get some startling or new
insights at this point. They literally see the
relationship differently. Don't rush clients here –
let the process take its time.

Position 4

Now again invite the client to move to a
position even farther away where, again, he or
she can see both chairs.
'So now in this position, I'm going to invite you
to see the relationship between Chris and Alex
in an even more resourceful way.
Focus on the two Chris's: what resources does
the detached Chris have that the engaged Chris
needs?
What other resources does the detached Chris
have?'

Position 1

Invite the client to return to Position 1,
gathering up all the resources he or she
experienced in Positions 3 and 4.
'So now you're Chris again, how does it feel
with Alex?
What are you going to do?'

Comments and variants

- Letting clients choose the distance between the chairs is important because it will contain some major clues about the relationship. Ask them when they return to the first position whether they now want to rearrange the chairs.
- Always ask clients to speak in the other person's voice, so, in the example above, Chris would say when sitting in Alex's chair: 'I see Chris as ... '
- You may want to invite clients to take up a fifth position even farther away – useful where it is a very fraught relationship.
- You can ask clients what the age difference is between themselves in the first position and the second position. It may be that the alternative self is older or younger. Older may mean older and wiser or older and more weary. Similarly, younger may imply more childlike and powerless or more energetic and playful.
- At the final stages, clients may get some benefit from returning to the second position.
- Always ask for a commitment to what will be different and what action will follow.
- Give clients ample time to return to equilibrium. Strong emotions are usually aroused. Suggest that you sit quietly together for as many moments as are necessary.
- Review the whole activity at the level of process as well as task: what was it like to be in those different positions? What has shifted? What is the experience of being a more resourceful self like?

This is a potent activity. I have used it many times with clients and there has never been an occasion where the client has failed to enter an intense and concentrated state. There is a stillness and deep absorption, which is quite unlike the usual run of coach–client conversations. Of course, there is no way of verifying the accuracy of our perceptions of what the imagined other person in the chair is feeling unless we check with them later – which some clients do – but my sense is that the insights from the perspective of the other chair are often spookily close. Most of us *can* actually access the cues others give us about their feelings towards us in the right circumstances, and this is what empty chair activities can provide. Perhaps most valuably of all, it allows us to understand and experience how we are contributing to the problems in a relationship.

Role play

This is another invaluable way of accelerating learning as well as of introducing a change of pace into the conversation.

Role play means that the client rehearses or revisits an important conversation. Normally the client 'plays' him- or herself and you 'play' the other person.

Some people have embarrassing experiences of role play from courses, where they claim that the artificiality of the exercise has created their extreme aversion for the method. Usually they are referring to staged and artificial scenarios where people who are not actors have to act. This is why it is probably safer not to label the activity 'role play' but just to do it without giving it a label at all.

Why role play is useful in coaching
- Some clients get psychologically jammed in one place, unable to move past their usual ways of behaving.
- Some cannot see how others see them.
- Role play is a safe way to experiment. The coaching room may be the one place where clients can try out different ways of behaving. Where you have grown the trust between you, clients can make themselves vulnerable without feeling that they will lose face if they get it wrong.
- It gives you opportunities for feedback to the client.
- It is the best way of rehearsing for a challenging conversation that clients describe as being on their agenda soon and also a good way of reviewing a difficult conversation in the recent past.
- Role play is invaluable for clients who describe many different types of people behaving in much the same way to them. In such cases role play is a useful way for clients to see that the response we get is as much to do with us as with the other person.
- For the same reason it is useful for clients who come to coaching to change another person. Role play is a way of finding out that the only way to change another person is to change ourselves first. It is often useful to remind clients of that old cliché, 'Behaviour breeds behaviour.'

How to do it
No real acting ability is required for role play to be successful, but it does help if you are able to change your own normal pace and delivery to become a little like the person you are playing.

Normally you will 'play' the other person and the client will play him- or herself, so you do any acting that is required.

Ask for a briefing:

> What kind of a person is this?
> What do they look like?
> How old are they?
> How do they typically respond when x or y happens?
> Tell me about a situation where there was a difficulty – give me some of the dialogue.

This briefing need not be extensive – a minute or two is all that is necessary.

Now say: 'OK, let's assume I'm the other person, and you're back in that situation. So you said … ?'

You then respond as you have been briefed the person would typically respond. Let the conversation run for a few minutes – or for however long seems useful. Three minutes is usually enough.

The debrief

Role play has no purpose without the debrief. Ask the client for permission to give him or her feedback.

- Ask for the client's view on how it went first; log how accurate the client's self-perception seems to be and explore any over-modesty or unrealistic self-acclaim later.
- Ask how like real life the role play was. Usually clients will tell you that the way it went was exactly like the real life incident went or could go. They will often say: 'You must know this person – you're just like him/her!' The later learning to be gleaned from this observation is that the client's typical behaviour is shaping the response he or she is typically getting.
- Tell clients how it felt to be on the other end of their style. You are not analysing here – just noticing and trusting your own emotional responses.
- Be very specific. You are looking here to feed back your micro as well as your macro observations, your objective as well as your subjective impressions, so you will need to note these while the role play is happening. Nothing is too small to be noticed and fed back. The objective impressions are likely to include posture, voice, facial expression, language and so on:

  > When you started telling me about the project being at risk, you leant forward and raised your voice. I felt you were really author-itative at that point, but only a moment later your voice dropped and I noticed you put your hand slightly over your mouth.

- Your subjective impressions are about the impact of the behaviour on you. To do this you imagine yourself in that person's shoes. Use 'I' all the time: 'When you did/said this ... the effect it had on me was ... ':

    So at first when you were looking authoritative I felt wary, but later at that point where your voice dropped and you put your hand over your mouth, I felt certain you would back down. The impact on me was that I felt if I hung in there I could get you to agree to what I wanted.

- Ask what the client would like to change or experiment with.

Always do a rerun if the role play has not gone well, to give the client the chance to experience success. Look for all the small and large gains which will tell you that the client is beginning to learn how to behave in a different way.

Swapping roles
Here you play the client and the client plays the other person. Again, I will typically introduce this activity without labelling it role play.

Felicity
Felicity told me that me that she couldn't understand why people were constantly hinting that she was *intimidating* when she met junior colleagues casually in walkabouts through the organization. 'I'm a friendly soul', she said. 'I just don't understand. I'm an enthusiast for my work – is that the problem?'

'OK', I said, 'so let's stand up. You and I have just met in the corridor. I'm a young colleague very new to your team. How do you greet me?' As we stood up, Felicity gave me her typical booming greeting, gripping my arm like a tourniquet and beaming her wide smile. As a physically big woman she seemed to take up a lot of space, including some of mine. She launched immediately into an intense discussion of 'my' work and how it was going.

We had no discussion of the behaviour at that point. Instead, I suggested reversing our roles.

'Right', I said, 'so let's swap over. Now I'm you and you're me.'

I then gave as good a version as I could without exaggerating, of what I had observed. Felicity was staggered.

'How did that feel for you?'

'Oh no', groaned Felicity, 'that is one overwhelming woman! Am I really like that? I felt you were interrogating me – and do I really grip people that tightly?'

Our debrief discussion then looked at other ways of behaving that were still true to Felicity – she was never going to be less than a powerful presence – but also likely to be less intense for the other person. After the discussion we then practised again, this time with Felicity 'playing' herself and me playing the casual corridor contact, followed by more feedback and discussion.

Role play as practice

A role play may last just a few minutes and be introduced with little fuss and no labelling. Alternatively there are circumstances where it can be usefully extended. In our firm we use it all the time for times where clients need extended practice and feedback. These will include areas such as job interview coaching, preparing to face the media and learning to enhance presentation skills.

Gareth

Getting on shortlists was easy for Gareth, but landing a Chief Executive job eluded him. After four failures in quick succession, he realized he needed help. First we worked on how he mentally approached the interview process. From his language, it was clear that he saw it as the equivalent of an academic examination:

JR: What is an interview like for you?
Gareth: It's a viva – it reminds me of the verbal grilling I had to go through to get my PhD.
JR: So you see it as a place to demonstrate your knowledge?

Gareth needed to learn that a job interview is a social and not an academic event. Interviewers would most probably take his knowledge for granted. Displaying it at such length was not answering the main question that potential employers had in their minds, which is always, 'What would it be like working with this candidate?'

Together we worked on a new set of skills for job interviews, this time emphasizing the social aspects of the interview situation as well as his leadership experience and skills, his approach to influencing, his motivation for wanting the job, and so on. There are only about eight core questions that can ever be asked in a job interview and we set about practising how to answer all of them. Working in five-minute blocks, I took the role of interviewer and he gave practice answers. Then we debriefed the answers with feedback from me, sometimes using video recordings. This way Gareth could see for himself how he was coming across. His own ruthlessly honest feedback, seen through the dispassionate lens of the camera, was all he really needed: 'I look too cocky there', or 'I seem a lot more confident when I sit up', or 'I'm more convincing when I answer the question more briefly and directly', and 'I seem like a nicer person when I smile.' Within two months Gareth had the Chief Executive job he wanted, has moved on successfully once more and is now a well-known figure in his sector.

For clients like Gareth, already very senior, it can take courage to make yourself vulnerable enough to come forward for help. *Talking* about the interview may be useful so far as it goes, but only practice will really make it clear what the blocks are and how they might be overcome.

Sometimes, the more specific a role play is, the more useful it can be. We will now routinely offer clients like Gareth the chance to rehearse micro behaviours: how you walk in, how you smile, what kind of handshake you have. Most of us have never had any feedback on these vital moments when first impressions are formed. Here is one client's view of what happened:

Beverley

Andy [the coach] suggested that we needed to work on the initial impression I make during an interview for a job. He'd already arranged with a colleague that the colleague would be a 'member of the panel' and that Andy himself would bring me into the room, just as typically happens in the first moments of a job interview. We went out of the room; Andy came in with me and introduced me to his colleague. To my surprise I got an enormous amount of detailed feedback – very straight and a bit hard to hear at first – for instance that my handshake was 'floppy' and that I stood sideways on to the other person. Andy also noticed that I seemed to do a silly little mini-curtsey, suggesting too much deference, and didn't smile enough. We must have rehearsed it about ten times before they were happy, but what a difference it made! The question in my mind was, 'Why has no one ever told me this before?!'

Similarly, a surprising number of clients describe themselves as handicapped by lack of social confidence. Inside their organizations, or in structured situations where they can feel in control, everything is fine. Put them in a room of strangers without the carapace of their role and status and they can freeze. Here, again, identifying from observation (this could be a homework assignment) or discussion of how socially confident people behave in such situations is the starting point, followed by bite-sized chunks of practice and feedback.

John

John was a senior police officer with a strong dislike for what he called 'tea and stickies' (sticky cakes). He defined tea and stickies as those apparently pointless social occasions where, dressed in civilian clothing, he had to be polite to people such as local politicians for whom he had scant respect. Even with people whom he might perhaps like in different circumstances, he felt gauche. I asked John to stand up and then to show me how he typically approached such a person at a tea and stickies event. I stood up too and became the local politician. John showed me how quickly his small talk dried up and also the awkward and barely suppressed hostility of his body language.

JR: How would it be different if you were in your uniform and talking to
         them about professional concerns?
John: Very different!
JR: Show me how different 'different' would be!

John immediately straightened his back, looked me square in the face, smiled
and seemed at least two inches taller and many percentage points more friendly
and confident.

Drawing attention to and experiencing the difference gave him his own
template for practising different behaviour along with some new scripts, which
concentrated on asking the other person about him- or herself, rather than
expecting to be asked himself.

At the end of this session, John's comment was, 'Why did it take getting to
this rank before I could see what is so glaringly obvious?!'

The truth is that it was not glaringly obvious until exposed in the safe place of
the coaching room.

Role play is useful in any area where the client needs feedback and
practice on skills. So it will be useful in working on areas such as running
meetings, delegating, influencing and negotiating, giving a presentation or
giving performance feedback.

Shadowing

Clients tell me firmly that they greatly prefer to come to our coaching rooms
than to have the coaching in their own offices or even on their premises. This
is because they relish the chance to make some space between the company
and the content of the coaching and they also know that it reduces the
temptation to indulge interruptions from a curious PA or from some apparent
'crisis' that will sap concentration. However, there is a strong case for seeing
the client at least once on his or her home territory. When you do this, you
meet the rest of the cast, people the client mentions who otherwise will
remain vividly described but fantasy figures to you.

Shadowing means that clients invite you to accompany them for a day or
half day, being with them as unobtrusively as possible. The idea is to see
clients in their own setting. In this way you will get to see how they interact
with others at the same time as getting a first-hand taste of the organization's
culture. Virtually all clients forget how weird the organization seemed when
they first joined it – they have become immune to its funny little ways.
However, you will notice. Feeding this back, along with everything else you
notice, can be an invaluable source of learning.

Setting up shadowing
It takes a brave client to do this. It will seem like a giant leap too far for any client whose organization still sees coaching as corrective training and where the coaching process therefore has to be kept secret. However, I have found that a surprising number of clients are up for shadowing.

Explain the benefits for the client. There are some benefits for you, but it's essentially for the client's benefit, not yours.

Discuss how the client will explain your presence to others. Total openness is really the only option. Most clients can see that their visible willingness to be open to such a high degree of feedback models exactly the behaviour that most organizations need so badly. Far from appearing 'weak', such clients appear robust and confident.

Be clear with the client – and others – that your role is observer.

Encourage the client to negotiate both permission and confidentiality boundaries with the colleagues who will be present during the day. Telling such colleagues that the spotlight is on the client, not on them, is usually enough to assuage any fears about being judged by the coach.

Ask the client on what he/she needs particularly to have feedback. Typical choices would be: delegating and briefing conversations; running meetings; interactions with a PA; time management; decision making. Leave plenty of time at the end of the shadowing (typically a half day) for feedback and discussion.

You may be able to organize some shadowing within a normal coaching session, depending on the client's issues. Here is an example of a coach who came up with an unusual piece of improvised shadowing by seizing the moment:

Ravi
Ravi grew up in a big family but described himself as chronically shy. Self-consciousness was the hallmark of his interaction with others when they were not part of his close circle of family or friends. In spite of his striking physical beauty, Ravi found it impossible to initiate conversations, so at the conferences which were an increasingly important part of his professional life he lurked on the perimeter of the room feeling miserable. Ravi's goal was to build his capacity to network confidently and this meant learning how to take the initiative with people he didn't know.

Ravi's coach seized the initiative, knowing that her coaching room was in an area surrounded by crowded sandwich bars. It was coming up to lunchtime. Ravi's challenge was the following:

Ravi, I challenge you to collect the lunch orders from others in the office, to go into six different sandwich bars, striking up a conversation in each with a complete stranger. It doesn't matter how banal the conversation is – it can be about the weather, the food, the sandwich bar – anything at all. I will be by your side, giving you feedback and encouragement on each one.

After recovering from his shock, Ravi accepted, collected the orders from the somewhat bemused office staff and set off with his coach trotting at his side. At each stage, his coach gave him encouragement and some further tips – for instance about his eye contact (sometimes avoided), his smile (dazzling when he used it), and asking him questions about what was working and what wasn't. The effect was astonishing. Within 20 minutes Ravi had discovered not only that he could overcome 30 years of waiting for others to speak first, but that he actually enjoyed it because of the response he got.

Observing

When you visit a client's premises, observe everything. Notice the state of the building: what is on the walls, the condition of the lavatories, the kind of food in the restaurant and how it is set out. Notice how you are treated as a visitor. Notice what surprises or impresses you. For instance, making a visit to a training college for one of our uniformed services, I immediately began to understand more about how my clients would be likely to think and behave.

The college is in the middle of soft and verdant countryside, but I was received by a uniformed guard who took a long time to verify that I was a legitimate visitor and then carefully issued me with a large car park pass and instructions only to park in a particular place. The grounds were crowded with people, most of them men, smartly turned out in full uniform, including hats – a shock to someone like myself, used to the sloppier informality that prevails in most training and development settings, even in formerly grand country houses. The noisy canteen was set out with long refectory tables topped by a high table with linen table napkins – a striking contrast to the cheap paper versions supplied for everyone else. The food was wholesome, plentiful and definitely in the school dinner mode. The room where I spent most of the day was spartan and distinctly cold, though there were also plenty of grand rooms on the campus. I was received with immense and elaborate courtesy by everyone and treated as an honoured guest.

This suggested a number of things about my clients' organization that helped me in working with them and also helped them to see their organization in the context of other organizations. There was an easy camaraderie to life in this organization – a hugely supportive network of colleagues who enjoyed spending time together. Hierarchy, clarity about roles, rules, and a smart appearance were also vital factors in the culture. The more senior you were, the more physically comfortable your life was likely to be, perhaps as a straight and visible reward for the notably stringent responsibilities for command you were expected to bear uncomplainingly.

I also understood that to appear to be threatening the camaraderie in such an organization would be difficult and painful. So, for instance, when one of my clients faced the ultra-tough challenge of having to investigate fellow officers, I immediately knew something of what courage and steadfastness this would take.

Real-time coaching

This approach to coaching is only for the bravest client and the bravest coach. It is possibly the most powerful single tool I discuss in this book. It involves you as the coach working 'live' with the client and his or her team and takes the process beyond shadowing. Here, you contract with clients to give them on-the-spot feedback about how they are working by coaching them in front of their team.

When to use real-time coaching
- Clients describe getting constantly snarled up in repetitive and unhelpful patterns.
- Clients do not see what these patterns are and will often blame others or express enormous frustration with their own lack of ability to make things happen on their terms, sometimes stepping up the very behaviour which has led to the problem in the first place.
- Clients espouse openness as an important value.
- Clients are self-confident learners, prepared to make themselves vulnerable.

James

James presents as dynamic and self-assured and has come to his role through his expertise and reputation in the sector rather than through a standard management route. Gathering 360° feedback for him reveals that his team sees him as talented, inspiring, enthusiastic, exasperating and capricious. The feedback suggests that he see-saws between involving the team on the one hand and then making what appear to be high-handed and inexplicable decisions on the other.

Initially, James cannot interpret this feedback – it baffles him. However, he accepts that there is also a high degree of dissatisfaction with the way he runs team meetings, and he feels it too. Mostly James tends to blame the members of his team for his own frustration. These meetings can, and often do, run for four or five hours at a time, with critical decisions left hanging and unresolved personal issues unnamed, leading to an unhealthy level of corridor conflict outside them.

As his coach, James and I identified what was at stake for the business if this dissatisfaction continued. We agreed that a lot was at stake: holding on to scarce talent was vital in the organization's competitive market, slow decision-making was paralysing the organization and the team's preoccupation with itself was sapping energy that should have been spent on beating off external competitors.

James and I had worked together for six months and there was a high degree of trust between us. We agreed that I would work with him in 'real time' during a meeting as a way of both spotting and then breaking whatever patterns he was using to maintain these unhelpful dynamics.

What real-time coaching is – and is not

It is important to be clear about what real-time coaching is and is not. You are not facilitating the meeting. You are not helping others in the meeting directly understand your client. You are not addressing any comments directly to any other person there nor eliciting their points of view. You are not taking decisions for the client. You are working solely with that client, but in front of his or her team. You are asking for 'time-out' space directly with your client, almost as if you are an invisible presence.

How to do it

- First you agree with your client what the goals for your session are. Two or three tightly defined goals are better than ten fuzzy ones.
- Next you contract for the degree of honesty that you will need. For instance, I will alert my client to the likelihood of my challenging him or her during the session, explaining that this will also help confront any scepticism that team members may feel about my role. It is important not to be seen as your client's creature, blindly supporting them whatever they do.
- Part of the contracting process is to discuss how my presence will be explained to the rest of the team. I will negotiate permission to augment or even contradict anything the client says at the time.
- Alert the client to how you will make your interventions by giving an example.
- Encourage the client to be explicit with the rest of the team about the goals he or she intends to work on in the real-time session, and also encourage him/her to ask the rest of the team to comment on the relevant behaviours during the meeting.
- Emphasize that your sole aim is to build the capacity of the client to solve his or her own problems, so you will be working in coaching mode throughout. Your role is to boost your client's authority, not to damage it.

- Offer the client the chance to back off at this stage if it all seems too scary.

James, continued

James invited me to his standard weekly management team meeting. His goals were to discover how to

- shorten these meetings without losing quality;
- involve people more evenly;
- make swifter decisions which everyone could endorse.

I sat immediately behind him and he explained the process to the group and also his goals: 'I want you all to help me with this – stop me and point it out if you see me doing things that go against these goals.'

They looked intrigued, puzzled and maybe a bit apprehensive. One of them later said that she was very fond of him and was afraid that he might be humiliated. The meeting got under way. Soon we had a vivid example of how James cut people off when they were in the middle of something that was important to them, but maybe was being put in a rather rambling way.

I intervened:

JR: James – did you notice that you just interrupted Sandie in mid-sentence?

James: Oh – yes, I did. Sandie was going on in so much detail, I just lost it.

JR: So how might you encourage Sandie to be briefer as well as letting her finish her sentence?

James: By tactfully telling her that – and by letting her finish.

As the meeting went on, I again stopped James at one point and said:

JR: James – what do you notice about who is doing the talking here?

There was a long pause.

James: It's just me and Simon, isn't it?

JR: Yes – and I notice you're really just talking to Simon's side of the room. What do you think the impact of that is on everyone else?

James: Well, of course, it's obvious isn't it – they're going to feel excluded!

JR: How could you involve the rest of the team?

James: By actually inviting them to speak or just by looking at them!

An hour into the meeting I asked James to consider what was happening to the energy levels in the room by looking around. He was able to see immediately what he had been blind to previously, that while his own energy level was high, others were looking weary and possibly bored.

> JR: What do you notice about how long the discussion on this topic has been going on?
>
> James: I suppose it must be about 40 minutes – that's too long. We've gone round the houses twice already. We need to move to a decision, don't we?
>
> JR: How could you do that?
>
> James: By establishing what everyone thinks then looking for what everyone can live with!
>
> This last was a real moment of understanding and change for James. Previously, as we had discussed at earlier coaching sessions, his model of decision making had been that everyone had to be 100 per cent happy with every decision. Since this is clearly impossible, looking for what people can live with (a different emphasis), even where there is discomfort, is far more likely to lead to swift and effective decisions. James knew this in theory but seeing it in real time was the breakthrough.

This type of coaching has enormous potential for change in the client. The stakes are high – for you and for the client. As with any kind of observation, you alter the dynamic simply by being there. However, by working in effect on the client's default behaviour, there will be plenty of material.

It is even more important than in any other kind of coaching situation to work respectfully and courageously. You have to keep yourself out of the way and yet be prepared to speak at just the right moment, possibly saying very little or maybe intervening a great deal, so exquisite judgement is essential. You certainly have to manage your own anxiety about being seen to add value, sitting on your hands if necessary.

Possibly the most powerful outcome of all is that in making themselves so vulnerable, and by making their commitment to change so public and specific, clients model boldness, openness and willingness to learn. The process itself demystifies coaching and also sends the most robust possible message to the rest of the team about what is expected of them in turn.

In general the way I think about any coaching session has been affected by my earlier career as a television producer. In any programme the producer knows that it is important to start with something that will grab the attention of the audience. This needs to be followed by subtle or overt changes in pace throughout the programme. There need to be fast parts and slow parts, points where there is laughter and places where there is room for sadness or thoughtfulness, light and shade, long sequences followed by short ones. Even the simplest kind of DJ-driven radio show will alternate fast music with slow, sweet ballad with upbeat cheeriness. Understanding that the same principles apply to any coaching session will immeasurably help both you and your client.

7 Practising professionally

Coaching is a relatively new profession. Many of us have come to it from allied disciplines such as management development, organizational consulting or therapy. In this chapter I look at what issues the professional coach needs to take into account and how some of those issues might be resolved.

Ethics

Coaching may present you with a number of dilemmas, none with easy, obvious solutions. There are few, if any, absolutes.

What alerts you to the presence of a dilemma? First, there could be a gut feeling that something, somewhere, is making you uneasy. Or there could be the knowledge that if whatever it was appeared in a newspaper, it would at the very least be embarrassing and hard to defend. Another symptom could be discomfort at the thought of having to defend it to a person whose moral judgement you respect and whose good opinion you prize. There may be the knowledge that a proposed action is against the law or a realization that you may be infringing a stated (or implicit) value for you or your practice.

Dilemmas may be around issues of priorities. Some possible ones might be: 'truth' versus 'sensitivity'; individual versus organizational need; organization versus community; business versus environment; short-term versus long-term impact; financial versus individual need.

Dilemmas in action

These are real examples.

- You are giving individual coaching to a management team of six people, excluding the boss. You make the usual promise of confidentiality. As the coaching progresses, it seems clear to you that there are some important systems issues emerging about the way the *total* team operates with its customers.
- The Chief Executive of a company with whom you want to build business has set up a coaching programme for one of his Directors. He accepts that you will not be able to give any feedback direct to

him. However, he asks you to let him know if the Director terminates the coaching or fails to turn up for a session.

- A client confesses to something illegal in a session with you.
- You are working with two people from the same management team. Their relationship is a hostile one. Both trust you and have a good relationship with you. Both tell you a large number of things about their own position, attitudes, hopes and fears, including how they feel about their colleague.
- You are coaching a Director and gathering 360° feedback on him from 10 people nominated by him through focused, structured interviews. You discover that all his colleagues appear to hold him in very low regard. The more you probe for some positive features and behaviour, the more detail pours out about the poor opinion his colleagues hold of him.
- You are working with a number of Board-level individuals in an organization. You are approached by the Board of their most significant competitor to undertake a similar programme.
- You realize that because of a blip in the way your tax is being dealt with, your practice could avoid a significant amount of VAT with no risk of discovery.
- As an external coach and consultant, you have found yourself a supervisor, another independent consultant, whom you pay at her going rate, meeting her every ten weeks or so to discuss your current issues. You get on well, so well that you ask her if she would like to be involved with you as a co-consultant on one of your projects.

There are no easy answers to most of these dilemmas and it is perfectly possible that different coaches would respond in very different but equally acceptable ways. For instance, some coaches will refuse to coach more than one member of the same team on the grounds that while the coach may be well able to keep the issues separate, the team members may not believe that this is so. In my own case, I will not now work as facilitator to a coaching client's team, though I used to do so. Now I will recommend a colleague on the grounds that the client's team will inevitably see me as biased towards the client, thus reducing my perceived value as an objective resource. Where I used to coach several members of the same team, I now avoid doing so, on similar grounds.

Susan and Thomas – team colleagues

Susan's coach was hearing a good deal about Thomas in his sessions with her. As a senior member of Susan's team, Thomas was a preoccupation: allegedly a poor performer. Susan was an enthusiast for coaching and asked her coach if he would also coach Thomas. Susan's coach demurred, feeling that Thomas would be unlikely to trust someone apparently so firmly in his boss's camp; he also anticipated feeling uncomfortable with the mutually hostile information that would in all probability be unloaded in the coaching sessions. Instead, Susan's coach suggested a colleague as Thomas's coach.

With permission from Thomas, this colleague brought the difficulties of the Thomas–Susan relationship into the open. In due course, Thomas's coach facilitated a meeting between Susan and Thomas, with permission to share the results with Susan's coach. The two coaches agreed that the coach to the more junior partner should be the one to do this work, to head off any feeling that it was a set-up by the more senior person. This meeting helped Susan see what she was contributing to Thomas's difficulties and vice versa.

It is difficult to mix roles, but not impossible. Where there seem to be boundary issues, it might be possible to resolve them through naming and facing up to any dilemmas that might be created. If it is not, then stick to one role.

Where organizations ask me for progress reports on a client as a condition of the work, I will refuse the work. This is because I believe that such a progress report will first of all be valueless because it is the client's judgement of progress that matters. Also, the real evidence of change is in the daily business where the client actually does his or her work. As coaches we do not witness this, so how could we judge our clients' performance? Most significantly of all, I know how impossible it would be to create trust if the client believes that the coaching is about *assessment* – a completely different process.

I will not work with direct competitor organizations simultaneously because it is inevitable that commercially sensitive information will be part of the coaching. I know that I can keep such secrets, but the client may still be concerned in spite of my assurances.

Where there is a triangular process of funder, client and coach, I ask for an initial meeting with funder, potential client and coach all present. If it is clear that the potential client is seen as a problem performer, I will float the possibility that the problem is with the relationship between the funder and the potential client (if they are in a line management relationship) rather than all the problems being with the behaviour of the potential client.

Where the relationship seems to be the problem, I will offer a facilitated meeting for the pair as an alternative to coaching for one of the pair. Assuming that this is not the case, this meeting often enables the line manager-funder to be candid for the first time with the client about what he or she sees the performance or career issues to be. I will facilitate this meeting, challenging any unrealistic goals and expectations on either side and explicitly clarifying the confidentiality issue.

My stand on this is that it is up to potential clients to disclose whatever they like about the coaching, but my own lips are sealed. After this meeting, I ask for thirty minutes alone with potential clients to discuss whether they are up for coaching or not. I cannot work with a reluctant client, so will usually say something like:

> Your organization has made this time and budget available, but it's up to you whether you take advantage of it or not. How do you feel about going ahead?
> What concerns do you have about this process?
> How will you report on progress to your sponsor?

If the sponsor wants a progress report, I will direct him or her to the client, as I find it seems to be impossible in practice for sponsors to avoid asking content questions about how the client is progressing. I raise this as a likelihood at the contracting meeting and explain that I cannot give progress reports, asking sponsors how they will manage the understandable anxiety they feel about how their money is being spent.

When the coaching is finished, I also negotiate a review meeting with funder, client and me. The purpose is to enable the client to point out to the funder what has changed, what has been learnt and how he or she proposes to embed the learning into everyday practice. This is often a crucial part of the process. Funders can have fixed ideas about the client, sometimes secretly believing that they cannot or will not change. This can be profoundly dismaying to a client who has made heroic efforts to change but has seen that these changes have not been registered by the funder. Again, I make no comment on the content or process of the sessions, but will help clients articulate what they believe has changed and will encourage funders to do the same.

The ethical situation is easier with whole-organization coaching programmes. Here we will ask all coaches involved to keep a note of the overall themes that are occurring in the coaching, eventually producing a brief report to the organization without giving any information that could identify individuals. This can provide the client organization with invaluable data on how the 'psychological contract' between a set of individuals in key roles and the organization is going – for instance, whether people feel that the balance between what they give to the organization in terms of time, effort and energy is well matched by what they receive in return – financial reward, status, promotion, and so on.

At the beginning of the coaching I explain to clients that confidentiality is not a blank cheque. In the unlikely event of clients confessing to something illegal or dangerous to themselves or others, I forewarn them that confidentiality rules would not apply. Our protocol here is that we would always try to persuade clients to take appropriate action themselves but if they refused we would do whatever we thought to be right, alerting the appropriate authorities while also doing everything we could to preserve the dignity of the client. Fortunately, I have never had to put this principle to the test.

We consider it is important to preserve client confidentiality, including the fact that people are actually clients. There are occasional exceptions. For instance, clients who have spoken openly about being clients, often on public platforms, can of course be named.

Sometimes events force you to choose between two equally unattractive options. I was coaching one member of a team in an eight-session programme. Towards the end of that time another member of his organization booked herself a coaching programme. By the time that programme had started, delays of one kind and another had meant that his programme overlapped with hers – not a problem, you might think, except that I discovered at her first session that she had unexpectedly become his boss. I then felt I had no option but to tell her that her new team member was a client with me and to ring him the same day to say that his new boss was a client, giving both the option of working with someone else.

So ethical guidelines are essential. We base ours on the guidelines suggested in *Co-active Coaching* (1998), which in their turn are based on the guidelines of the International Coach Federation and are similar to those of the European Mentoring and Coaching Council. We aim to keep them as simple as possible, without underestimating the complexity of the issues:

1   You act at all times to protect the public reputation of coaching, avoiding doing anything which could reflect badly on how the public perceives the coaching profession.
2   You clearly describe your levels of competence and experience and will never overstate your qualifications or expertise.
3   As a coach, you believe in the resourcefulness of each and every client with a matching recognition of the fact that all clients make themselves vulnerable in the coaching relationship. You recognize and protect this vulnerability.
4   Clients must be volunteers. If there is any element of coercion you decline the work.
5   You clearly set out the terms of the coaching contract at the beginning of the relationship and confirm it in writing: times, fees, cancellation policy and limits, if any, on telephone and email contact between meetings.
6   You will protect clients from exploitation of any kind: sexual, financial, emotional. The purpose of the coaching is the client's well-being and growth and as a coach you demonstrate this in all your dealings with the client.

7   You make every effort to protect the client's confidentiality, though this is not a blank cheque. Confidentiality will be fully discussed at the beginning of the coaching contract and will be raised with the client whenever it could be an issue. The coaching relationship is not privileged under law and clients need to be told that this is so. In the extremely rare cases where the client discloses something dangerous or illegal, you may be obliged to inform the relevant authorities with or without the client's permission. You will encourage clients to take appropriate action themselves, without the intervention of the coach. There is no obligation under current UK law for a coach to disclose such matters.

8   Confidentiality involves preserving the names of clients unless they have given active assent to disclosing them. The confidentiality rule applies to third parties who are funding the coaching: recipients of the coaching can decide what they disclose, for instance to a funding sponsor, but the coach will not do so without the explicit consent of the client.

9   The data that you collect for a client belongs to that client: he or she has a right to hear it, however uncomfortable it might be for you or the client.

10   Where there is the possibility of a conflict of interest, for instance over boundaries or roles, you and the client will discuss it and look for a fair resolution. You will always look for a way to preserve the client's best interests. If there is any appearance of a conflict of interest which could damage the coaching relationship you should consider withdrawing, explaining why to the client in a way that protects the client's dignity.

11   Where you have a business relationship with a third party concerning referrals or advice, you will disclose it.

12   Where you feel that the coaching is not appropriate for the client or is not working effectively for some reason, you are obliged to discuss it with the client in a way that preserves the client's dignity and protects his or her vulnerability. Where the solution involves referral to another professional, you will make every effort to avoid injury to the dignity and feelings of the client.

13   You manage your own issues in a way which means that they do not intrude into the coaching relationship.

14   You have regular sessions with a supervisor or mentor to review and reflect on your practice. 'Difficult' sessions or clients should be discussed as soon as possible with another coach or supervisor. You commit to regular training and updating.

Supervision

Coaches need supervisors. But what is supervision for?

What a strange word *supervision* is, when used in the context of professional development. A supervisor in the managerial world is someone who has direct line management responsibility for your work. This is the very thing that a coaching supervisor does not and cannot have. There is also a distinction between a coach having *coaching* – a place where the client-coach can discuss any and every issue, and *supervision*, where only professional issues are on the agenda. In some of the many rival schools of therapy, a therapist is expected to have a lifelong commitment to receiving therapy and a major commitment to supervision as two separate but parallel streams.

A supervisor offers a space and place where professional concerns can be discussed with a more experienced practitioner. Supervision operates on coaching principles – that is, the supervisee brings his or her agenda to the sessions and the supervisor works without giving advice. It should also offer the coach a place where stress and burnout can be anticipated and prevented. It should be possible to declare mistakes and to discuss dilemmas without fearing being judged.

How frequent should supervision be? Supervision is more useful at more frequent intervals when you are in training or a relatively new coach than it is when you are more experienced. However, there is also a good case for supervision when you are very experienced indeed. The long-serving coach may be equally in need of supervision to guard against the potential jadedness or complacency of burnout. For instance, a coach who becomes invested in being a *clever* coach may be in urgent need of challenge and refreshment.

Watch out for signs of burnout both in yourself and in fellow coaches with whom you work on a regular basis and deal with them quickly. Clients notice these differences, possibly before the coach does. Any incongruity between what we claim and how a client actually experiences us is immediately apparent. Such signs might include:

- feeling messianic – you can save your clients from their own failings;
- feeling wonderfully insightful all of the time;
- boasting about your expertise as a coach;
- failing to experience at least a quiver of apprehension before meeting new clients;
- believing that you know exactly what clients are going to say long before they open their mouths;
- claiming that you have acquired special powers of problem-solving simply through people being in your presence;
- noticing a high degree of irritation and distraction with your clients – reverting to Level 1 listening a lot of the time;

- knowing that you are seeking new gizmos, 'tricks' and 'techniques' to jazz up your coaching to keep boredom at bay;
- realizing that a higher than usual percentage of your clients are opting for fewer sessions than originally booked, matched by a smaller percentage than usual of people who are extending their programmes.

These dangers can be overcome by applying some realism and common sense and discussing them openly with a supervisor. It is also invaluable to have an experienced practitioner with whom to discuss difficulties and triumphs. It is not a guarantee of perfect practice, but it makes poor practice a lot less likely.

Getting best value from a supervision session

- Choose your supervisor carefully. Liking and mutual respect are important. It takes about 1000 hours of practice to become experienced enough to handle the range of everyday coaching situations and about 3000 hours to be equipped to work with virtually any client. Regardless of the actual amount of experience, it probably takes at least a chronological year to become reasonably adept as a coach and another three or four years to operate at a high level with any client most of the time. This is the level at which you would be acceptable as a supervisor with another coach. This is because 3000 hours of coaching and several years of practice implies a successful coach with a high level of repeat business based on word-of-mouth recommendations. A good working assumption is that someone who is a successful coach will also be an effective supervisor.
- Prepare for a supervision session carefully, constructing your agenda in just the way you expect your clients to do.
- It is fine to blend supervision with coaching, bringing life, career and personal issues to the supervisor as well as professional issues. Clients do this so why should it be different for coaches?
- Notice your own reactions to the sessions. It is highly probable that you will be feeling apprehension combined with excitement, pleasurable anticipation and interest. This is useful – it reminds us that our clients make themselves vulnerable in their work with us. Similarly, in order to get value out of a supervision session, we also make ourselves vulnerable by being willing to own up to doubts and mistakes and to receiving feedback.
- Offer your supervisor feedback and build the relationship on candour and trust, just as you would expect from one of your own clients.
- Expect to get non-judgemental comment. Your supervisor was not

with you when you made those quick decisions about what to do in the moment and there is a literally infinite number of ways any coaching session could go. There is no one right way.

- Concentrate on you and your coaching style, not on yet another intellectual analysis of your clients' issues. To me the greatest potential flaw in some supervision is the danger of second-guessing. The sessions can come to be about the supervisee's clients rather than about the supervisee. Just as your clients may try to lure you into discussing people who are not present in your coaching sessions, so you could do the same with your supervisor. There is only you and your supervisor – you are the raw material, not your clients. The questions should be, 'My dilemma with this client is x', not 'this client's problem is y'.

- Good questions for supervision sessions include:
  - Which clients am I finding it most enjoyable to work with? What does that say about me?
  - Which clients am I finding it tough to work with? What does that say about me?
  - What is the best/worst coaching moment that has occurred since we last met?
  - What ethical issues am I troubled about?
  - What dilemmas am I facing (with particular clients, or in general)?
  - What issues do I find recurring with my clients? What might this suggest I am noticing or ignoring? What does that say about me and my practice?
  - Which skills and techniques do I find easy?
  - Which skills and techniques am I avoiding because I find them difficult?
  - What concerns do I have about my coaching practice?
  - What feedback have I had from my clients? How should I be addressing the themes that come out of this feedback?
  - How is the relationship between us going? What does the answer to that question suggest about my coaching style?
  - How am I growing as a coach?
  - What else is going on in my life that could shed light on the above issues?

- Alternatives to a paid supervisor can work well. These will include a co-coaching arrangement with another coach or a learning set – a group meeting where coaches will take it in turns to have air time to explore their issues, coaching-style. Some learning sets also usefully do live coaching with each other for review and feedback. This is another invaluable way to benchmark your practice and to get skilful and thoughtful feedback from people in the same business. The downsides of these approaches is that where coaches share the same weaknesses or gaps in experience, these might be reinforced rather than challenged.

Evidence

In coaching itself, we know that the value of the process is immeasurably increased when it is based on observation and external data rather than just on storytelling from the client. The same principle applies to your own development as a coach. There are a number of ways you can seek such evidence:

- Ask a willing client for permission to record a session, using it as the basis for your own reflection and then as the basis for a supervision session. Reassure the client that the purpose is your own professional development and the recording will only be heard by your supervisor, perhaps offering the client the tape after your supervision session is over. It would be rare for clients to refuse this permission. This enables a supervisor to get first-hand evidence of your coaching practice rather than just relying on your account of it. Making this the basis of a supervision session transforms its value.
- Ask a trusted and experienced colleague to sit in on a session with you as a strictly non-speaking observer. Choose the client carefully, backing away immediately if he or she show any signs of reluctance. Reassure the client, as with a taped session, that the focus is on you, not on them. Allow plenty of time for a debrief after the client has left, accepting that the observer's presence will have altered some aspects of the session.
- Ask a willing client to write a reflective diary after each session, matching it with one of your own. Topics could include: highlights and low lights of each session; useful and less useful coach behaviours; thoughts and feelings that it was difficult to express in the session itself, and so on, exchanging the diaries towards the end of the coaching programme. This is a humbling and challenging experience for any coach, usually revealing a wide discrepancy between what the coach and client believe has happened.
- Ask a third party to run a simple emailed questionnaire for you with clients who have completed their coaching. Ask them for feedback on how useful the coaching has been, what changes they have made in their lives as a result of the coaching and any suggestions they have about what you might do to improve your effectiveness. The reason for asking a third party to perform this service is that you will

get more truthful answers that go beyond conventional politeness. Where you work for a coaching firm, it is good practice to conduct such client surveys from time to time. If you do not, you may be able to offer a mutual exchange with another coach.

Being realistic about supervision

What can supervision actually do, compared with the claims that are sometimes made for it as a process? In the UK, many of the professional therapeutic bodies insist on a high ratio of therapy-giving hours to supervision hours, sometimes as high as 8:1. Similarly, I have seen some coach-training organizations suggest a ratio of 25:1 for coaches. That also seems high. In my own case, since on average I give 18 hours of coaching a week, I would need to be employing a supervisor every week and a half – but of course I do not.

In practice, inflated claims are sometimes made for supervision, confusing it with *audit*, a different process which involves the actual measurement of one professional's results against an objective benchmark. Other professions do not demand that there is such a high level of supervision, so what makes coaching so special? We could argue, for instance, that any profession in which there is 'emotional labour' should offer supervision. This would include anyone in any kind of therapeutic role where one-to-one working is the norm. This would include, for example, chiropody, physiotherapy, nursing, beauty care, some kinds of legal work, medicine and probably many other kinds of personal service work where there is a brief but intense kind of exchange between client and professional which can leave the professional exhausted or the client crushed in some way. Supervision, in the sense of a non-line-management relationship, is now a routine part of the nursing profession and increasingly becoming so for the medical profession, but is not the norm for many others.

I am troubled by some of the claims made for supervision as a process. For instance, I cannot see how supervision *guarantees* either the quality of the coaching process or protection for the client. In the social work profession, there is an elaborate and careful system of supervision which has been in operation for at least forty years, yet the dreary and predictable round of child protection scandals continues. Whether supervision fails or succeeds depends to a large extent on the honesty and self-awareness of the supervisee. A dishonest or un-self-aware supervisee could, in theory, fool a credulous supervisor.

A supervisor is also assumed to have access to greater wisdom and experience, but there is no certainty that this is the case. Supervisor and supervisee could well share the same blind spots, especially if they have been trained in a school where such blind spots are built in because of the theoretical bias of that school. Some supervisors may criticize supervisees over their lack of adherence to such theory rather than looking at whether the coaching is actually working for the client. In some parts of the therapeutic world, there seems sometimes to be almost as much supervision as there is therapy – an ever-reflecting series of supervisor–supervisee mirrors, including supervision for the supervisor. All this adds to the costs that have to be borne by the client.

Perhaps the ultimate heresy where supervision is concerned is my doubt about how far we can truly hurt a client. We might damage ourselves, yes, but clients? We may waste a client's time. We may bore clients. We may annoy them. We may deluge them with unwanted and inappropriate advice. We may do embarrassingly poor coaching, but real, lasting injury? As with everything else in life, the principle of choice applies. The client most likely to claim damage is probably also the one who has well-honed and ultra-sophisticated defences, perfected over many years. This client will probably be the first to say that our coaching is terrible, thus rightly and paradoxically denying our ability to cause any real harm. There may be exceptions with the sexual abuse of very vulnerable clients (see page 222) but in the ordinary run of coaching it is hard to see how real and lasting harm could result from it.

In general, I see supervision as one part, an important one when done rigorously, of the continuing professional development to which all of us need to commit. We may need it in different ways and at differing levels of frequency at different stages of our coaching careers. We also need to seek out other forms of development such as training to update our skills and qualifications, attending conferences, reading and simple networking with other coaches.

Keeping notes

As a coach you absolutely must keep and file notes on each client. As your practice grows, you will begin to forget details of what your clients have said at their earlier sessions. Similarly, you may forget how many sessions a client has had and paid for, or there may be confusions between you about this. A professional coach spends time before a session reviewing notes from the earlier sessions as a way of getting in the right frame of mind to work with a client. It is also a useful way of reviewing your own practice and of preparing for supervision sessions. Finally, if by any unfortunate chance your notes were subpoenaed by a court, you would want them to be immaculate.

New coaches often want to know whether you should write notes during the session. My own practice is that I rarely do, but I respect other coaches who make the choice to write at the time. It is a matter of personal choice. These are the various arguments for and against.

Taking notes during the session

For	*Against*
It is a reliable way of remembering what the client has said and of recording details accurately	You may find you have jotted down the inessentials, or have written notes that are too full to be read quickly next time
It looks as if you are taking the client seriously	The client may wonder what you are writing
You don't have to spend time later reconstructing the conversation	You have to break eye contact with the client in order to write; the notebook forms a barrier between you

Making notes after the session

For	*Against*
You can concentrate wholly on the client	You may forget some of what has been said or remember it inaccurately
There is no barrier between you	Not taking notes may worry the client – may think you are likely to forget vital details
Writing the notes later makes it easy to edit down to the essentials	You have to spend time after the client has left writing up the notes
It sharpens your listening skills when you know you are going to have to write up your notes later	Your listening skills may not be as good as you think they are.

If you coach using the telephone, you may be able to have the best of both worlds.

Basic principles

- Keep notes short and simple: a page and a half of bullet points is usually more than enough.
- Keep judgements out of your notes – keep them factual and descriptive.
- Always write notes in a way that would not embarrass you if they were seen by clients – which clients have the legal right to do.
- Leave out acronyms which could be misinterpreted. For instance, a doctor's patient, who saw her notes, made a formal complaint about

being called, as she thought, 'Son of a bitch'. The doctor had written SoB, meaning *short of breath*.

- Store the notes in a secure, locked cupboard or filing cabinet.
- Tell a trusted colleague how to gain access to the notes if for any reason you are unable to run a session or need to get access to your notes when you are not in your office.
- It is best practice to keep the client's contact details separate from the actual notes of each session. This enables a PA or admin assistant to contact a client without having to risk breaking confidentiality by accessing session notes.
- Store 360° feedback reports with the notes.

Use the notes to record:

- Client's name, date, session number and time taken at each session (e.g. *Jane Smith, session #3, 14.1.01, 1 hour 45 minutes – client 15 minutes late*).
- How much time has been invoiced, or when an invoice is due.
- Presenting issues for the session.
- What was discussed.
- Outcomes of any forms you used – e.g. the Balance Wheel or psychometric questionnaires.
- Any handouts you gave the client or book-reading suggestions.
- Agreed action points and accountabilities.
- Next steps/any items agreed for discussion at the next session.

Some coaches prepare simple forms to help create order with their notes. Feel free to do this if it will help you.

Chris

Client   Chris Scott   Invoice submitted March 21

Session # 2 of 6

DATE   *APRIL 24*

ISSUES

- Review of action points since last session

  Experimented with new type of departmental meeting – i.e. with 'show and tell'/fun elements; project reviews; etc as agreed. 'Went brilliantly' – lots new energy in team. High approval rating. Will do now as routine.

Had conversation as agreed, with Nigel (boss). Tried offering him feedback – 'semi worked'. Did work when was assertive and interrupted him. Didn't when let him have all control.

- Goals for this session

1 Improve ability to say no to inappropriate demands.

Offered saying no protocol. Practised with me asking for quick-fire series of ludicrous things. 'I find this so hard – hear my mother saying got to be good girl.' Gremlin territory – reminder – she agreed. Got better with more practice. Offered feedback on where she comes across as determined, where still tentative. Confirmed that did NOT seem 'rude'.

2 Tackle B— - poor performer in team.

Discussed evidence of B's performance. B 'gets away with it because believes organization won't ever sack anyone' . Brief discussion organizational culture. My challenge: 'what are <u>you</u> doing to sustain this?' Answer: 'ducking it!' Explained feedback principles. Did initial practice. NB: return to this again next time with tougher scenarios.

3 Feedback on FIRO-B

Fed back her scores with interpretation

	Inclusion	Control	Affection
Expressed	5	2	5
Wanted	2	6	7

Discussed light this shed on assertiveness and leadership feedback she's already had.

ACTION

- Return to Nigel and reopen discussion; get assent to study leave
- Find one opportunity a day to say 'no' using techniques practised today
- Practise giving <u>positive</u> feedback using feedback principles to praise min. one person per day between now and next session

Training and development for coaches

Training can make a significant difference to your effectiveness as a coach. It can offer you a framework for understanding and assessing what you are doing as a coach, feedback on how you are doing it and the chance to swap bright ideas with other participants. One issue may be where you can find high-quality training, especially as more and more providers enter the field, some of them of dubious merit.

There are many ways in which training can now be delivered: by open/ distance learning, by electronic means and through the telephone with teleclasses where there could be many dozens of learners on the line with one tutor. These methods are by and large a great deal cheaper than doing the same thing face to face. Where written materials are concerned, once the development cost has been recovered, there is far less cost to the training provider than there is with face-to-face training. They have the great advantage of being flexible – with open learning materials, for instance, you can work at your own time and pace. As with any kind of learning delivered at a distance, everything depends on the quality of the written materials. Some of this is deplorable, some excellent.

Delivering face-to-face training is expensive for both provider and student, and I am a supporter of open learning in the right place and for the right purpose. However, my own belief is that face-to-face training is easily the most effective way of learning how to coach. This is because you can read descriptions of coaching but, until you actually do it, you have no idea whether you are going to find it easy or difficult.

Training for coaches is often about challenging ingrained poor practice as well as finessing an already sound style. Without that instant individual feedback from a practice partner or experienced tutor, bad habits can become chronic handicaps, simply because they are never challenged. Some of the most common mistakes we see trainee coaches make, for instance, arise from lack of awareness. This includes: not realizing how intrusively long a coach's typical question is; unawareness about asking advice-in-disguise questions, wrongly believing them to be innocent, open questions; failing to notice how often rapport is broken when the coach's anxiety subtly changes the dynamic, and so on. This is the kind of thing that would be hard to spot when you are one of thirty people on a telephone line or just reading an open-learning text.

In choosing a training provider, these guidelines may help you reject the charlatans and identify the quality providers:

- Look for realism and modesty in what providers say about their training. Anyone promising the full, once-and-for-all authoritative guarantee that they can turn you into a fully-fledged coach within a few short days will be misleading you. A training course starts, rather than ends, the process of growing as a coach.

- Look for a low ratio of participants to tutors: 1:10 is about the maximum that can be guaranteed to provide enough individual attention.
- Four days of face-to-face training is the minimum for serious learning about coaching.
- Look for providers who are also successful practising coaches with a demonstrable track record in the field in which you intend to practise. Some training companies save money by employing recent graduates of their own courses, thus possibly perpetrating the Chinese whisper effect of poor-quality training. Ask how many years of successful practice as coaches the actual course tutors have.
- Look for a high ratio of practice to lecturing.
- Look for an emphasis on personal feedback.
- Ask how your participating in the training links to accreditation and who will be doing any accrediting. Press for information on how strictly the verification process is handled. Many accrediting bodies have only the most notional part in maintaining quality.
- Specialist training will become increasingly likely – for instance courses that offer to turn therapists into coaches; fast track courses for already-experienced coaches; courses aimed exclusively at life coaches, and so on. Courses aimed primarily at managers are not usually suitable for people who want to work as professional coaches, and vice versa.

Other types of training

Many coaches find that they need to acquire licensing in a number of parallel skills and areas such as psychometric testing or Neuro-Linguistic Programming (NLP). It is no longer a competitive advantage to have such qualifications as so many people already hold them, but it may be a competitive disadvantage not to have them. See page 92 for some suggestions concerning particular questionnaires. It may also be useful to acquire training or qualifications in your own niche. For instance, one of our actor-coaches holds a specialist qualification in voice training. This has deepened an already impressive expert knowledge as well as making her more credible to potential clients. Two of our associates are also qualified psychotherapists, enabling them to blur the boundaries between therapy and coaching, if they wish.

Accreditation

Assessment of your actual coaching through observation or recordings should be at the heart of any accreditation process rather than writing essays or asking your clients to fill in a questionnaire about you, useful though these processes can also be as back-up to the main question: How good a coach are you? For instance, some training providers accredit students solely on the basis of a 'dissertation'. Interesting and challenging though this no doubt is, it does not prove anything about their likely quality as coaches. You could write a brilliant essay about coaching and be a terrible coach or be a brilliant coach and be unable to write an essay about it.

As a new profession, many people are interested in the question of accreditation. The demand for it may come from different quarters.

Coaches may want to be able to use it as part of their marketing and may also want to be certain that they are properly trained against a national or international standard. Increasingly, coaches may want credits towards a master's degree. I also notice how much more frequently clients ask for evidence of training and accreditation. Clients may assume that there is some national or international standard and hope that, if there is, this will protect them against employing rogues. At the very least, clients are seeking some reassurance that their coaches have been rigorously trained and look for it as a sign that a coach is serious and not just a well-meaning amateur.

Comparisons

The greater the potential for danger to life, limb, soul and pocket, the more important this issue becomes. The key issue is accountability. Thus the professions where there is strong professional accountability include medicine and its allied professions, the law, religion, accountancy and flying. So, for instance, you cannot pilot a plane solo, practise medicine, call yourself a nurse, be a priest in the Anglican Church, or call yourself a solicitor unless you have passed examinations controlled by a professional body. In these cases, *licensing*, which can include active re-registration and continuous retraining (now compulsory in some professions), controls access to the profession.

The situation in coaching

Although there is considerable interest in accreditation, the current situation is confused and patchy. The International Coach Federation (ICF), a US organization, offers accreditation. This works by the ICF scrutinizing courses offered by providers. To become fully accredited, an individual coach has to clock up an agreed large number of hours with clients and be supervised and observed. The ICF is the nearest we have worldwide to a proper accrediting body. However, it is not particularly well known and there seems to be a shortage of ICF-accredited providers and assessors. Some training providers accredit their own coaches.

However, this is a more complicated question than it first appears.

To have real control over quality there would need to be a national body – say the equivalent of the various Institutes in financial services (Chartered Accountants, Secretaries, etc). To be effective, these bodies need:

- the power to control entry to the profession, backed up by statute;
- money – to set and test standards;
- consensus on what constitutes a good outcome of a professional intervention;
- a complaints mechanism and accountability procedure;
- teeth – to discipline and if necessary expel miscreants;
- public support and agreement that the profession is important enough to be worth controlling, i.e. has the potential to do significant harm as well as good;
- the support of all practitioners;
- staff – to administer all the above.

There is no national body in the UK which can deliver all of this at the moment, and frustration is leading many people to follow their own paths.

At the moment the existing accrediting mechanisms do not and cannot control access to the coaching profession. This is easy. Anyone can call themselves a coach regardless of whether they have been trained or hold a coaching qualification. It is impossible to identify misdemeanours because there is no widely agreed analysis of what constitutes success in coaching, let alone what constitutes failure. There is no effective means of disciplining a coach who has been accredited but who is guilty of a professional misdemeanour, because there is no way to prevent a poor coach from continuing to practise.

The actual *knowledge* content specific to coaching is relatively small, though there is a substantial sister-field in therapy and counselling. This compares with, say, the knowledge of tax law needed by an accountant. An excellent coach has *wisdom and skill*. Real success as a coach is the result of a great many hours of practice with real clients and commitment to continuing professional development rather than the accumulation of factual knowledge which can be tested fairly straightforwardly through an exam.

Parallels with other professions

The nearest parallel is with psychotherapy. There are many university-accredited courses leading to qualifications in psychotherapy. However, there are a number of rival psychotherapeutic bodies in the UK and there is no universally agreed approach. Indeed, there is sometimes a high level of unseemly squabbling, reminiscent of the bickering between religious sects about who has real access to the true faith. You can call yourself a therapist and practise as a counsellor or a therapist without licensing or training, though this is becoming increasingly difficult. The existence of training and of professional controls does not prevent corrupt therapists having sexual relationships with their clients nor prevent other kinds of inappropriate behaviour. This suggests that controls are weak.

Even in professions such as medicine with the tightest controls, it can be notoriously difficult to expel a poor performer. For instance, constant rudeness and arrogance are not normally bad enough behaviours *on their own* to justify being struck off the medical register, however many patients complain. By contrast, a coach who was rude and arrogant would not stay in business very long.

This situation may improve over time. However, I notice a similarly hostile press developing around coaching as it did about psychotherapy twenty years ago. For instance, in a recent newspaper article about a coach specializing in parenting skills, the opening paragraph contained a reference to coaches *preying on* clients. This casual insult contradicted the content of the long article that followed. This was entirely positive about the coach who was the focus of the story and contained glowing testimonials to her skill from a number of satisfied parent-clients.

Return on investment

With coaching now becoming a familiar part of management development, the question of whether coaching delivers a good return on investment becomes ever more pressing. It is common for commissioning clients to ask: 'How do we know it will work? What can you tell us about how you assess success?' This is a tricky question. If we fail to take any of the credit for the apparent successes of our clients, we do not honour the coaching process. If we take it all, we do not honour our clients. It is an infrequently discussed danger of coaching that we can be over-keen to see our clients 'succeed' as a way of proving to ourselves and others that we add value. For instance, if I coach a client for a job interview, how much of the credit can I claim if that client is successful? And am I helping that client in some way to 'cheat'?

My approach is always to answer that I work with a client to bring out what is already there rather than in any way subverting the selection process. A client who wanted interview coaching once asked me straight out as a condition of hiring me what percentage of my interview-coachees did actually get the jobs they apply for. If the percentage is at the level of chance, then what does that say about my coaching? But if it is high, then that may say more about the poor quality of the selection process than about anything I do in the coaching room.

Learning from coaching is also not a smooth, steady process. Instead, it typically proceeds in fits and starts, often with fast progress at the beginning followed by lulls and apparent lack of progress. These lulls often precede another major leap forward, but it is impossible to identify this except retrospectively.

Coaching is, or certainly should be, a voluntary process. So any clients who seek coaching could be different in some way from clients who do not – for instance, they may already be more self-aware and probably therefore already more successful. This makes it difficult to compare a coaching cohort with a control group unless there is also a large waiting list group. Knowledge and skill may also leak from individuals getting coaching in an organization to individuals who are not – in fact we have to hope that it does.

Asking clients after the event can be difficult because memories fade, even where the coaching has been successful – the lessons are internalized to such a high extent that the client forgets their origin. Then, too, success in work or in life is never down to any one factor. There are usually far too many variables to be able to say for certain that it was the coaching that made the difference. For instance, in any large-scale coaching project, there are not only many clients, but many different coaches. It may be impossible to establish how much of the success or failure of the coaching was because of the strengths and weaknesses of any individual coach. Clients themselves may be no better able to assess this than supposedly objective researchers. It is common, for instance, for clients to say, 'I did it myself, and I do know I couldn't have done it without you – but I don't really know how or why.'

Concern with measurement may also lead to attempts to measure the only things that can be measured. Dismayingly often, these are the most trivial things. For instance, you can easily measure how many sessions any individual client attended, but how far does this tell you whether or not that client had value from the process?

It helps to be clear what commissioning clients actually want because a number of separate processes may be wrapped up in a request for proof that coaching works:

- *Research* could be a separate process, involving looking at long-term outcomes, coaching style, and assessing the value of different theoretical and practical techniques.

- *Audit* may involve benchmarking costs and outcomes with those obtained in other ways or in other organizations.
- *Evaluation* may try to measure what tangible and intangible benefits have been obtained by the individual and the organization. Few robust studies have been carried out here, though those that have do suggest both tangible and intangible benefits to both individual and organization. One example is the study carried out by Merrill Anderson in 2002 with 43 participants on a leadership development programme in the United States and Mexico. This study looked at evaluation from a four-level framework. First, what did individuals feel about the coaching, second, how were they applying the learning? The third level asked for third-party validation – how others had seen this learning applied. Finally, clients were asked for causal connections between the coaching and measurable changes in the performance of their units. Even when results were adjusted to exclude relatively 'easy' measures such as staff turnover, 77 per cent of the participants cited coaching as having had significant impact on bottom line results. Altogether, the return on investment was calculated at a staggering 700 per cent (Anderson 2003).

As a coach you will be unlikely to be able to create such convincing proof of your effectiveness. However, there are a number of actions you can take to ensure that there are answers to the legitimate concerns of the commissioning organization about how its money is being spent, or indeed any individual client of a life coach:

- Ensure that the goal-setting process gets enough time at both the outset of the coaching and in every session.
- Make your goals measurable.
- With executive coaching, ensure that you link business results with the relationship and skills issues.
- Ask for feedback all the time on how the client is progressing towards achieving these results. Ask what and how the coaching is contributing.
- Where you are involved in a large-scale project, look for ways to build evaluation in from the start.

8 The heart of coaching: the coach–client relationship

> I see you
> I am here
> (West African greeting – and reply)

What actually goes on between coach and client? Why does coaching work? What makes the difference between an averagely acceptable coach and a brilliant one? How far is coaching actually the partnership of equals that so many of us say we create?

I have hesitated about writing this chapter. The subject can seem so nebulous, yet it is probably at the heart of why, when coaching works, it does work. Finding simple and direct ways to describe that heart is not easy. I once spent some time at a conference about coaching where many of my fellow delegates were enthusiastically exchanging words and phrases like: *global visionary*; *majestician*; *non-moralistic attunement*; *creationist compassion*; *coaching as an act of love*; *self-structuralization*; *spontaneous wholeness*; *quantum leap into new consciousness*; *profound spiritual passions*; *transformative alchemy*; *vibrational awareness*; *world-changing potential*, and so on. At one session to discuss these concepts, I had to confess to the convenor that while I heard her words I had very little idea what she was talking about. I don't want the same fate for my thoughts here.

It is easy to make coaching seem as if it is technique and nothing else. As a coach, you must have techniques because without them there is little understanding of what coaching can do and achieve and you will not have all the tools you may need. Yet the best coaches go a long way beyond technique. This is the paradox: you have to learn technique in order to bypass it.

Many years ago I was making a television programme about textile craft as art. My programme consultant ran a large and successful textile department at a leading university and she was showing me around her first-year students' work stations, bedecked with what to me looked like dazzlingly accomplished and original art. My consultant looked at me with tolerant pity while I expressed my wonder. She explained that virtually everything I was seeing was a technically expert and clever pastiche of some outstanding contemporary artist's work and was therefore without any great aesthetic merit. First-year students, she explained, have to do this before they find their own style. They have to perfect their techniques through copying others. It was encouraged and expected. By the second year it was steadily discouraged and by the third, work of true originality was demanded.

The same is true of learning to act, to play a sport or a musical instrument. In acting you have to acquire and then go past methods to get to the meaning of the text. To inspire the orchestra, a conductor has to be an accomplished musicologist before going beyond what is simply written in the score. A jazz musician must acquire a thorough grasp of musical technique before being able to improvise successfully.

It is the same with coaching. You have to learn the techniques in order to discover where they fit into the true learning that comes about through coaching. This learning can only happen in the crucible of the coach–client relationship. This is because the coaching client is not an *object* to be worked on but a *subject* to be worked with by another human being. There are some useful clues from the world of therapy. The Gestalt therapist and writer Martin Buber wrote astutely:

> The deciding reality is the therapist, not the methods. Without methods one is dilettante. I am for methods, but just in order to use them not to believe in them. Although no doctor can do without a typology, he knows that at a certain moment the incomparable person of the patient stands before the incomparable person of the doctor; he throws away as much of his typology as he can and accepts this unforeseeable thing that goes on between therapist and patient.
>
> (Hycner and Jacobs 1995: 17)

A colleague and I were assessing would-be coaches in order to fulfil a contract we had won. We set up a process where we observed the candidates through a session with willing guinea pig clients. One would-be coach broke every suggested guideline in this book and many more. This coach, as it turned out, had never had any training, though she claimed a track record of successful coaching. In our practice session, she intruded grossly into her client's physical space, at one point almost sitting in her lap she was so close; she continually pressed her pet solution onto the client; she talked too much.

And yet ... and yet her client, correctly identifying that we would probably not be offering this coach a job because of this behaviour, said wistfully, 'In spite of all that, I really liked her and it was actually helpful. I will do some of the things she suggested because I knew how much she wanted to help me.' I am not advocating this artlessly naïve and unskilled coaching, as I am certain that this coach would soon have floundered helplessly with many of the demanding clients we had in the pipeline. However, the intention to help in this session was so strongly conveyed that some decent coaching did actually take place.

Power in the coaching relationship: the outer signs

Talking about coaching as a relationship of equals has become a mantra in coaching. It is one of my own – and my company's – basic principles and values (see page 7). Working in partnership is what gives coaching its power. How far can this pious hope be true in practice?

When you contrast coaching with some other professions, there are some startling differences. For a start, where many of the traditional professions are concerned – accountants, lawyers, doctors – most people would much prefer not to have to consult them. Almost all are associated either with an actual crisis or a potential crisis. Coaching clients are always facing change, but they may see this as bracing rather than threatening. Once they get into the swing of it, clients may look forward to coaching sessions rather than approaching them with the dread that a visit to a lawyer could involve.

The traditional professions are selling the superior knowledge that their specialism gives them. Sadly, this has often led to conveying an attitude of superiority. The more obviously service-based and possibly more overcrowded professions (think of financial advisers, architects, interior designers) have always had to take a more client-centred approach. Similarly, a coach may rate his or her specialist skill very highly while underplaying the knowledge that goes with it.

Most coaches will go to considerable lengths to live equality in the relationship as well as talking about it. This contrasts with the way many of the traditional professionals treat their clients. So, for instance, I have never once been on mutually first name terms with any doctor to whom I was a patient, indeed most commonly have been talked at as an anonymous 'you'. By contrast, I work with many doctor-clients, use their first names from the start and expect them to address me likewise. I always offer tea, coffee or water, thus introducing the social nuance of guest and host – also a relationship of equals.

There are some ways in which the relationship favours the coach. Many coaches insist that the client comes to them: we do in our firm, unless we are coaching on the phone. When the client comes to us we have already disturbed the balance of power. The client is on our territory and, a bit like being a guest in our house, knows that he or she is expected to play to our rules. We set the method for the coaching, including, paradoxically, the method that says the agenda is the client's. We set the time frame for the length of each session. We set the fees.

Against this, we may offset a number of factors that play to the client's power. The client can and often does negotiate fees downwards, depending on the state of the coach's order-book. The client will probably take a far more active role than the coach in deciding the appropriate number of sessions.

Apart from the initial session, where most coaches will have a well-rehearsed protocol, the format of the sessions is entirely in the client's hands – in theory. And, as in any profession, all clients know that there are many other coaches out there eager for business.

In his devastating critique of therapy, Jeffrey Masson (1990) suggested that even the best therapists cannot avoid creating an exploitative and controlling climate because it is so ingrained in the profession. The critical difference with coaching is that our clients are mentally healthy, and where they are not, their 'symptoms' are the ones of familiar minor dysfunction.

Also, certainly where executive coaching is concerned, we are dealing with robustly successful, senior and well-paid people used to having their own way and dealing with suppliers of all sorts as part of their daily lives. For many coaches in the most obviously elevated end of the market, their clients could be earning ten times or more the salary of the coach. Many are also well-known public figures. This makes a world of difference – the coach will usually approach the client with at least some vestige of the world's respect and may even be unconsciously basking in power borrowed from the client. None of this, of course, may be true of life coaching, where a dynamic more like that of therapy might apply.

There are other, more subtle ways, in which the coach–client relationship is not one of equals. For the most part, as a coach, you set aside a great many of your opinions during the course of the conversation. The client is allowed to express opinions. The coach is willingly more restrained. It is the coach's responsibility to reach out to the client, not the client's to reach out to the coach. The coach is responsible for setting the climate of the conversation – not the client. The client is invested in his or her own learning – not the coach's. The coach has to affirm the client, but the client has no such responsibility towards the coach.

These are the outer signs, and in coaching the outer signs suggest a rough and ready power-neutral relationship where a balance of sorts is possible. Far more important is the kind of transaction that takes place in the actual working relationship.

Bringing your true self to the coaching

Mature, mutually reciprocated relationships are rare indeed in our society. In spite of some of the puzzles and dilemmas I describe in what follows here, that is what we are seeking in coaching. As a coach, how can you do your best to ensure that this is what actually happens rather than it remaining an aspiration?

Coaching works because of who the coach is as well as what the coach does. However, clients judge by what they experience, and the outer sign of this is in what you, the coach, do. Everything you do has to be consistent with the values you espouse. As Anon wisely remarked, 'People may not believe what you say, but they do believe what you do.'

When you start coaching, and certainly in all decent coach training courses, you will learn about the critical importance of keeping yourself out of the way. One sign of this is the detailed guidance you should receive on many of the areas covered earlier in this book – for instance, keeping your own agenda banished, learning to ask powerful non-content questions, and so on.

Now think about your image of one of the most famous listeners of all time, Sigmund Freud, and a founding figure in the professions that became therapy and coaching. You probably instantly call up a stern, passionless figure with perfect self-control who schooled himself in blankness so that the client could project on to the empty screen which the therapist thus provided. You probably imagine that the room in which this blankness was provided would itself be a neutral and austere space.

All of this was indeed what Freud advocated in his books and papers. However, in practice this was far from what he actually did. He shouted at his patients, visited them at home, lent them money, gossiped with them, cajoled, laughed and joked. Famously, he waved his cigar in triumph when he believed that he had found some special solution to the patient's problem. His consulting room was a richly patterned and densely ornamented place, full of clues to his personal taste.

Freud's actual practice shows the reality. It is a myth that you can or should hide yourself and be some kind of void. You will be making a statement about yourself before you even open your mouth, for instance through the clothes you have chosen to put on that day. Are you giving the impression of dippy-hippy with carefully untended beard (if male) or lusciously flowing ethnic skirts (if female)? Are you dressed for comfort rather than for style? Are you in a dark business suit? How far does your dress match the dress in which you expect your client to appear for the coaching? Although voice and accent can be worked on, they will most likely still say something about your regional or class origins and your education.

Your coaching room will convey the atmosphere you expect to engender in your client. When our practice was expanding and we needed to hire extra coaching rooms, for a time we took occasional rooms in an alternative therapy centre. This did not last long. Having a massage bed in one corner of some rooms always had to be apologized for (thus of course drawing attention to it), the lack of natural light felt oppressive and the cloying smell of aromatherapy oils was embarrassing.

Neutrality is impossible. A library wall of books may intimidate a client who missed out on university or impress one who respects academic achievement. If you have certificates up on the wall that will convey that you think certificates are important. Your choice of pictures will tell the client what kind of art you admire – or think suitable for a coaching room. Having no pictures or ornamentation of any kind will also convey a message. If you are coaching from a room in your home, evidence of your domestic life may be a plus or a minus to the client. Too much intimacy too soon might also be off-putting. A woman client whose previous coach ran their sessions from his home told me that in his small flat she was too embarrassed to use the lavatory because she thought he might be able to overhear her.

Think hard, then, about your coaching room and what you want it to convey about you and your coaching. At the very least you need two chairs able to accommodate people from the thinnest to the fattest for up to two hours. Women need to be able to sit in such chairs without having to worry about whether you can see their underwear. People with short legs do not want to have them dangling during the session and people with long legs should be able to stretch out comfortably. The chairs need to be identical in shape, size and covering. A sofa for the client while you sit on a matching chair may seem like a generous gesture, but it will feel wrong to the client, as will any differences in the height of chairs.

Taking the mystery out of coaching – and out of you

In any relationship where helping is involved, there is always a strong possibility of both sides tapping into the deepest roots of human longing. Psychology as a subject has its roots in philosophy, medicine and religion. Magic, superstition, spiritualism and mysticism are peeping just around the corner. When something is wrong, we can crave some magic, whether it is a wonder-crystal with the power to ward off danger, faith healing to save us from death, ley lines which will explain puzzling events, or an exorcism which will banish evil spirits. The power of belief in this respect can be overwhelming. Several studies have shown that placebos (pills that contain no drugs) and placebo procedures (for instance opening a patient's chest and sewing it up again without any other surgery having taken place) can have almost as much positive benefit as conventional drug or surgical treatment.

It is only 150 years or so ago that mental illness was widely believed to be possession by the devil, and there are some religious faiths where people still believe that. The idea that there are people with special powers seems to be something we can all find potentially appealing. It is comforting, if also a little scary, to think of giving yourself up to someone who can reassure through their links to the Divine, or through their special insight ... sliding smoothly into *second-sight* and *psychic*.

Beware of letting your coaching become contaminated with the same ideas. It is easy, believe me. In my early days as a coach I several times heard clients introduce me to colleagues at a social event as 'witch', or slightly less alarmingly as a 'white witch'. 'She put me together again – and I don't know how', or 'There's a kind of magic there.'

Now, I go to some pains to demystify the process. You cannot work as an equal with someone who believes that you are some kind of secular priest or shaman. Clients may not always welcome this at first – it might be more comforting to believe in the wizardry. But long term this cannot be right. I was once training the executive team of a large hospital in coaching techniques – the aim being to add to their tool-kit of managerial skills. One person in the group was also a long-standing client of one of my colleagues. We came towards the end of the second day of the course. 'Oh no', he groaned, 'I'm finding out what lies behind the magic and I don't know that I want my illusions shattered!'

There is power in the coaching relationship and I want my clients to believe in that power. However, the power is invested in the relationship itself and in the coaching process, not in the supposed supernatural powers of the coach.

Negotiating the partnership

In your first meeting with a client, it is important to negotiate the partnership explicitly.

This fulfils several functions. It emphasizes to clients that coaching is indeed different and allows you to explore how the client wants to be coached. It creates an opportunity to flush out any different ideas and hypotheses the client may have about coaching – for instance that it is like therapy or that you have a pre-planned agenda (as a trainer might). It also allows you to find out what assumptions the client is making about you and gives you the chance to take the mystery out of coaching – and out of you.

- Briefly explain the history and philosophy of coaching and the concept of partnership.
- Emphasize that all coaching starts and finishes with the client's agenda, not yours, and talk about the motivation for coaching being about making changes that the client feels are important in his or her life.
- Explain the importance of honest speaking.
- Explain that coaching is about the whole of life, not just work.
- Demonstrate that coaching may include unusual behaviours from you, such as interrupting and offering feedback, explaining why this may be important.
- Explain the importance of questioning and of avoiding giving advice – give some examples; do a brief three-minute coach on one of the client's topics and show how you have asked questions and maintained a non-judgemental attitude.

- Ask the client for comments on this.
- Now ask a series of questions such as: 'Have you been in a one to one relationship at all like this before?' Many clients have had therapy or previous coaching. If so, ask: 'What helped the relationship work then?' 'What should I avoid or try?' 'How would you like to be coached?' 'If you could give me some tips on how to coach you, what would you say?' If clients are puzzled here about what you mean, discuss issues such as how hard they like to be challenged, how candid they would like you to be, and so on. This always produces useful material for the coaching. Interesting answers clients have offered include:

    > Tough but not too tough: soft cotton boxing gloves!
    > I need to be challenged, but you'll see me resisting. Wait with me while I get adjusted!
    > Give me honest feedback on how I strike you – I can't get it anywhere else.
    > I don't know – can we work it out together?

    You could also ask: 'What's the most effective way to get around blocks and difficulties for you?', 'What are your views on how fast or slowly we should go?'
- Explain that coaching sometimes hits a plateau after the first few meetings. Ask the client: 'How would you like us to cope with that?'

It is also important to ask clients what, if anything, they need to know about you. Often the initial answer will be 'nothing' – and at one level, of course, that is fine. The client has come to deal with his or her own issues, not yours. However, an apparent total lack of curiosity troubles me. In fulfilling a contract for coaching with one organization, there was a 'meet the coach' preliminary event at which, unlike three colleagues, I could not be present. I joined the group the next day for the first of their coaching sessions, held within the timetable of a five-day course.

One of the managers in the group who had selected me 'blind' to be his coach told me that he had done so precisely because I had not been present the previous day. His reason, he explained, was that he wanted me to be a 'totally neutral coaching machine' and the less he knew about me the better. In my early days as a coach I would have accepted that.

Today I realize that this is too interesting a piece of data to be ignored. So in discussing this wish for neutrality, it quickly became apparent that this client felt that the more he knew about me, the more he dreaded that I would judge him. I found the idea of being a *neutral coaching machine* distasteful and I also know that this is not how coaching works. In my refusal to stay at the level of coaching cipher, I was able to show him that he could both explore his issues with a real person and be accepted for who he was.

So, in that first conversation:

- Take a few moments to say how you came to coaching and how long you have been doing it (your credibility as a coach – the doing part of you), including any qualifications you hold.
- Tell the client something about who you are – the being part of you; why coaching matters to you; and a little about your personal life.
- Keep it short – three or four minutes only.
- Ask 'Is there anything else you'd like to know?' Note, this is a closed question which expects the answer 'no'.

It is also vital to ask why those clients have chosen you. What do they already know about you? What are they expecting from you? How does the reality compare with what they expected? How are they feeling now, this minute, about being here? What are their first impressions of you?

When you ask these questions you begin to break through the fantasies and polite conventions that will hold up the process of coaching. As long as you and the client stay stuck in a mutual role play of objectivity, nothing of much value can actually happen. The real value of the coaching is in the relationship you and the client create. So it is vital to know what is already in the client's head and heart. Asking this type of question will often reveal that clients:

- do not understand what rules of engagement will govern the conversation;
- are worried about being shown up as incompetent;
- fear exploitation or colonization;
- may be more worried about their presenting issues than they want to admit;
- worry about being made to do things they don't want to do;
- have concerns about confidentiality;
- fear finding out things about themselves that they won't like;
- worry about the coach finding out that they are really repugnant: the coach will see through them;
- doubt whether they can actually change, even though that is the stated reason for undertaking the coaching;
- have concerns about the competence of the coach;
- may see the coach as an authority figure, bringing all the assumptions that go with past encounters with such figures.

Being able to reveal some or all of this is what starts the process of change. It is the beginning of discovering that if you do fully reveal yourself and then, despite your worst fears, do not get judged, learning and change is possible.

Throughout the coaching process, there may be some unconscious processes going on which may explain phenomena which are otherwise inexplicable. For instance, why do you instinctively like some clients more than others (or they like or dislike you?). Why do some clients seem to bring odd expectations to the coaching relationship? Some ideas from therapy may help explain at least some of what is happening.

Replaying family dynamics

For all of us, our primary experiences of relationships were formed as children in a family. Our main responses to authority, and our typical responses to the feelings of dependency this created, were probably set here. Being in a coaching relationship can reawaken such feelings at an unconscious level. Clients may behave as they did as children, perhaps wanting to be the cleverest, the nicest, the most loved. Former family roles may also be replayed in the relationship: family clown, responsible eldest child, naughty boy or girl, and so on.

In exactly the same way, your own experiences will have affected your own attitude to power and dependency and will have had a radical effect on your feelings of comfort or discomfort with the coach role. It may be useful to ponder on this from time to time, perhaps with a supervisor. Do you, for instance, want to be 'one of the gang' with a client as a way of recreating the feelings of *us against them* that you had with your siblings against your parents? Do you, perhaps, relish the feeling of power that the coach role gives you because in that way you recreate the enjoyable feeling of being the trusted and responsible eldest? Do you like to transfer power to the client as quickly as possible because that feels comfortable in the same way that it did when you were the carefree youngest in the family?

Projection

As a coach you remain non-judgemental and unattached to your own ideas about what might be good for the client. This is why self-awareness about the phenomenon known as projection can be so useful. Essentially the assumption is that we all have dark sides which we may not acknowledge about ourselves. We say to ourselves, in effect, 'I don't like this about myself. I'll project it on to someone else and that way I can criticize it because then it's nothing to do with me.' Or there can be positive projection where we fantasize the ideal person we might like to be on to another person. The phenomenon of projection may take a number of forms:

- At its simplest, we may project an emotion we are feeling on to someone else. This is because we cannot or will not own the feeling in ourselves. So, for instance, I might say to a friend, 'You seem worried', when actually it is I who am worried, but don't want to face my worry.

- As coaches, we might start thinking, 'This client is hostile to me', when in fact, you are feeling hostility towards him or her.
- We may see others as the cause of our problems, especially those closest to us.
- We imagine that another person possesses the ideals and qualities we fail to incorporate into ourselves and our lives.
- We may create cycles of unrealistic infatuation which then turn to bitter disappointment in jobs and relationships, leading to cynicism and resentment.

When we criticize other people, what we criticize may be the very thing we most fear could be true about ourselves. Where you find yourself having these judgemental thoughts, it can be a useful discipline to stop and ask yourself, 'Are these feelings or behaviours that are actually true for me?'

Perhaps the most powerful single idea relating to projection is that how we speak about others always says a great deal about how we see ourselves. This of course applies equally to clients and to coaches.

Transference and counter-transference

Again, these are concepts from psychotherapy. The idea is that clients unconsciously project on to you and the coaching relationship patterns and assumptions from earlier relationships in their lives. These projections will be distortions – they are preventing the other person from seeing you as you think you really are. Most usually, they may transfer to you feelings they have had or still have about significant figures from their past. So a client who constantly rebelled against an authoritarian father may see male figures such as a coach in the same light as he saw his father, even though the coach concerned is a mild and pleasant person who is totally unlike the father. Older women may create expectations of being *mother* or *teacher* to a client and this could trigger off both rebellious adolescent behaviour and expectations of being nurtured.

Counter-transference may also be going on – that is when you as coach do the same on to the client. So a challenge from a client may painfully reawaken ghosts from an early relationship. For that moment, the client is standing in for the ghost and you respond as you might have to him or her in the past.

Some coaches believe that if you are in transference territory, it means that your client needs therapy. Others might counsel simply ignoring the signs that it is there.

I take a more pragmatic view. The more transparent you are in your working with the client, the less likely these phenomena are to derail the process. For instance, Glenda is a client who appears to be resisting delivery on the actions she and her coach have agreed. Her coach takes up the story:

Glenda

Glenda told me that she just hadn't had time to do her 'homework'. This was our fourth session and in each of the last three the same thing had happened. I said, very calmly, 'Glenda, I'm really puzzled and intrigued. I'm also feeling a bit stuck and wondering if you're not doing this stuff because I'm not coaching you properly or in a way you can relate to. When we started the coaching, you said you were keen to make changes and we discussed how important it would be to try out the new tactics that we developed in the sessions. This is the third session where you've said you haven't had time to do that. I'm wondering what's going on here for you . . . ' Glenda looked sheepish and then annoyed: 'You aren't my headmistress you know!'

Coach: No, I'm not. But I'm wondering now if I remind you of one you used to know!

There was a pause and Glenda's face changed colour.

Glenda: Well, yes. You're about her age when I knew her and I was constantly in trouble for not doing my homework and when I left I swore I'd never let anyone boss me about again.
Coach: How else do I seem to remind you of her?
Glenda: You don't – except that you seem very confident and together.
Coach: What else?
Glenda: Can't think of anything else!
Coach: What would you like to say to that headmistress if she were here?
Glenda: Please respect me. Don't come down on me like that – it wasn't fair, though I know I was a right little pest.
Coach: In what ways am I different?
Glenda: Far, far more – in fact you're not like her at all really!

We then had a truly breakthrough discussion about our relationship and what needed to happen to make it work. I, for my part, was of course quite unable to promise that I would be anything other than myself, including not being like her head teacher. Glenda was able to look at all her troubled relationships with authority in this light. The candour and the intimacy it created were remarkable and a real turning point.

The power of now

When I was relatively new to coaching I acted on an unstated belief that I did have to remain in some kind of positively neutral gear throughout the conversation. The client could get upset but I couldn't. The client could be boring but I had to simulate interest. The client could give me feedback at the end of the session but I had to be restrained.

I see now how wrong that was.

The real catalyst for change is in the coaching relationship itself. What the client does with you, he or she will be doing everywhere else. Therefore possibly the most important data you have about that client is how he or she is with you. This is the data that possibly 90 per cent of coaches ignore. Does this client create feelings of fear in you? That is what she will be doing at work. Does this client lose you in his rambling descriptions of what is happening with his team? Ten to one he will be a poor communicator with others. Does a client try to exert inappropriate control in the conversation with you? That's what others will experience too.

This data is every bit as important as what the client tells you about events and people outside the room. It is pricelessly valuable. Ignore it at your peril. It is far more important than intellectualizing or analysing either on your part or on the client's part. How are they affecting you? Here are two examples.

George

George was a puzzle. Sunny, charming and good looking, he had been asked at what he himself described as 'the fag end' of his career to take on a Director's role in his company. He came for coaching saying that he had to have a coach because everyone else in the Director-team had one, so why shouldn't he? What were his goals for coaching? Ah, that was where things began to get a little vague. He thought the goals would emerge after we had done some psychometrics – he knew that his fellow Directors had found these useful. What did he want in his job? There he was clear – his role was to transform customer relationships in a culture where for too long customers had put up with second-rate treatment. He was finding this task an uphill struggle – the culture was defeating him, even though he had brought in expensive consultants to help.

I began to feel increasingly baffled. George smiled, was super-courteous and professed himself grateful to have the chance to talk in such privileged circumstances, but I felt there was no passion or commitment there. I noticed that my attention began wandering. Instead of ignoring it and thinking that this must be my fault – I was a bad coach for allowing myself to be distracted so easily – I raised it with him.

'George, I find I'm wondering what's going on here for you. I'm finding that I'm distracted and feeling at a distance from you. I'm puzzled by what I think I'm seeing and hearing which is that while you talk about the importance of improving customer relationships, I don't experience that importance in how you're describing it to me. It feels as if you're talking about a neutral activity which you could take or leave. I find that I'm asking myself, what does George really care about?'

This was a breakthrough. George was astonished at the candour of my feedback and amazed that I cared enough to mention it. He told me he did care passionately about customer service but had never expressed that passion. His going along with things, whether being asked to take on a new role or to have a coach, was a symptom of a trend in his life where he assumed that events would look after themselves. You could detach your real self quite happily – there would be no consequences. Discovering that you cannot detach yourself from your job and that talking openly and in public about your real values could unleash energy in yourself and others was a major learning.

Candice

Candice was a reluctant client who had been enrolled by her boss. Candice was proud of her track record in production management, had an MBA, and was pleased to have won her job against stiff competition. But soon her boss was regretting the appointment, complaining that Candice was unable to speak or write without recourse to jargon and was generally unaware of her impact on others. Candice was both annoyed and hurt by this accusation, believing that the fault lay with others for not being clever enough to understand her.

Both Candice and her coach understood that Candice's job was on the line here. Candice's coach negotiated an agreement that the coaching room was one place where she could expect real objectivity. When Candice began to use convoluted sentences with her coach, the coach found himself as baffled as colleagues. Instead of glossing it over and pretending to understand, the coach stopped her every time.

'Candice, can I stop you here? I notice how many very long words and sentences you are using. Just now you described *production flexibility analysis* and *Kanaban* with *JIT systems* and *Economic Value Added*, and a lot of other stuff that followed and I had no idea what you meant. Instead of concentrating on what you went on to say I was still puzzling about those sentences. Then I began to feel stupid and that I somehow should be understanding you and it was my fault for not being able to. I wonder if this is an example of the effect you have on colleagues?'

After several more examples along the same lines, Candice began to realize that her coach was no different from her non-specialist colleagues, and that stepping back to ask 'What does a non-specialist really need to understand here in very simple terms?' would significantly change her impact on colleagues. Because no one else had felt able to take this intrusively detailed and high-risk approach, Candice had resorted to the all-too-human defence of denial. She simply had not understood the problem or how deeply rooted it was in her communication style and personality. To Candice, being an expert mattered to her above all else and this is what had led to her over-reliance on technical jargon. This investment she had made in being an expert also became rich territory for the coaching.

To use this approach, a number of things have to be in place. You have to:

- intend to look – at everything: how clients greet you, how they come into the room, what they say in the first few moments, how they treat you, the language they use, the feelings they arouse in you throughout the session;
- recognize the data when you experience it and know the difference between how much of this data is generated by you and how much is being created by the client. This requires the deepest kind of self-knowledge from the coach;
- be able to give the client skilled feedback.

Giving feedback

This is probably the single most significant way in which a coaching conversation differs from any other conversation our clients are likely to have. Unlike the client's line manager, we have no power to hire and fire. Unlike the client's partner, we have no wish to create or destroy love. Unlike the client's friends, we need not feel we could be putting the friendship at risk if we speak candidly. Coaching is one of the few occasions where anyone is permitted, even encouraged, to comment on the immediate behaviour of the other person. Being able to do this with the honest intent to help the other person learn and with no wish for self-aggrandisement endows the act of giving feedback with enormous power.

Just to be clear, *feedback* is not the same as *criticism*.

Being on the receiving end of criticism is devastating. In many years now of working with people on how to give feedback, I have collected their comments on what it has felt like to be the focus of criticism. It's always the same, regardless of people's age, seniority or experience:

> Made me feel like a naughty child.
> Felt really frightened – wondered whether my career was on the line.
> It was so unfair! I was obsessed by the unfairness – couldn't hear what
> lay behind it.

Criticism attacks the person by making generalized judgements. Criticism is an opinion: *you are* [usually something unpleasant]. This brings out all the defensive and aggressive reactions described above because it contains hurtful generalizations: *you are a poor communicator; you are sloppy; everyone thinks ...* Criticism is tough on the person, where feedback is tough on the issues. Feedback is given for one reason only: to help the person learn, and is given at a point where the feedback-giver judges the other person can hear it. Feedback is also about the things that we can change – it would be pointless, for instance, to give someone feedback about their height, their racial origins or their gait. Criticism looks to hurt and is usually a way for criticism givers to unload their anger.

In giving feedback:

- Negotiate the expectation that you will offer it from the very beginning of the relationship. Explain how it can be valuable and ask the client how he/she feels about getting it.
- Ask permission every time: *may I offer you some feedback here?*
- Stick to descriptions of what you have seen, using phrases like 'I noticed ... ', 'I saw ... ', 'I observed ... ', 'I heard ... '

> I noticed that when you were talking about X, you seemed agitated. You leant forward and thumped your papers.
> I heard you giving X a really straightforward explanation of what she needed to do to fulfil your expectations of her – and I noticed how her face relaxed immediately.

- Don't interpret. Describe what you have seen without attributing a motive. So avoid saying something like

> So I knew you were angry with X ...
> I saw that you wanted to leave the room straight away.

Instead, ask a question, using phrases like 'I wonder ... ', 'I'm curious about ... ' This asks the client for his or her motivation rather than you making a guess at it, so say something like: 'I wondered what was going on for you at that moment?'

- Describe the impact on you:

> When you leant forward like that I felt alarmed just for a second. I wondered if you were angry with me!

You started your presentation with a story and I was completely absorbed in it – I wanted to know what happened next!
You touched your face a lot while you were talking and that had the effect on me of making me wonder whether you were really confident about what you were saying.

- Look for opportunities to offer more positive than negative feedback, especially where a client can show you how vastly improved some skill or behaviour has become.
- Choose your words carefully. It is better to say something like 'I ended up feeling a bit alarmed about what you might do next' rather than 'you were intimidating'. There is a fine line between feeding back how the client has had an impact on you and seeming to have taken it personally. The whole point about your feedback is that you are not taking it personally even while you are describing the personal impact of the client on you.

Being open to influence: receiving feedback

The feedback process in coaching is two-way. It's not just you pronouncing on the client. You will also be inviting the client to pronounce on you. Again, this is unusual in virtually all professional relationships except perhaps coaching's close cousins, therapy and training. I have just once been asked to fill in a questionnaire by our legal firm on the quality of the service we experienced, but never once been asked directly by any lawyer, accountant or doctor how I felt about the service I was receiving. In fact, the only time I have ever encountered it in a professional relationship where I have been the client has been with my own coach.

In asking for feedback you will again be modelling how sincerely you believe in the two-way nature of the relationship.

There are two kinds of feedback you can ask for and expect. The first is about the content and style of your coaching:

How have you found this session?
What worked especially well for you?
What worked less well?

When people offer you feedback, they may be uncertain how you will receive it, or they may just not know how to do it properly because they have never had any training. So the feedback may take any of these forms:

Apparent attack (criticism) – 'You asked a lot of questions but I didn't get any of the advice I need.'

Apparent compliment – 'You're brilliant at seeing beneath the surface.'
Vague hints – 'You're a bit hard to understand at times.'

Don't: get angry, defensive or self-justifying.
Don't: immediately confess 'guilt'.
Much better tactics are to follow this protocol:

- Repeat and summarize the feedback (look back at the section on summarizing for a reminder of how to do this): 'So you mean I let that first part of the session go on too long?' This shows that you have understood and gives the client the chance to correct you if you have not understood.
- Ask for evidence, whether it is of positive or negative points: 'When you say I'm "brilliant at seeing below the surface", what do you mean exactly – can you give me an example of something that worked especially well for you?' 'When you say I make too many assumptions about what you might already know, can you give me a specific example?'
- Ask for ideas on how you could improve: 'So if I use too much jargon for you, could you tell me what would be better for you?'
- Give your side of things, if necessary: 'The reason I had to cancel that session at such short notice was that my daughter was suddenly taken ill and I had to go to hospital with her.'

This method of receiving feedback has a number of advantages, especially where it is feedback you have actually asked for:

- You will get some pleasant surprises.
- It demonstrates the two-way nature of the relationship with clients.
- Feedback is one of the best ways to improve your practice.

The second kind of feedback is about the quality of the relationship. Here, again, you are doing what few people do in the context of a professional relationship. Examples of questions to ask here are:

How are we doing – you and me?
What's remaining unspoken that might usefully be said out loud?

These questions are so unusual that the quick and maybe self-protective client response – is to say 'fine' in answer to the first question and 'nothing' in response to the second. Allowing a thoughtful pause may encourage more reflective and interesting responses that are tentative at first and then become more confident as the client sees that you are indeed up for some honesty. Interesting and useful answers I have received in the last few months to this question have been comments such as:

Client: I have to be careful I don't treat you as an authority figure.
JR: What would happen if you did?
Client: There's a danger I wouldn't be honest or that I'd meekly agree to something I thought you were suggesting without actually intending to do it!
JR: What am I doing that's creating that danger for you?
Client: You seem very calm and composed and you're obviously very experienced. I think it's because I'm in my first Chief Executive role and I'm unconsciously worrying about whether you'll be comparing me with other Chief Execs you've worked with who might be 'better'. [Pause. Laughs.] Actually, having said it out loud I don't think it's really a danger. It's my stuff, isn't it?
JR: Maybe, but let's keep it in mind!

Client: What's remaining unspoken is that I'm gay and I think you've already guessed.
JR: [Smiles] Yes. [Pause]
Client: So you asking me that has enabled me to say it. I'm glad. I need to talk to you next time about me and my lover because I think we're through.
JR: Yes, of course we can. What's the question you're asking yourself?
Client: How to end something that's been over for a long time really without upsetting him or me too wildly – how to have a happy-enough ending in the circumstances.
JR: So perhaps to add to the homework we've already agreed, you could think about what criteria you'd like to use to judge that happy-enough ending and we can talk it through next time. What prevented you saying that earlier in the session?
Client: I wasn't sure how far I could trust you because I'm only sort of half 'out'.
JR: But you decided you could.
Client: Yes – I took the risk. And it feels great. Thank you.

Humility

I was working with a client who was in long-term remission from cancer. In talking calmly and optimistically about his treatment, he remarked that the single most therapeutic part of his many visits to the hospital were the conversations he had with his oncologist. This woman had acknowledged the limits of her knowledge as well as stressing her confidence in what did work. I know her to be one of a handful of leading specialists in Europe, doing superb research as well as her hands-on clinical practice with patients. She has adopted the position of treating patients as fellow adults, mixing judicious optimism with honesty about her own and her profession's limitations.

This is a hard act to carry off. Do it too much or in the wrong circumstances and you destroy your client's confidence in you. But act all-seeing and all-knowing and you will miss many critically important opportunities to nudge clients towards change. Coaching is full of paradoxes and this is one of the most profound: we have to be powerful and powerless simultaneously.

The critical test is: is this in my client's interest? If yes, then

When you are puzzled, say so:	*I'm feeling puzzled about the connection between what you've said about x and what you've said about y: what's your take on that?*
When you feel confused about where the conversation or session is going, raise it:	*I notice we've spent nearly an hour on what you've done since we last met – and we still haven't set any goals for this one! How do you feel about that?*
If you feel caught in a dilemma, describe it:	*I'm in two minds here about what to do,* or *I'm caught between a number of different ways of responding here.*
When you have made a mistake, acknowledge it and apologize:	*When we met for our last session I feel I pressed you too hard on x issue. I did notice that you seemed uncomfortable but I still carried on didn't I? I'm sorry. That was a mistake.*
When you feel out of your depth, declare it.	

Owning up to weakness may have more impact than you realize. As a coach you need a high degree of self-management. You must be centred, self-aware and with a high degree of all the many intelligences that the role requires: analytical intelligence, emotional intelligence, spiritual intelligence, systems intelligence. Yet at the same time you are human; there are things you don't know and areas where you are uncertain. Conveying these to clients whose lives have often been lived in dread of such 'weakness' may have only beneficial effect.

Acknowledging

We are often the only witnesses to enormous acts of courage and learning. What may seem like small steps to others are often huge leaps for a client. So a client who has overcome her genuine phobia and fear of HIV infection to have much-needed electrolysis may only have you to tell. A client who has given up what to him was the scaldingly shameful and lifelong habit of biting his nails may only feel able to glory in his achievement with you. You may be the sole recipient of an email from an apparently confident senior executive who wants to tell you joyfully about having overcome her fear of giving a presentation to her Board. A client who has experienced the death of a profoundly disabled child may not be able to tell anyone else that this death was welcome, received with relief, and was not the tragedy that the rest of the world assumes.

Acknowledging is yet another way in which coaching is different from a 'normal' conversation. In *acknowledging*, the coach recognizes an important aspect of who the client is rather than noticing what the client has *achieved*. The coach is acknowledging the being self, not the doing self.

> **Peter**
>
> Peter is a client who has struggled with an enormous amount of personal and professional change. He has had to start a new job, recruit a new team and get to know a new boss at the same time as coping with three bereavements.
>
> Peter: These last few months have been the toughest I can remember.
> Coach: Yes, I'd like to acknowledge your courage and resolution in keeping going.
> Peter: [surprised and pleased] Oh, thanks. Gosh. I feel great!

In *acknowledging*, the coach notices and mentions positive qualities in the client: humour, energy, clarity, courage, doggedness, willingness to learn, humility, and so on.

Useful phrases include:

> I'd like to acknowledge
> Let's just mark your [quality] here
> I'd like to salute your [quality] in doing [   ]

Note that, in acknowledging, we are not giving empty compliments. If it is not authentic that will be immediately obvious to the client.

When it's always someone else's fault

There are some clients who can seem fixed in the role of victim. They have adopted the life position of 'I don't value me and I don't value you either' (see page 40). You are likely to find such clients occasionally, even in very senior roles in organizations. I personally find them taxing because they test to the limit my assumption that everyone can be resourceful. To have a client determined to blame others for their own disappointments invariably takes me to the boundaries of my skills. Suggesting therapy is always a possible alternative, but many clients are not so obviously extreme in their distress as to warrant this tactic.

> **Carys**
>
> At the time we worked together, Carys was a disappointed woman. As a senior accountant in the City she had expected to get the Finance Director job in her organization. It had gone instead to a colleague whom she liked but whom she also judged to be less competent than herself. Our work initially focused on getting another job as Carys felt she could not stay in the original organization – it would have felt too humiliating.
>
> I encouraged Carys to contact head-hunters and to alert her networks to her wish to move. Soon there were two potential offers on the horizon, both of which paid much the same as the job she had failed to get. Carys took one of these jobs, but as our coaching went on into her new job, it was clear that a sense that 'it was unfair' still pervaded her life. Her marriage began to suffer and she contemplated leaving her husband. She complained about the new job – it was lonely, the office was stiflingly hot, the Chief Executive did not appreciate her. In every session it seemed that we would inevitably come back to the unfairness of not getting the FD job in her old organization, even a year later.

What can be done for clients like Carys?

Some possible approaches

First you must *notice the pattern*. The give-aways are:

- Coming to coaching looking for a way of changing someone else.
- Evading questions about what he or she, the client, has contributed to the situation.
- A lot of sentences beginning
  - If only they would ...
  - If only it hadn't turned out like it did ...
  - My life would be fine if only others would let me ...

- Generalizations suggesting that mostly other people are getting things wrong around this client: 'They always … '; 'They never … '
- A constant sense of weariness and disappointment, whatever good things seem to be happening – nothing is ever quite good enough.

The next step is to *offer the client feedback*:

> Carys, I notice that in this session as in so many others, we keep coming back to that old sore of the FD job. You've mentioned it twice in this session, just as you did in our last one. What's going on here for you?

In Carys's case, she was ahead of me. 'I must be a very annoying client because I'm always blaming someone else, aren't I?' So Carys could intellectualize her dilemma but still could not move on.

Experiment with *outcome-based thinking*.

Many clients can benefit from being shown the difference between victim-thinking, or problem-based thinking and resource-based thinking. For instance, ask a client mentally to identify any current problem, then silently to respond while you read out these questions:

> Whose fault is it?
> Why haven't you done anything about it yet?
> What's stopping you doing something about it?
> What does having this problem say about you as a person?
> What does having this problem say about you as a professional?
> What forces outside of your control are contributing to this?
> What are the negative consequences?
> What further problems is this leading to?

If you now ask, 'How do you feel?', the chances are that the client will report that his or her feelings of helplessness are reinforced. The general effect of questions like these is to rob the client of power. They increase the chances of the client staying fixed in victim mentality.

Outcome-based thinking is very different. It empowers the client. When you ask outcome-frame questions, you can often see a visible difference in the way clients respond – for instance, they may sit up straighter, stop frowning, or look somehow lighter. So if you ask the client to stay with the same topic, this time referring to it as an *issue* not a *problem*, you will probably get a very different response:

> What do you want?
> What else will that do for you?

What will it look, sound and feel like when you have what you want?
What resources outside of you do you have to get what you want?
Who else can help you?
What will getting what you want confirm about you as a person/
professional?
What further benefits could there be?
What is the first step to getting what you want?

Discussing the different mental and physical effects of these two types of approaches to the same issue can often offer startling clarification to this kind of client, especially when you follow it up with discussion about how much either pattern is a feature of their everyday thinking.

Identify the pay-off.
However miserable clients are about their feelings of being victimized, there is always a pay-off. The prison of misery may be horrible but at least it is familiar. Asking the client to identify how the pay-off works can often be a moment of enlightenment. Typical pay-offs may include:

- controlling and manipulating others by engendering guilt;
- giving away your power means that you can't fail any more because you can always say that if you'd tried you could have succeeded;
- forcing others to take responsibility for you means that you never have to blame yourself if something goes wrong;
- avoiding facing up to actual weaknesses.

Ask the client what he or she is contributing to staying stuck.
Some clients will deny that they are contributing anything. The therapist and author Irvin Yalom suggests saying something like, 'OK let's accept that 99 per cent of this is someone else's fault. Can we work on the 1 per cent that's yours?'

Expose the fallacy of devoting time and energy to the goal of having a better past.
The past has gone and can never be rescheduled, reworked or remodelled. There is only now.
For most clients one or all of the tactics I describe here will work, one way or another. If they don't, I will have one last shot in my locker:

Expose the client to your own dilemmas about how to help them. So with a client like Carys, having tried all of the above tactics without any apparent success, I might say,

Carys, I feel at my limit here. I really want our coaching to succeed for you yet I'm feeling frustrated by my inability to help. We've tried a number of things, yet I notice you still seem attached to that original dream of the job you didn't get. What would you advise me to do?

Note that the risks here are of a client like Carys believing that I, too, am persecuting her and will be about to reject or abandon her. I will refuse to play that game, stressing my continuing support for her as well as putting half the responsibility for our relationship back on her.

In the end it is the client's choice whether or not to move on. When confronted in the ways described here they may ultimately prefer to stay psychologically where they are. Carys did eventually move on, but I have worked with a number of other clients who could not.

Roger

Roger was a highly self-aware person, but, like Carys, he had received what he saw as a crashing disappointment in his career. He had already worked with two other coaches and a therapist. He had told me mournfully that he was not a rich man and although he had found the therapy helpful, he had not been able to afford to continue paying his therapist for the weekly sessions. (Our programme was being funded by his organization.) In fact this history should have alerted me to the unlikelihood of success with me, and with the benefit of hindsight I should have taken a lot more time than I did to explore his previous experience of both coaching and therapy. After four sessions of frustration and a strong feeling of no progress, I eventually challenged him and said:

Roger, I've reached the end of what I think I can do. We keep coming back to the same point where you seem to be trying to rewrite your history. I think we ought to stop.

'Funny you should say that', said Roger, and then in a moment of real candour, 'I got to exactly the same stage with Lucy [his therapist] and she told me that unless I was prepared to stop "sitting in my own shit", as she put it, she couldn't go on with me.'

JR: So are you prepared to stop sitting in your own shit?
Roger: Yes, yes, and I'm finding these sessions really helpful.

I felt dubious, but we made another date. Roger failed to show for this date. When I rang his office he was apologetic.

Roger: I'm terribly sorry, I completely forgot it.
JR: Well, when you're ready, ring me again.

He never did.

Tough speaking

Most coaching will involve some use of confrontation from time to time. If you never confront clients, then you need to ask whether you are colluding – going along with their view that everyone else is at fault but them or that it is impossible for their situation to improve.

Confronting needs to be done with extreme care: you can destroy the client's trust in a few seconds if it is done clumsily. Even if done well, it may dismay the client. Confrontation may also lead to denial, making the resistance more extreme than it was in the first place.

Reasons for confronting

Many senior executive clients are never confronted about the very behaviour they most need to change. Your intervention may be their best hope of getting honest feedback. Also, all of us who work with senior people are familiar with the exceptional pressures that a senior role may involve. It is not surprising that senior leaders often respond by concealing the extremity of their anxiety with long hours at their desks, or with impatience and irritation.

For all of us it can be true that we are part of the problem – coaching is a way of finding out in what ways this is the case. The coach is someone who can help by exploring this with the client. Finally, coaching is about change. Clients may say they want to change but also resist it in a number of ways – for instance saying that they are unable to do so, or that 'now isn't the right time', and so on. The only way to help them move on may be to confront this discrepancy between saying and doing.

Usually there are three types of situation that you and your client could explore:

- Discrepancies between espoused values and values in action. This is where, for instance, the client says one thing but does another. An example might be a client who says she believes in equal opportunities but actually recruits and selects people on the basis of stereotype or old boy/girl networks.
- The client agrees that a change needs to take place, but postpones the moment when it will happen. For instance, the client may say he or she is fed up with the current role and wants to leave but makes no actual attempt to seek another job.
- You have serious doubts about whether the client's proposed course of action is actually wise or desirable. For instance, the client may be overwhelmed with anger about a boss's behaviour and be prepared to storm into the boss's office the next day. You feel certain that this will not get him the outcome he says he wants.

For confrontation to be successful your own motivation has to be a sincere wish to help. If there is even a smidgen of feeling that you want to get at the client, or teach him or her a lesson, don't do it. You must also have reliable data to back you up. Rumour, gossip and scuttlebutt do not amount to reliable data. Ideally you need to have experienced whatever you are talking about at first-hand. There must be a relationship of trust and liking between you and the client, so confrontation is not usually a technique to be used at the early stages of the process. You must have a high level of skill in giving feedback, including the ability to create real rapport and to manage any fallout from the conversation.

How to confront

- Introduce the subject straightforwardly.
- Make the link to the stated results that the client wants and show your own commitment to these results.
- Alert the client to the possibility that you are going to say something which could be difficult to hear.
- Stress how much you value and want to support the client.
- Base what you say on data; keep it descriptive and non-judgemental; talk about 'what is', not 'what should be'.
- Keep it short.
- Ask how the client sees it.
- Explore the implications with the client.
- Ask what will happen if the situation does not change.
- Brainstorm solutions, including offering any bright ideas of your own about alternatives.
- Make it clear that you assume the client has the resources to change if he or she wants to.
- Make it clear that it is the client's choice whether or not to make the changes.

Knowing when too far is too far

The coaching relationship is a tightrope. Too much pressure on the client and you and they will fall off. Too little and the coaching will feel inert, suggesting that it will not lead to the changes the client wants to make in his or her life. Knowing when to press and when to hold back is a matter of the finest and most split-second judgement.

Robert

Robert was a miner's son, left school at 16 and began teaching himself some of the principles of para-legal work while he worked in a solicitor's office. His employer spotted his potential and sponsored him on an escalating number of qualifying courses. At the age of 40, by now an experienced solicitor, he had done brilliantly well and had become head of legal services for a local authority. His starting issues for the coaching we embarked on together were to bring more finesse into his managerial style – a nice, safe topic.

Soon, however, it became clear that the underlying issues were his profound lack of self-confidence and his acute social isolation. He had no friends at work and no social life. He had married his childhood sweetheart at 19 and his wife had opted to stay at home, even though they had no children. The relationship was one of mutual dependency but at the point where Robert started the coaching, he was expressing a strong wish to break out of the stifling pattern he and his wife had created: 'I want to get out at weekends, go to football, meet more people, but if I do she will feel it's a threat. She just wants me there so that we can do the garden, watch a video, just the two of us together.'

As his coach, I felt we had reached a crossroads.

JR: What do you really want?
Robert: I do want to have a better social life and one that's outside this charmed circle of just me and her.

Robert describes how this would look sound and feel in response to the question, 'If you could have this ideal life what would be happening?'

JR: So how could you set about this?

There is now a long pause – perhaps twelve seconds. Robert looks at me, looks tense, wrings his hands slightly and looks at his feet. Very slowly he says: 'I can't. If I discuss it with her, she'll panic. It will raise the whole question of the relationship and I can't do that to her.'

What does a coach do in these circumstances with a client who has described what he wants so vividly yet also describes the total block to action? Challenge? Suggest a tiny first step? Withdraw? After a few moments more of silence, I asked how Robert felt about staying with the idea of doing nothing: 'Fine – for now', was his reply.

Later I thought long and hard about this exchange, pondering whether I might have pressed him harder, but feeling in the end that it was right to hold back. Eight weeks later, Robert called me, devastated, to tell me that totally out of the blue with no warning or previous threats, his wife had killed herself, swallowing a lethal dose of paracetamol. He discovered that she believed she had had terminal cancer (she didn't). Robert's judgement about his wife's fragile mental state was totally correct, including a diagnosis of agoraphobia, which he had not shared with me. What he had not anticipated was how violently her feelings would implode. His weighing up of what he could cope with if he had confronted his wife was also correct. And my judgement about what would have been too far was correct, though I did not have anything like all the relevant data at the time.

Subsequently, in training new coaches, I have seen how easily the coach's eagerness to help can stray into too much intimacy too soon, ignoring the warning signs from the client which say 'keep off'. When this happens, the client's energy goes into repelling what he or she perceives as an attack, rather than into learning and change. I was on the receiving end of such clumsiness myself during a practice session at an international conference on coaching.

I was the client, working with another coach and an observer for a ten-minute piece of coaching. The observer had met me for the first time a few minutes before. In the review session, in the grip of what she obviously sincerely believed was a profound intuition about what I needed, she immediately plunged into what felt like the most unwarranted and impertinent comments on my marriage, deluging me earnestly with advice about 'not being exploited'. Only the iciest British politeness prevented me from telling her to shut up because she knew nothing about me or my marriage, had seriously misinterpreted what she thought she had heard and, most important of all, had absolutely no permission from me to go into such private places after a few moments of superficial acquaintance.

Handling these moments

- When the client tells you straightforwardly that they want you to stop, stop.
- Be alert to the evidence from the client – small frowns, a tapping foot, looking away.
- You can't go on with a task-based agenda when this happens – the pause or the resistance becomes the agenda.
- Name it: 'I notice we seem to have hit a pause here. What's going on for you?'
- Agree jointly how to handle it.

When the client cries

A box of tissues is an essential part of the equipment in any coaching room. This is because clients do cry; they are often unprepared for crying and as a coach you have to be prepared to give them the wherewithal to mop their tears. Even more importantly, you have to be mentally prepared yourself.

Trainee coaches often express considerable and understandable anxiety around this area. It is unusual for a relative stranger to break down in front of you. Also, adults may feel that crying is childish or it shows that you are out of control or incompetent and can't cope. It certainly exposes the vulnerability of the person who is crying and some clients may find it humiliating.

However, in my experience, the person who is most likely to be worried about the crying client is the coach. The reasons may be a mixture of embarrassment at seeing an apparently well-adjusted person break down, or a fear that the client may discomfit themselves then or later by their tears, regretting having shown apparent weakness. Some coaches describe a fear that they may feel so much empathy that they will join in.

As coaches we may also worry that we have in some way caused the tears through clumsiness in our coaching – for instance through asking the 'wrong' question or probing too far. The language here is often telling: 'I made him cry', implying that it is our responsibility. My own view is that crying is one of the multitude of choices that clients make during their work with us as coaches. Coaches cannot *make* clients cry – any more than they can make them laugh, or bored, or command them to feel any other emotion. The client chooses, unconsciously perhaps, but chooses none the less. Often the coach's worry about whether the client can cope is just a way of projecting our own worry – 'Will I be able to cope with a client who cries?'

When you look at an uncaptioned photograph of a human face clearly showing strong emotion, it is often impossible to tell whether the person is laughing or crying. We use most of the same muscles for laughing as we do for crying. We can cry with laughter – or with sadness. We can laugh with anger or with joy. Crying is just at one end of the spectrum of human emotion and since we are dealing with the whole person in the coaching room, it is inevitable that we will see tears from time to time.

The biggest trap for a coach with a weeping client is to imagine that your role is to fix the tears. If you know, or feel, that you might fall into this trap, first ask yourself what your motive is in trying to fix the feelings. The chances are that it will be one of the list I have given above. Then ask what message it would give your client to do anything at all which implied that their tears are not legitimate. Tears are legitimate and the client is giving you a privileged opportunity to understand more about them and to help them work through whatever underlies the tears. Platitudinous there-there-ing does not help, nor does any of the range of mumbled clichés about time healing, or 'a good cry does you good'.

The second biggest trap is to join in. There is a place for your own emotional reaction, but if you are crying as helplessly as your client you will be in no position to help.

Better tactics start with the first session, where part of the preparation you can do with a client will be to discuss the possibility of strong emotion bubbling up from time to time, including the possibility of anger and tears. Explain that though this is not an everyday occurrence, it can and does happen. If it should happen, ask the client how the two of you should deal with it. Keep your briefing low-key here otherwise you may unwittingly convey that you are actually eager for tears.

Tears can seem to appear out of nowhere, or they may develop more slowly where clients will alert you through clear signals that they are struggling not to cry. Some clients may alert you verbally – 'This is a difficult area for me – I may cry', or, 'I can feel tears starting.'

Your most appropriate response depends on that split-second moment of judgement that only you can make:

> You're looking upset – do you want to go on?
> Of course you can cry – this is one place where you can.
> If it would help to cry, that's absolutely fine.
> These feelings are so strong – of course they will produce tears.

Clients who prefer to contain their tears will stop at this point. Clients who do not may let the dam break. It is always a good idea to invite clients to manage the moment with you. A possible response here is: 'Take as long as you like – tell me when you're ready to go on.'

Far from feeling that tears are an embarrassing intrusion into the coaching, to be airbrushed out of sight as soon as possible with both coach and client conspiring in the illusion that nothing happened, the skilled coach realizes that tears are wonderfully useful material for the work.

To touch or not? So much has been written about sexual abuse in therapeutic relationships that many coaches hesitate to offer a touch or a hug to a seriously upset client. My instinct is to reach forward and hold the client's hand – or sit alongside and put an arm around their shoulder – and this is what I typically do. But this depends on the client and the circumstances. For instance, in some cultures, any kinds of touching between two people in a professional relationship may be frowned on. Use your judgement.

When the crying has subsided a little, I will often ask: 'What was the trigger for the tears?' followed by 'And what is it about that thought/event/ memory that has such power?' Answers could be anything at all: a sweet remembered sadness at some loss, a childlike frustration recalled, the desperation of a chronic disappointment, fear over the diagnosis of a serious illness, unresolved grief, unresolved loss, anxiety, rage, and so on. It's all grist to your joint mill.

A useful question taken from the therapist's repertoire is: 'If your tears had a voice, what would they say?' Consider sharing the emotion the tears arouse in you – as long as you are certain that this is for the benefit of the client. For instance, a client told me about the bitter disappointment of six failed attempts at IVF and her heartbreak at coming to terms with the reality of never having children. She cried harsh tears all the way through her story and I told her how moved I was by her courage in coming to terms with it and by her account of the whole affair.

Whatever else you do, it is always worth exploring how the client made the decision to cry in front of you. For instance, I will ask: 'It takes courage to cry and be vulnerable. What made it possible for you to do that here today?' and 'How does it feel now, having done it?'

Again and again when I meet clients some time after the coaching has finished, they will tell me that these moments are the ones that stick in their heads as among the most helpful in the entire process:

Marie

Marie had lost her job as a result of a scandal in the hospital at which she was Chief Executive. An enquiry later exonerated her. Although in subsequent sessions we worked on how to frame her CV, how to prepare for an interview, how to network and how to settle into the new job she soon got, at our first session she wept more or less continuous, angry, hot tears as she told her story.

> Letting me cry was the most amazingly healing thing. I got it out in that room in a way I couldn't do anywhere else. I couldn't worry my husband by letting him see how devastated I was because I was and am the bread-winner. I knew I just had to do that howling before I could move on. By letting me do it you conveyed far better than any words could that how I felt was legit. You conveyed that I was OK and I would get over it.

Martyn

Martyn and I worked together on and off for a number of years through a variety of jobs and roles. He remembers the moment when he wept for the first and only time during one of our sessions.

> I'd suddenly fallen out of love with my job. I'd been dreading bringing it up because I felt that it was important for you to see me as always on top of things. You encouraged me to name the anxiety and I took the risk of letting my emotion show. I trusted you with that and realized it was OK to fail sometimes because you accepted that it was, and you accepted me in spite of my seeing myself as a potential failure.
>
> Our discussion later of why I felt that, and your response that it would in no way affect your view of me, was one of the best moments in our work together – a real moment of learning because I realized I did not have to be

> a brilliant performer or totally optimistic all the time. We had looked toge-
> ther into what felt like an abyss at the time. In a weird way, crying released
> the anxiety and straightaway afterwards I'd got it into more perspective.

What these stories show is the cathartic effect of tears, especially when they
have been long held back. By accepting the intensity of the moment and the
legitimacy of the emotion, you show that you accept the legitimacy of the
person. Where the tears recur and indicate some deeply traumatic experience,
remember that you may be in therapeutic territory and be prepared to
recommend the client to a colleague trained to handle it. (See also page 19.)

Other cathartic moments

There is sometimes a case for encouraging a degree of catharsis. This would
typically be when clients are telling you of some deeply hurtful or provocative
scenario, yet their description seems curiously bare of emotion. The words
may be dramatic but the face and body are blank. My response will be to
notice and then raise this interesting contradiction, as in this case with a
client whose relationship with her boss was problematical:

Melanie

JR: Melanie, may I interrupt you here? I'm really curious about what you're
saying and how you're saying it. You describe your boss as making
sexist jokes and appearing to glory in your discomfort, yet as you're
telling me about it you seem perfectly calm, but I notice your voice has
gone flat and tight and your hands are clenched.

Melanie was silent for what felt like many seconds. Then she burst out
with,

Melanie: Oh – yes, I really hate him.

JR: And yet, even now, as you're saying those strong words, I hate him,
you still seem calm.

Melanie: I'm not calm at all!

JR: So how do you feel right now?

Melanie: Mad, angry, humiliated!

JR: So show me how mad, angry and humiliated looks, feels and
sounds ... If you had him here now, what would you say?

Melanie stood up sharply, put her hands on her hips and shouted:

Melanie: You horrible person, you bully, you think you're being funny but it's
always at someone else's expense, you disgrace to your profession!
[and continued for at least another minute]

This was a turning point for Melanie. It released her rage and also her energy and determination to deal with the erring boss. The next week one very astonished manager received a crisp, cool and measured set of instructions about how he was to treat this particular team member in future, instructions which, as far as history can tell, he obeyed to the letter.

Talking about yourself

Coaching is a unique kind of conversation. It differs from other close, intimate kinds of conversation in very many ways. One of those ways is that in a conversation with a friend, we often aim to demonstrate our kinship with the other person by emphasizing that we, too, have had a similar experience. For instance, here is a sample conversation we might have with a friend:

Friend: I'm really worried about my scan results. Perhaps I've got cancer.

You: Oh, don't worry too much about that. I had a similar thing a few months ago and it was nothing to be concerned about. Yours is probably just the same.

Friend: Oh, that's a comfort, perhaps mine will be all right too!

A coaching conversation would be different:

Client: I'm really worried about my scan results. Perhaps I've got cancer.

Coach: Yes, I can understand that concern. Say more about the worry ... ?

New coaches often ask how appropriate it is to talk about your own experience. The urge to do so can be strong. It could help create empathy. It could show that we, too, have our vulnerable side and it could help discharge the emotion that a distressed client can create in the coach.

Coaching is about the client's issues, not the coach's. Talking about yourself will readily distract the client into discussing your experiences and concerns – or even trying to coach you.

Your experience could trigger a powerful emotional reaction in your client, and not always a helpful one. For instance, the client may, at that stage in the coaching, feel that he or she needs to see you as someone above the hurly-burly of human emotion.

A client once told me towards the end of our coaching programme that the reason she had selected me rather than the other two coaches she had considered was that I had appeared 'very calm and therefore probably a whole person, not a fragmented mess like me'. This client's starting-out issues concerned managing what felt like the turbulent emotions she experienced in her workplace. In other words, if I had appeared to burden her with any of my emotion then it could have implied that there was no hope for her either. Later, after I had shared some of my own doubts and struggles, she came to see that if I could have such doubts and still be functioning pretty well, then there was hope for her too!

Sometimes, the wish to share a client's pain can seem overwhelming, particularly where the client is describing a loss or trauma that you feel is akin to something you have experienced yourself. Sometimes there seem to be some eerie coincidences when the very issues you are struggling with yourself are apparently being brought to you by your client.

There are two related points to make here. The first is that you will be making assumptions that your experience is actually a close parallel to the client's – never the case, however similar it might seem. The second is that you may appear to be making a bid to usurp the client's experience – 'my tragedy is worse than yours'. Alternatively, the client may interpret your comment as 'Well I've coped with my difficulty, so you can jolly well cope with yours – forget it – move on!' It will also be harder to re-establish coaching conventions – the conversation may veer towards a nice friendly chat.

Ask yourself when tempted to share your own experience, 'What's my motive here?' If there is a soupçon of doubt that your motives could include any of the following, don't do it: showing off; indulging your own emotion; insincerity; avoiding getting to the heart of the client's issue; wanting to put the client down; embarrassment.

In the initial 'Hullo-and-how-are-you?' part of the session, a client will virtually always politely ask you how you are. Ninety-nine per cent of the time a conventional 'fine' or 'very well' is the appropriate answer. Exceptions could be when you know the client well enough to share a major triumph or upset in your life and feel that the client has the right to know that he or she may observe tiny changes in your usual demeanour. Without hearing your explanation for such changes, the client might well misinterpret your behaviour as being some reflection on him or her. Equally, giving yourself brief permission to talk about it will, paradoxically, help you manage its impact on you.

With experience, you may feel that, as in these very rare cases, the benefits of talking about your own issues and experience could outweigh the disadvantages and benefit the client. When you are still building your experience don't risk it.

However, when there is profound challenge in your life, it must be right to share at least some of it with your clients.

In 1996 I experienced a great personal sadness. In living through this experience, I not only learnt a lot about the appropriateness of bringing some of this pain into the coaching relationship but also learnt some enduring lessons about the limits of professional detachment. In the spring of that year my 22-year-old honorary god-daughter, Charlotte, succumbed to influenza, quickly turning to pneumonia, then to septicaemia. She was in the Intensive Therapy Unit of the London Hospital, sedated and unconscious on a ventilator, for 30 days, but, in spite of their impressive care, she died. The eight of us very close to her in life, including her parents Chris and David and her sister Emma, spent that time in a round-the-clock vigil at her bedside – not all at once, but in shifts of two to four at a time. We were all with her when she died: a quiet ebbing away of a life that had been vibrant, noisy, argumentative, funny, loving, independent and clever.

When a young person dies, especially when their illness comes without warning and is inexplicable, it overturns all our illusions about 'living on' through our children and forces us to face our own anxiety about death. This was certainly true for me, especially since I have no religious faith and cannot take refuge in comforting ideas about eternal life.

I suppose that the sensible thing to have done would have been to cancel everything: to have looked after myself by taking time out and to have demonstrated my care for Charlotte and the other seven people by devoting myself full time to the vigil. I did ask myself whether I should, and many other questions. For instance, was it appropriate to mention this personal crisis to clients, or would it seem as if I, the coach, was turning for support to the client? Wasn't a coach supposed to be strong and impersonal? Would clients think that it was unfeeling of me to be continuing to work as if everything was normal? Would they feel embarrassed or fearful that I might start crying, displaying emotion that I would regret later?

When Charlotte's death was imminent, one of the nurses, Gail, came to fetch us to her bedside. 'It's time to say goodbye', said Gail, her cheeks a chalky white and her usual cheerful lipstick long since bitten off. Gail was unashamedly weeping, too, but she held my arm and offered me paper tissues. Later, she and Anne, the other nurse on duty that bleak night, laid Charlotte out and did everything else that clinical care demanded. Three of the team that had nursed her travelled 240 miles on a day off to be at her funeral. Their utter professionalism, for me, was defined by their ability to shed tears with us at the same time as being able to do a technically and clinically demanding job to a very high standard.

After Charlotte died, I responded for some weeks to virtually every client who routinely asked 'how are you?' by giving a brief account of what had happened. Their kindness and sensitivity was immense. None recoiled in embarrassment – as far as I was aware – and of course I might not have been aware of any embarrassment they did feel. All made gentle murmurs of regret with a few further enquiries into the circumstances before we moved with absolute naturalness to the rest of our session.

A client whose session had to be cancelled was among five or six who wrote compassionate notes, sent emails or left supportive messages on the answerphone. I valued this: it went beyond what was necessary.

I believe I did good enough work during this time. It took hugely more effort to do virtually everything in the way of essential preparation or record keeping. But once I was with my client, I gave myself up wholeheartedly to being there. Contrary to the rune that only by remaining detached can you be helpful, I confirmed my belief that the opposite was true. I took the risk of disclosing some of the rawness of my emotion and asked for some modest support back: empathy, understanding, tolerance. As a result, I increased the amount of empathy, understanding and tolerance I could offer those clients: take some, give some.

Client relationships in coaching are fragile flowers. 'I'm paying you to be nice to me', said one client sternly, 'but I do think you mean it'. They are not purely 'professional' in the sense that I do what one former mentor advocated and forget them the moment they are gone; nor are they friendships. They grow somewhere in that delicate territory between the two. Turning to clients, however briefly, for a moment of trustful comfort and understanding felt entirely right.

As coach with a client, my basic belief is that we are all in this together. I don't want to be an omnipotent, detached coach. I want to be there in the middle of the human struggle along with my clients.

Can a client become a friend?

Just occasionally a client may become a friend. In our firm, two former clients have become colleagues as well as friends. Clients are often drawn to us and we to them because there is some essential like-mindedness. As coaching becomes increasingly specialized, this will become even more likely. As coaches we operate most successfully, in the business sense, in the worlds we understand from our own past experience. This is where our networks, contacts and expertise are rooted and this is what gives us credibility with our clients, even though we may indeed pride ourselves on being able to work with a wide range of people. The research on which the Strong Interest Inventory (see page 99) is based tells us that people who are happily working in jobs and sectors they love have similar interests to others in the same jobs, both vocationally and – perhaps surprisingly – in their leisure interests. So all of this makes it more probable that some of our clients will be drawn to us because they have a lot in common with us psychologically and by history.

Signs that a client has become a friend could include events that encompass any two or three of the following on either side:

- invitations to a Christmas party;
- sending a birthday card;
- sharing gossipy emails;
- socializing on home territory;
- going to sporting, cultural or other events purely for fun, not because it is 'corporate entertaining';
- being invited to weddings;
- spending time together out of liking rather than out of duty.

When this becomes the pattern, you cannot be coach to that person. He or she has crossed the line from client to friend. Friendship is a coach-free zone, just as family is. Coaching is about outcomes, learning and change. The client pays for the empathetic objectivity that the coach provides. None of this is true of friendship. When I am with friends I am off duty as a coach – it's what I do all day; I don't want to do it in my leisure time and I hope my friends do not expect it of me. I will make one exception here. With colleagues who are also both friends and trained coaches, any of us will occasionally ask for 'ten minutes of coaching please', on some bothersome issue. The coaching is clearly demarcated from the rest of the conversation, its end as precisely signalled as its beginning. This is possible because both sides understand the rules. In most circumstances it would be unfair to expect a former client, now friend, to do the same.

When a client becomes a friend, it is best to draw attention to what has happened and to explain why the coaching relationship cannot continue, rounding it off gracefully. In practice it is unlikely that the client-friend will want to continue and a bigger danger is that the coaching will just peter out. If there is still a need for coaching, you might want to make a recommendation about another coach, but of course the decision rests with the other person. Be chivalrous about your replacement. Don't ask about the coaching and do control any irrational twinges of jealousy you may feel about your successor.

Is sexual abuse possible?

One of the reasons that therapy has acquired a bad name in some quarters is that it has become clear that there are some therapists who have inappropriate sexual relationships with their clients. The current evidence is that those who do so are a very small number but that they are serial abusers – that is, they do it often. All the regulatory bodies for psychotherapists explicitly warn against it. As with doctor–patient sexual relationships, it is grounds for being struck off. This is because where the relationship is one of healer–afflicted there is a power differential, and to cross the boundary from healer to lover is thus rightly regarded as abusive. Virtually all of the abusers are male. They justify their behaviour as acts of altruism. The relationships take place, they say, out of pity for the client, usually when the female client believes she is unattractive. As with all abusive relationships, the core of the abuse is in the exploited vulnerability of the abused person.

Remember, too, that power has aphrodisiac qualities and if our clients attribute power to us or us to them, then this dynamic may be at work – see any scandal in which a famous politician's bedroom secrets are revealed. When the press ponders aloud, 'How did someone as physically unattractive as X draw a beautiful women like Y?' the answer is usually his fame and assumed power.

Although I believe it would be rare indeed for anything similar to happen in coaching, it is still possible. As in therapy, clients may reveal matters to us that they have told no one else. Several clients have told me that I know more about them than anyone else except their partners, and sometimes they have shared secrets with me that they have not shared even with a partner. Where this is linked through the coaching with permanent and positive change, it is perfectly natural for the client to have feelings of gratitude and warmth towards the coach and for the coach to delight in being on the receiving end of such feelings.

The intensity of the one-to-one relationship in these circumstances may often have some erotic undertones. When you take a whole-life perspective, you will inevitably get to know something about the client's personal life, and this may include his or her sexual relationships. Talking about it puts it on the agenda. So where coach and client get on well, that powerful instinctive drive to love and be loved may well be in the air, especially if one or both of the parties has some sexual dissatisfaction in their lives.

Examples might be a coach and client of the same age and background finding that there is some sexual chemistry between them at a time when both have unhappy marriages. Another example might be an older male client who may not often have the experience of being listened to intently by an attractive younger woman – and in this case she happens to be his coach. An older female client may enjoy being coached by a younger man for the same reasons. One of my own recent trainee coaches told me that her previous supervisor had spoken openly of enjoying bringing *flirting* to the relationship with his clients, whether they were men or women. Ultimately she found this uncomfortable, intrusive and distracting, especially since he was a strikingly good-looking man.

There is the same potential for disaster lurking here as there is in therapeutic relationships. Being listened to with unconditional acceptance is a rare event for most people: it is gratifying. Just as in therapy, a woman client with low self-esteem, or who has been abused in the past, may believe that sex is her only gift or that a sexual exchange is the reliable way you find affection.

An older male coach could in theory be as tempted to 'rescue' a vulnerable young woman client with sexual reassurance as his misguided therapist counterpart could do. Some clients undoubtedly do seductive behaviour and this can be destabilizing, especially at times of upheaval in your own personal life. Beware especially of wanting to seem attractive to your clients in the absence of feeling attractive to your own partner, friends or family. If you find strong sexual feelings intruding into your coaching, it is time to stop.

A sexual relationship may indeed be possible after the coaching relationship is well and truly over, but it is not possible while it continues.

Note that a client may also abuse a coach. This is even rarer than a coach abusing a client. However, it is possible. Just occasionally my colleagues and I encounter clients whose distress is overpowering and where the coach becomes the target. One colleague describes such a client:

> **Anna**
>
> Anna arrived for her session with the stated aim of getting coaching on finding a new job. She spent most of the first hour crying, telling me that her life was a mess and that she was sure I couldn't help her. As she warmed to her theme of how I couldn't help her she became angry and agitated, shouting at me, telling me that my fees were outrageous, her employer was mad to pay them, that I was enjoying the spectacle of seeing her cry just as everyone else in her life had done. I assured her that I was not enjoying it, suggested we stop the session if she was finding it distressing but also offering to carry on once the initial storm had passed. I realized afterwards that I was receiving the displaced vengeance from years of disappointment and sadness. I was probably the first-ever target of her rage who just sat still without retaliating.

This coach terminated the coaching, suggesting therapy as the proper alternative. However, an American contact once described to me the ultimate horror: being stalked. The client in this case, through her own well-thought-through decision in work with her coach, had ended her partner relationship. The rejected partner had stalked the coach, blaming her for the decision. Ultimately this man plea-bargained his way to five years on probation and supervised medication but only after subjecting the coach to over a year of terrifying threats.

The saving grace in coaching, and the reason abuse is bound to be so much rarer, is that the power is so much more evenly balanced. Our clients do not come to us for healing and are therefore less likely to regard us with the awe that could lead to abuse on the part of the coach.

The place of insight

It matters as a coach to have psychological insight. Feeling that you have useful insight into others is probably one of the main reasons that people become coaches. Insight is closely linked to curiosity about people, another important qualification for being a coach.

However, it is also important to keep the question of insight in proportion. Mind reading is a very inexact art. There are two principles here. First, the best and most valuable insight to have is into yourself. Second, it is far more important for the client to have insight into him- or herself than for you to do so. This quote from Carl Jung's book *Modern Man in Search of a Soul* says it all:

> Nothing is more unbearable for the patient than to be always understood. It is relatively unimportant whether the psychotherapist understands or not, but everything hangs on the patient doing so.

Also, while you are searching for insights, you will be distracted from your main task of listening at Levels 2 and 3 to your client. You will be worrying about yourself and how to ask *clever* questions. The point about coaching is to ask *wise*, not clever questions and to keep out of the client's way.

This means that:

- You do not have to labour to make connections for the client.
  Instead, say 'What connections do you see between x and y?'
- You do not have to read a client's motivation.
  Instead, say 'What was your motivation then?'
- You do not have to grasp all the content of the client's issues – effort spent on trying to discern all the nuances will tend to pull the client's effort into helping you understand what they already understand. This will pull you away from *experiencing* what the client is telling you – a very different emphasis.
- You do not have to offer insights to the client.
  Instead, say 'What insight do you have now into that incident?' Or you can ask 'What learning did you gain from that?' – another way of asking the same question.

This does not prevent you from having insights – sometimes a coach will experience an intuitive moment when an insight appears which is potentially useful to the client. My rule here is that I try never to present it to the client as a profound truth. Instead, I might say something like 'Can I offer you a potential insight here? It may or may not be right, but it's occurred to me that . . . ' – and then I describe my insight. 'How does that seem to you?' If you are wrong, the client can then tell you so. If you are right, then the client has the benefit of your ideas.

Often, insights that seem inspired and brilliant to the coach are about the coach's gratification and rarely have meaning to the client. What seems clever to the coach is often blindingly simple to the client, whereas the insights and connections that clients make for themselves are part of what coaching is all about.

Endings

Many coaches overestimate what the client needs to get from the coaching. By and large the client needs straightforward instrumental outcomes and is not looking to reinvent him- or herself as a person. So coaches who offer the equivalent of lifelong coaching where the grandiose aim of 'self-actualization' could be accomplished will probably be disappointed. Six or eight sessions, sometimes fewer, are often enough. Having a sensible and mutually agreed number of sessions at the outset will usually prevent this happening.

Offering a longer programme is possible and can be useful – for instance, with a higher fee in return for unrestricted access over a year-long period. This constant support can be useful to clients who are taking on a major new role that they know they will find challenging. However, such a programme needs monitoring and managing. Some coaches find that, like Mr Colman and his mustard, they make their money through the sessions that are not taken up. When this happens, coaches can feel both guilty and rejected. Where the coach wishes to end the coaching but the client wants to carry on, the client may feel rejected and hurt. Clients may also feel guilty where they do not really need or wish to carry on, but do so out of fear that they may hurt the coach's feelings. Sometimes both coach and client may continue to meet when both would really like to stop – so, in this way, both end up doing what neither really wants.

A alternative tactic may be to agree an initial set of sessions with a review point half way through, matched by an invoice point. The review point will include the mutual opportunity to assess

> How far are you toward reaching your goals?
> What tangible evidence is there that there is change in your life?
> How are you and I doing in our coaching relationship?
> How much more coaching do you feel you would find useful?

Some clients like to keep one final session in the bank – for a rainy day. I don't discourage this, but I do also look for a cut-off point, even if it is an intermediate one, telling every client that I never regard a coaching relationship as truly over. Clients frequently return when they have new jobs or challenges, or email me with their news sometimes years after the formal coaching has finished. However, I do like to mark the final session of any one stage with a review. In this review I will ask clients to think back to the issues they initially presented and to look at what has changed, including any feedback that they have solicited from colleagues. I will also ask for their feedback on the coaching process and on me, always asking:

> What were the real high spots for you?
> What were the low points?
> What encapsulates the learning?
> What have you learnt that you will never forget?
> What would you advise me to go on doing, adapt and change in my coaching?

After that session I will normally email clients with a friendly note, expressing the hope that they will keep in touch. All clients get our regular newsletter, and this, too, will often prompt further communication from them.

In general, managing and marking the ending is a lot better for both sides than letting it peter out. An email or letter from the coach will often be followed by a matching note from the client with some memorable or amusing insights into how the client has perceived the coaching.

Finally

In general, as a coach, your best instrument is yourself. You will need all the tools and techniques and many others described in this book, but if you cannot use your authentic self, you will be consistently disappointed in the work you do.

As with so much else in coaching, this is the central paradox. You have to be fully present, yet not intrude too much. You have to bring the full force of your personality into the coaching room, yet it must never overwhelm the client. You have to know all the techniques, yet restrain yourself from using them except when they are totally appropriate. You have to be able to form a relationship of intimacy with the client, yet it must never cross the boundary into a friendship while the coaching is continuing. You have to be vigilant about yourself and your own interventions while simultaneously maintaining a high level of alertness to everything the client says and does. You have to keep a degree of control over the overall process, yet allow the client to take control as well. Coaching is about feeling and acting in a more powerful way, yet, to work, both coach and client have to stay together in powerlessness.

Being centred

As a coach, you need to be as centred as possible. This means that your own concerns and anxieties have to be banished during a coaching session. This is difficult, but it is a state to strive for. If you are not centred, you will find intrusive thoughts affecting your behaviour and therefore your effectiveness with your client. These might be thoughts such as:

> Am I good enough? Am I asking clever enough questions?
> I don't like this client.
> I'm afraid of this client.
> I'm too important to be working with a junior/young/not very bright client like this.
> I need to take control to prove who's in charge here,

and so on.

One way of putting this is that there is a spectrum of possible 'places' to be during coaching. At one end is the anxious, defended, protected ego, described by Thomas Crane in his book, *The Heart of Coaching* (1998), as 'Fortress Me'; at the other is the centred person who can stay relaxed and alert. Fortress Me is self-conscious rather than self-aware, critical and judgemental rather than accepting and discerning, arrogant rather than self-confident, spiteful rather than inquisitive and controlling rather than adaptable. Fortress Me tries to be perfect. The centred coach will accept good enough as the norm but with the aim of keeping on learning. The paradox is that you cannot really have the aim of being a brilliant coach without a self-serving element creeping into your work, though you can have the aim of doing excellent coaching.

Becoming, and staying, centred

There is no one right way. Each coach has to find his or her own path. Experienced coaches find that any or all of these help: meditation, prayer, yoga, listening to music, gentle physical exercise such as walking, cycling, jogging or swimming, when the mind can be suspended.

Most of the world's great religions are about releasing the grip of the ego on the personality. You do not need to subscribe to any of them to find your own path, but as a coach you do need to be able to detach yourself from the needs of your ego, to set your own needs aside and to listen deeply and non-judgementally.

We meet ourselves time and again in a thousand disguises on the path of life.

Carl Jung

In the West African greeting I quoted at the beginning of this chapter, there is a wonderful acknowledgement of the importance of two people meeting and seeing – really seeing each other; being present – and being fully present. That is what the best coaching is all about.

Bibliography

Anderson, M. (2003) *Bottom Line Organizational Development*. Oxford: Butterworth-Heinemann.

Bandler, R. and Grinder, J. (1979) *Frogs into Princes*. Moab UT: Real People Press.

Bandler, R. and Grinder, J. (1982) *Reframing*. Moab, UT: Real People Press.

Berne, E. (1964) *Games People Play*. London: Penguin.

Berne, E. (1975) *What Do You Do After You Say Hello?* London: Corgi.

Bevan, J. (2002) *The Rise and Fall of Marks and Spencer*. London: Profile Books.

Block, P. (1981) *Flawless Consulting*. San Diego, CA: Pfeiffer.

Bridges, W. (1991) *Managing Transitions*. Reading, MA: Addison-Wesley.

Briggs Myers, I. with Myers, P. (1980) *Gifts Differing*, Palo Alto, CA: Consulting Psychologists Press.

Bryce, L. (2002). *The Coach*. London: Judy Piatkus Publishers.

Carson, R. (1987) *Taming Your Gremlin: A Guide to Enjoying Yourself*. London: Harper and Row.

Casement, P. (1985) *On Learning from the Patient*. London: Tavistock Publications.

Clarkson, P. (1995) *The Therapeutic Relationship*. London: Whurr Publishers.

Cockman, P., Evans, B. and Reynolds, P. (1999) *Consulting for Real People*. Maidenhead: McGraw-Hill.

Covey, S.R. (1992) *The Seven Habits of Highly Effective People*. London: Simon and Schuster.

Crane, T. (1998) *The Heart of Coaching*. San Diego, CA: FTA Press.

Egan, G. (1998) *The Skilled Helper*, 6th edn. New York, NY: Brooks Cole.

Farwagi, P.L. (1998) *The Life Balance Programme*. London: Orion Publishing Group.

Feltham, C. and Horton, I. (eds) (2000) *A Handbook of Counselling and Psychotherapy*. London: Sage Publications.

Flaherty, J. (1999) *Coaching: Evoking Excellence in Others*. Oxford: Butterworth-Heinemann.

Frankl, V. (1959) *Man's Search for Meaning*, New York, NY: Pocket Books.

Gallwey, T. (2000) *The Inner Game of Work*. London: Orion Publishing Group.

Goleman, D., Boyatzis, R. and McKee, A. (2002) *The New Leaders*. London: Little, Brown.

Harris, T.A. (1973) *I'm OK – You're OK*. London: Pan Books.

Harvey, J. (1988) 'Eichmann in the Organization', in *The Abilene Paradox*. Lexington, MA: Lexington Books.

Hazler, R.J. and Barwick, N. (2001) *The Therapeutic Environment*. Buckingham: Open University Press.

Hycner, R. and Jacobs, L. (1995) *The Healing Relationship in Gestalt Therapy*. Highland, NY: The Gestalt Journal Press.

Jackman, J. and Strober, M. (2003) 'Fear of feedback'. *Harvard Business Review*, April.

Jung, C.G. (1923) *Psychological Types*. New York, NY: Harcourt Brace.

Jung, C.G. (1963) *Memories, Dreams, Reflections*. London: Fontana.

Kline, N. (1999) *Time to Think*. London: Ward Lock.

Lewin, K. (1935) *A Dynamic Theory of Personality*. New York, NY: McGraw-Hill.

Lewin, K. (1948) *Resolving Social Conflicts: Selected Papers on Group Dynamics*, edited by Gertrude Lewin. New York, NY: Harper and Row.

Luft, J. (1970) *Group Processes: An Introduction to Group Dynamics*. Palo Alto, CA: National Press Books.

McLelland, D.C. (1985) *Human Motivation*. Chicago, IL: Scott, Foresman.

Martell, Y. (2002) *Life of Pi*. Edinburgh: Canongate Books.

Masson, J. (1990) *Against Therapy*. London: Fontana.

Mearns, D. (2003) *Developing Person-Centred Counselling*, 2nd edn. London: Sage Publications.

Mearns, D. and Thorne, B. (1999) *Person-Centred Counselling in Action*. London: Sage Publications.

O'Neill, M.B. (2000) *Executive Coaching with Backbone and Heart*. San Franciso, CA: Jossey-Bass.

Orbach, S. (1999) *The Impossibility of Sex*. Harmondsworth: Allen Lane, The Penguin Press.

Palmer, H. and Brown, P. (1998) *The Enneagram Advantage: Putting the Nine Personality Types to Work in the Office*. New York, NY: Harmony Books.

Rogers, C.R. (1951) *Client-Centered Therapy: Its Current Practice, Implications and Theory*. Boston, MA: Houghton Mifflin.

Rogers, C.R. (1980) *A Way of Being*. Boston, MA: Houghton Mifflin.

Rogers, J. (1998) *Sixteen Personality Types at Work in Organizations*. London: Management Futures; Milton Keynes: ASK Europe.

Rogers, J. (1999) *Facilitating Groups*. London: Management Futures.

Rogers, J. (2001) *Adults Learning*, 4th edn. Buckingham: Open University Press.

Samuels, A. (1985) *Jung and the Post-Jungians*. London: Routledge.

Schutz, W. (1984) *The Truth Option*. Berkeley, CA: Ten Speed Press.

Schutz, W. (1989) *Profound Simplicity*. San Diego, CA: WSA Bantam.

Senge, P. (1994) *The Fifth Discipline Field Book*. London: Nicolas Brealy Publishing.

Stacey, R.D. (1996) *Strategic Management and Organizational Dynamics*, 2nd edn. London: Pitman Publishing.

Tolle, E. (2001) *The Power of Now*. London: Hodder and Stoughton.

Ward, P. (1997) *360-degree Feedback*. London: Institute of Personnel and Development.

Waterman, J. and Rogers, J. (1997) *An Introduction to the FIRO-B*. Oxford: Oxford Psychologists Press.

Whitmore, J. (1996) *Coaching for Performance*, 2nd edn. London: Nicholas Brealey Publishing.

Whitworth, L., Kimsey-House, H. and Sandahl, P. (1998) *Co-Active Coaching*. Palo Alto, CA: Davies Black Publishing.

Yalom, I.D. (1991) *Love's Executioner and Other Tales of Psychotherapy*. Harmondsworth: Penguin Books.

Yalom, I.D. (2002) *The Gift of Therapy*. London: Judy Piatkus Publishing.

Contact details

For feedback on this book, email Jenny.Rogers@managementfutures.co.uk

For information on training courses please consult the Management Futures website, www.managementfutures.co.uk

Index

Diagrams and charts are indicated by page references in italics. Case studies are not indexed but can be found using subject references.